# PRACTICING ORAL HISTORY AMONG REFUGEES AND HOST COMMUNITIES

*Practicing Oral History among Refugees and Host Communities* provides a comprehensive and practical guide to applied oral history with refugees, teaching the reader how to use applied, contemporary oral history to help provide solutions to the 'mega-problem' that is the worldwide refugee crisis.

The book surveys the history of the practice and explains its successful applications in fields from journalism, law and psychiatry to technology, the prevention of terrorism and the design of public services. It defines applied oral history with refugees as a field, teaching rigorous, accessible methodologies for doing it, as well as outlining the importance of doing the same work with host communities. The book examines important legal and ethical parameters around this complex, sensitive field, and highlights the cost-effective, sustainable benefits that are being drawn from this work at all levels. It outlines the sociopolitical and theoretical frameworks around such oral histories, and the benefits for practitioners' future careers. Both in scope and approach, it thoroughly equips readers for doing their own oral history projects with refugees or host communities, wherever they are.

Using innovative case studies from seven continents and from the author's own work, this manual is the ideal guide for oral historians and those working with refugees or host communities.

**Marella Hoffman** is a Fellow of the Royal Anthropological Institute and has held positions at Cambridge University as well as at universities in France, Switzerland and Ireland. A former chief editor of a public policy magazine, her projects with communities have been taught as positive practice by government. Her other books include *Practicing Oral History to Improve Public Policies and Programs* (2018), *Asylum under Dreaming Spires: Refugees' Lives in Cambridge Today* (2017), and *Savoir-Faire of the Elders: Green Knowledge in the French Mediterranean Hills* (2016). She runs a Writers' Retreat Centre in southern France; visit www.marellahoffman.com.

## PRACTICING ORAL HISTORY

**Series editor, Nancy MacKay**

Museums, historical societies, libraries, classrooms, cultural centers, refugee organizations, elder care centers, and neighborhood groups are among the organizations that use oral history both to document their own communities and to foster social change. The *Practicing Oral History* series addresses the needs of these professionals with concise, instructive books about applying oral history best practices within the context of their professional goals.

Titles fall into one of three areas of applied oral history.The first format addresses a specific stage or skill within the oral history process.The second addresses the needs of professional communities who use oral history in their field.The third approach addresses the way oral history can be used to make an impact. Each title provides practical tools, ethical guidelines and best practices for conducting, preserving, and using oral histories within the framework of acknowledged standards and best practices.

Readers across a wide array of disciplines will find the books useful, including education, public history, local history, family history, communication and media, cultural studies, gerontology, documentary studies, museum & heritage studies, and migration studies.

Recent titles in the series

**Curating Oral Histories**
From Interview to Archive
*Nancy MacKay*

**Practicing Oral History in Historical Organizations**
*Barbara W. Sommer*

**Practicing Oral History with Immigrant Narrators**
*Carol McKirdy*

**Story Bridges**
A Guide for Conducting Intergenerational Oral History Programs
*Angela Zusman*

**Practicing Oral History to Improve Public Policies and Programs**
*Marella Hoffman*

**Practicing Critical Oral History**
Connecting School and Community
*Christine K. Lemley*

**Practicing Oral History to Connect University to Community**
*Beverly B. Allen and Fawn-Amber Montoya*

**Transcribing Oral History**
*Teresa Bergen*

**Practicing Oral History among Refugees and Host Communities**
*Marella Hoffman*

For more information, or to place orders visit Routledge, Practicing Oral History, www.routledge.com/Practicing-Oral-History/book-series/POHLCP

# PRACTICING ORAL HISTORY AMONG REFUGEES AND HOST COMMUNITIES

*Marella Hoffman*

NEW YORK AND LONDON

First published 2020
by Routledge
52 Vanderbilt Avenue, New York, NY 10017

and by Routledge
2 Park Square, Milton Park, Abingdon, Oxon, OX14 4RN

Routledge is an imprint of the Taylor & Francis Group, an informa business



*Library of Congress Cataloging-in-Publication Data*

Names: Hoffman, Marella, author.
Title: Practicing oral history among refugees and host communities / Marella Hoffman.
Description: New York : Routledge / Taylor and Francis, 2020. |
Series: Practicing oral history | Includes bibliographical references and index.
Identifiers: LCCN 2019034965 (print) | LCCN 2019034966 (ebook) |
ISBN 9781138541306 (hardback) | ISBN 9781138541313 (paperback) |
ISBN 9781351011334 (ebook)
Subjects: LCSH: Refugees--Interviews--Handbooks, manuals, etc. | Oral history--Handbooks, manuals, etc.
Classification: LCC HV640 .H56 2020 (print) | LCC HV640 (ebook) | DDC 305.9/069140722--dc23
LC record available at https://lccn.loc.gov/2019034965
LC ebook record available at https://lccn.loc.gov/2019034966

ISBN: 978-1-138-54130-6 (hbk)
ISBN: 978-1-138-54131-3 (pbk)
ISBN: 978-1-351-01133-4 (ebk)

Typeset in Bembo
by Swales & Willis, Exeter, Devon, UK

For Karmapa,
a refugee on this earth, but at home in the universe[1]

The refugee crisis is about us, not just about them.

David Miliband
Head of the International Rescue Commission

# CONTENTS

*Figures* *xii*
*Series Editor Foreword* *xiv*
*Preface: What This Book Provides* *xvi*
*Acknowledgments* *xxi*

**PART I**
**What Is Being Done Around the World** **1**

**1 How Oral History Can Improve Outcomes for Refugees and Host Communities** **3**
*A Global Surge of Innovation* *4*
*Whole Populations on the Move* *11*
*The Unthinkable Costs of Failing, and Why We're All Invited to Help* *14*

**2 The Importance of Listening to Host Communities** **21**
*Two Types of Host Communities, and Why We Must Listen to Their Concerns* *21*
*The Spectrum of Political Reactions among Host Communities* *24*
*Recent Oral Histories with Host Communities* *26*
*How This Book Enables You to Engage with Host Communities* *30*

**3 The Tradition of Oral History with Refugees, and How It's Radically Changing** **35**
*A Century of Tradition, and Changing Fast* *36*
*The World's Political Responses to Refugee Populations* *37*

*Who Is Interviewing Refugees, and How?* 40
*Publicizing Refugee Oral Histories through the Arts* 43
*The Tech Industry's Innovations with Refugees' Oral Histories* 50

**4 Case Studies of Oral Histories with Refugees: Transforming Lives and Outcomes** 60
*Oral Histories with Refugees* 61

**5 Case Studies of Oral Histories with Host Communities: Letting Discontent Be Heard** 73
*Oral Histories with Host Communities* 74

**PART II**
**Doing Your Own Oral Histories to Improve Outcomes for Refugees or Host Communities: The Step-by-Step Guide** 95

**6 The Ethics, Risks and Legalities of Doing Oral History with Refugees or Host Communities** 97
*Six Important 'PIECES'* 97
*Legal and Ethical Protections* 106

**7 Strategically Planning an Oral History Project that Will Improve Outcomes for Refugees and Host Communities** 117
*What Do You Want Your Project to Achieve?* 117
*Gathering 'Useful Messages' that Will Make a Real Difference* 124
*Selecting Narrators Strategically* 125
*Planning How to Publicize Your Project's Findings* 128
*Planning Your Project's Logistics* 130

**8 Doing Interviews that Will Make a Difference** 135
*Preparing Interview Questions* 136
*Doing Your Interviews* 139

**9 Editing and Publicizing Narrators' Interviews in Ways that Help Improve Outcomes for Communities** 146
*Designing Your End Products* 147
*Editing and Extracting from Your Interviews* 150
*Quantifying and Communicating the Financial Value of Your Applied Oral History Projects* 153

**10 Soaring Refugee Numbers, a Twenty-First Century '*Mega-Problem*': Applied Oral History Skills as Part of the Solution** **158**

*Why Now Is the Time 158*

*Intervening at the Pressure Points 159*

*Bringing Oral History to the Populist Identity Crisis 160*

*Oral History as Part of the Problem-Solving Frameworks of the Future 162*

*Appendices* *173*

*Glossary: Some Key Concepts Used in this Book* *197*

*Index* *201*

# FIGURES

1.1 The eight gains from using oral history to improve public policies and programs 9
1.2 Eight fields where applied oral histories are being used to assist refugees and host communities 10
1.3 Extremes of variation in refugees' education, transferable skills and internationalism 13
1.4 Spectrum of variations in individual refugees' finances 13
1.5 Curve of causal relationship between refugees and terrorism 16
2.1 The spectrum of host communities' political positions on migration 25
3.1 The tradition of refugee oral history, and its evolving methods 36
3.2 The *Four Golden Pillars* of the oral history method 41
3.3 *Ten Variables* in the methodology of refugee oral histories 42
3.4 Arts and multimedia publicizing refugee oral histories 45
4.1 Case studies of oral history projects with refugees 62
5.1 Stages of economic migration where oral histories can communicate the truth back to those considering migrating in the future 83
5.2 Case studies of oral history projects with host communities 89
6.1 The spectrum of political activity among refugees before fleeing 98
6.2 Extremes of variation in the amount of trauma refugees experienced before escaping 101
6.3 The range of traumas that refugees may experience during their escape journey 101
6.4 Extremes of variation in long-term outcomes for refugees 103
6.5 Spectrum of ways that your oral history work could harm your narrators 104
7.1 Planning your project's aims, target audiences and intended effects 118

7.2 Seven aims a refugee or host oral history project could have, from modest to ambitious 120
7.3 Groups that your oral history project could (a) interview and (b) reach with its findings 121
7.4 Refugees' typical preoccupations at each stage of the refugee journey 122
7.5 Host communities' typical preoccupations along their spectrum of responses to refugees 123
7.6 Five categories of 'useful messages' that an oral history project could carry to its chosen audience 124
7.7 Some of the ways that you could publicize your findings 129
8.1 Types of interview questions to capture specific 'useful messages' 137
8.2 Five chronological levels of an applied oral history interview 140
9.1 Analyzing interviews to extract the most useful material 151
9.2 Quantifying the equivalent financial value that your work saves or gains for organizations 154
10.1 The 'ripple' relationships between climate crisis and increasing waves of refugees 160
10.2 Populism, environmental crisis and refugees: the chains of cause and effect 161

# SERIES EDITOR FOREWORD

In late 2016, when Marella and I began discussing the idea for this book, the United Nations High Commissioner for Refugees (UNHCR) reported **65.6 million displaced people around the world**, a 20 million increase over the previous two decades. The most recent UNHCR statistics, about late 2018, show the figure has grown to over 68 million, 25.4 million of them identified as refugees and 31 million of them children. (As a point of reference, the population of Shanghai, China is about 24 million; the population of France is slightly more than 68 million.) As Marella mentions, this number is expected to explode over our lifetimes, as the effects of climate change make large population centers unlivable.

Alarming as they are, refugee statistics no longer surprise us; in fact, hearing them on the daily news has become a ho-hum event for most of us. That's the difference between statistics and stories. Sixty-eight million is perceived by humans as simply a large, rather meaningless number, but the voices of one or six or ten refugees or hosts telling their story in their own words will touch the human heart.

*Practicing Oral History among Refugees and Host Communities* begins with a reminder that refugees, as opposed to economic migrants, are

> a whole population on the move, with the same spread of age groups, finances, education levels, professions and personalities that any ordinary settled population would have. The only thing refugees have in common with each other is that, unlike economic migrants, they didn't want to leave home in the first place.

And that is only half the story. Refugees, by definition, end up in the homeland of others. Though it is always awkward, the reception refugees receive from their new communities varies, depending on the resources, cultural attitudes, and political climate of these host communities. We hear less about communities hosting refugees than about the refugees themselves, and when we do, it is usually about a confrontation, culture clash, or fight for scarce resources.

Neither the refugees nor their hosts asked to be in such a situation, but they are thrown together willy-nilly and need to learn to live as neighbors. Sometimes the relationship works relatively smoothly, sometimes it takes generations, and sometimes it never happens. Despite all the variations, a couple of things are universally true: one is that the refugee–host relationship is far more complex than portrayed in the media, and, second, oral history methodology has been proven to foster a range of social, political, and economic benefits for easing the relationships between refugees and hosts.

This is what *Practicing Oral History among Refugees and Host Communities* is about. It makes a case for using oral history along with other methods to forge a path of positive change for both refugees and their hosts. Then it offers a flexible methodology for accomplishing this in a variety of situations.

In doing research for this book, Marella discovered much less attention has been given to the experience of communities hosting refugees than to the refugee experience itself. Yet the experience of the hosts is every bit as important as that of the refugees in achieving integration. She fills this gap by devoting Chapter 2, The Importance of Listening to Host Communities, to the experience of host communities and throughout the book integrates the experience of both hosts and guest refugees.

Marella's preface calls readers to action, explaining that 'the sheer scale of the crisis means there are – and there will be – unlimited opportunities for you to use the applied oral history skills that you'll learn in this book to improve outcomes for both refugees and for host communities'. And as she so skillfully advocates, these stories, collected as oral histories, ignite the fuel to stir communities into action.

I am pleased to add *Practicing Oral History among Refugees and Host Communities* as the ninth title in the series and the second by Marella Hoffman. In this book she builds on the methodology she presented in *Practicing Oral History to Improve Public Policies and Programs*, applying it specifically to relations among refugees and host communities. I am sure it will touch the hearts of readers and inspire them into action, as it has me.

Nancy MacKay<br>
Austin, Texas<br>
July 2019

# PREFACE

## What This Book Provides

The world's growing refugee crisis can feel daunting. And the thought of future climate change refugees joining the millions already displaced can feel even more so. The World Bank predicts that over the next 30 years alone, 143 million people will be forcibly displaced by climate change.[3] But the sheer scale of the crisis means there are – and there will be – unlimited opportunities for you to use the applied oral history skills that you'll learn in this book to help improve outcomes both for refugees and for host communities.

Across the book, you will see that applied oral history with refugees is a rapidly growing, transdisciplinary practice that is set to keep mushrooming, due to the sheer demand for it worldwide. By 'applied', we mean that our oral history interviews are not just preserved or published: instead, findings, insights and recommendations extracted from them are also used to measurably improve public-interest projects and services for communities. Both inside and outside academia, aspects of this work are also sometimes called *contemporary* oral history, or simply oral *testimony*. This is because their temporal focus is often on events and experiences of recent weeks, months or years, rather than on the more distant past. This kind of contemporary oral history can also be understood as a 'history of the present', being captured as the present unfolds and spools away in front of us, before it disappears into the past.[4] As we know, this important firsthand witnessing can often be lost or dissolved in that past, suppressed or misrepresented by authorities who have the power to record 'history' the way *they* want it remembered, rather than the way that their powerless victims actually experienced it.[5]

This book is designed to be equally helpful for two audiences, namely:

- Professionals or volunteers who already work in any way with refugees, and need some oral history skills to help with their work.
- Oral historians (experienced, fledgling or would-be, starting from scratch) who would like to use their oral history skills to help make a difference to the refugee crisis, whether locally or globally.

Whichever side you're coming from, and whatever your previous level of experience, the second half of this book is a comprehensive how-to guide that will leave you fully equipped to deliver such a project yourself. The reality is that hundreds of thousands of people worldwide are already doing just that. They have dived in, in response to the need, and are already busy with this sort of work. Across our case studies you'll see that they include, among others:

- public sector professionals and charity staff responsible for processing refugees, delivering services to them and resettling them around the world;
- community workers responsible for improving integration with host communities long-term;
- ordinary people in host communities doing projects that challenge anti-refugee prejudice and assist integration;
- crime prevention agencies responsible for preventing radicalization and homegrown terrorism among poorly integrated refugee communities in the future;
- researchers, teachers and students of academic fields like Refugee Studies and Migration Studies.

Audiences are calling out for a rigorous but accessible methodology that includes guidance on legal parameters and ethical standards for this work. Importantly, this is the only publication to date that:

- defines applied oral history with refugees *as a field*, summarizing its ethics, impacts and future potentials;
- insists on, and explains, the equal necessity of doing applied oral history with host communities;
- shows the cost-effective, sustainable benefits that are already being drawn from this work, from grassroots to the highest levels of policy-making;
- presents innovative case studies from around the world and from the author's own work, which has been taught by government as a positive practice model;
- teaches a comprehensive, step-by-step methodology for doing your own applied oral history with refugees or host communities, at home or abroad;
- situates this work in a sociopolitical and theoretical framework for the future.

This book doesn't seek to give a comprehensive survey of who and where the world's refugee populations are, nor of the conflicts that got them there. Such information is available on the website of the United Nations High Commissioner for Refugees (UNHCR), in further detail in UNHCR's *Statistical Yearbooks*, and in fine detail in their *Online Statistical Database* as well as on their website, www.refworld.org.[6] However, by the end of our opening chapter, you will have an overview of the sheer diversity of the refugee world, the work being done there and how applied oral history is helping.

That first chapter will show you that, in terms of the backgrounds they're coming from, individual refugees are as diverse as the rest of us. It will explain, for instance, the difference in likely future outcomes between a refugee who, back home, was an educated, internationally minded professional with English as a second language and a refugee who was an illiterate subsistence farm labourer knowing little of the wider world beyond her own tribal culture.

Chapter 2 will explain the two very different types of host communities – the poor in the developing world who host 85% of the world's refugees, and societies in the Western world who proportionately host very few. The chapter gives an overview of the limited, though important, oral history that has been done with host communities, and explains why we'll need a lot more of it with both types of host communities in order to tackle the world refugee crisis ahead.

Chapter 3 gives an accessible overview of the major waves of refugee populations in modern times, and the century-old tradition of refugee oral history that has accompanied them. You'll see the tradition's twists and turns, its methodological variations and its current surge of innovations.

Chapters 4 and 5 each bring you case studies from around the world, with an analytic table showing how each project differed, and the impact it had. Chapter 4 examines applied oral histories with refugees, while Chapter 5 looks at applied oral histories with host communities.

From there on, the rest of the book is your how-to manual, coaching you through every detail of doing your own applied oral history project, big or small, local or international, to improve outcomes for refugees or host communities. This includes Chapter 6 that gives a unique guide to some of the ethical parameters of this complex, sensitive field and Chapter 9 that supplies another unique tool that can revolutionize your applied oral history projects by quantifying the added value they bring for organizations and communities in financial-equivalent terms. The final chapter will situate your new refugee oral history skills within the theoretical, sociopolitical and professional currents ahead.

But before we embark on this journey together, I want to mention my qualifications for being your guide. I've worked as an academic in social and political science, published on migration and identity and written books of applied oral history with communities. But I've also been employed at length by government to proactively involve communities in improving public policies and programs. So I have worked on both sides of the policy 'fence'. As an applied oral historian, I have listened to communities and service-users, gathering their needs and insights. And, as a policy insider, I had to apply those insights in ways that measurably improved public policies and services for communities.

Both for oral history and for policy, my work has included outreach with ethnic, migrant and refugee communities, both settled and in transit. On field trips to the ports of northern France where refugees and illegal migrants congregate, I witnessed unaccompanied African boys aged 14 or 15 taking hideous risks over and over, flinging their slender bodies onto British-bound lorries that accelerated and swerved to avoid them. And I watched up close the complex dance of interactions between (in that instance, kindly) French border police and those utterly determined young travellers with nothing to lose.

My book *Asylum under Dreaming Spires: Refugees' Lives in Cambridge Today* presents some of my work with refugees, which was taught by government to public service officials as a positive practice model.[7] That project provides one of our case studies in Chapter 5. The book about it is a real-life, very human account of how we, in one city, used applied oral histories to improve public policies and services around refugees in the community. One challenge I always welcome when working for government is that you are under constant scrutiny to demonstrate how your activities genuinely benefit society in concrete ways that give value for taxpayers' money. I hope that spirit of practical public service pervades this book too.

My 2018 book *Practicing Oral History to Improve Public Policies and Programs* (like this present one, part of Nancy MacKay's *Practicing Oral History* series at Routledge) is a comprehensive manual that teaches how to do oral history to improve public policies or nonprofit projects in any field, from elder care to land management. It gives a thorough grounding on how to apply oral testimonies to measurably improve public or nonprofit services of any sort, with any end-user group. This book you are reading now meets a demand raised by the other two, namely for a step-by-step manual teaching how to do applied oral histories with refugees and host communities specifically, so as to improve outcomes for both.

I have never been a refugee but I did emigrate alone at 19 from my home country – then an underdeveloped economy – to find work in a more prosperous country and, necessarily, in the foreign language spoken there. I've since spent my whole adult life working abroad as an economic migrant. The politics of my own migrations (politics of class, economics, decolonization, ethnicity and gender) twine through my published work alongside the much more dramatic migratory pressures on my refugee narrators.

At moments across this book, we will need to refer in passing to right-wing and left-wing politics, because the fate of refugees is often decided by the tug of war between those two forces (neither of which have excelled at the task in recent years). The tools that this book will give you are intended to be equally useful to any moderate person on either the right or the left of the political spectrum. Oral history has traditionally listened more to communities on the left (and my own private inclination happens to be to the moderate left). But the methods in this book must be applied to listen empathically to right-wing communities too, not least because they deserve to be heard. Applied oral history is capable of delivering a deep listening that can help bridge social and political divides. Across this book you will see many exciting examples of such work being done. We will also witness the increasing dangers of extremism in any ideology. And we'll see why the ability to really listen and engage meaningful dialogue with an increasingly right-wing populism will be so important, not only for managing the refugee crisis but for maintaining world peace in the future.

## Notes

1 Tibetan refugee Ogyen Trinley Dorje, one of the spiritual leaders of the Tibetan people in exile.
2 Thanks to Routledge for permission to reproduce adapted versions of the following figures from my 2018 book *Practicing Oral History to Improve Public Policies and Programs*: in Chapter 1, Figure 1.1 (The eight gains from using oral history to improve public policies and programs); in Chapter 3, Figure 3.2 ('The *Four Golden Pillars* of the oral history method'); in Chapter 8, Figure 8.2 ('Five chronological levels of an applied oral history interview') ; and in Chapter 9, Figure 9.2 ('Quantifying the equivalent financial value that your work saves or gains for organizations').
3 Kanta Kumari Rigaud et al., editors, *Groundswell: Preparing for Internal Climate Migration*. Washington, DC: World Bank, 2018.
4 Michael Roth, 'Foucault's "History of the Present"', *History and Theory*, 20(1), 1981.
5 Ronald Fritze, *Invented Knowledge: False History, Fake Science and Pseudo-Religions*. London: Reaktion Books, 2019.
6 Urls are given in the references at the end of this preface.
7 Citations for sources already named in the text are given in the references at the end of each chapter.

## References

Fritze, Ronald, *Invented Knowledge: False History, Fake Science and Pseudo-Religions*. London: Reaktion Books, 2019.

Hoffman, Marella, *Asylum under Dreaming Spires: Refugees' Lives in Cambridge Today*. Cambridge: Cambridge Editions in Partnership with the Living Refugee Archive, University of East London, 2017.

Hoffman, Marella, *Practicing Oral History to Improve Public Policies and Programs*. Abingdon: Routledge, 2018.

Rigaud, Kanta Kumari et al., editors, *Groundswell: Preparing for Internal Climate Migration*. Washington, DC: World Bank, 2018.

Roth, Michael, 'Foucault's "History of the Present"', *History and Theory*, 20(1): 32–46, 1981.

UNHCR, *Statistical Yearbook 2016*. Geneva: UNHCR, 2017 [Available at www.unhcr.org/uk/statistical-yearbooks.html; accessed on 21-6-2019].

UNHCR, *Online Statistical Database* [Available at www.unrefugees.org/refugee-facts/statistics and www.unhcr.org/uk/figures-at-a-glance.html; accessed on 21-6-2019].

# ACKNOWLEDGMENTS

Thanks to:

Nancy Mackay, the far-seeing editor who welcomed this topic – her guidance and corrections then went on to make this a much better book;

Paul V. Dudman, University of East London's Archive Director and convenor of the UK's Oral History Society Group on Migration, who advised on the manuscript;

Norma Buckley, community activist in Glenville, Ireland, who read the manuscript, improved it with her contributions and has always supported my work.

# PART I

# What Is Being Done around the World

# 1

# HOW ORAL HISTORY CAN IMPROVE OUTCOMES FOR REFUGEES AND HOST COMMUNITIES

Kurdish refugee Behrouz Boochani – a gifted journalist, filmmaker, human rights activist and poet – was unlawfully imprisoned by the Australian government from 2014 onward for four years. His crime? Applying to them for political asylum. His prison was cut off from the world, on the very remote Manus Island in the Pacific Ocean. Almost miraculously, he managed to smuggle out his irrepressible words and images to the wider world via his mobile phone, and they have been meticulously stitched back together by others to produce his award-winning book, *No Friend but the Mountains* and his award-winning film *Chauka, Please Tell Us the Time*. In an interview, Behrouz explains:

> I always imagine the world map. I imagine a tiny island and a prison on the tiny island. It is where I am at this moment. Three years ago, when the local people attacked our prison and killed a person and injured 100 people, the guards took us to a soccer ground outside the prison. That was the first time we had been out. They gathered 900 men on the soccer ground for a night. On that dark night I was looking at the sky, and I felt that there was no place in the world for me. They even took away my prison. I felt that I do not even belong to the Earth, and I was looking to the sky and imagining another planet …
>
> I think we are human and do not have any shelter but humanity. We have to trust in humanity (…) I belong to this world and to the humans beyond the political borders (…) I am a stateless person, but I am a free man because the Earth is for me, I belong to nature, belong to mountains, oceans, seasons, jungles, deserts and I belong to those societies where I have breathed with them, smiled with them, cried with them or lived with them. I am a free man.[1]

I had the privilege of contacting Behrouz to tell him that his words would reach you, reader, here on this page of this book. A powerful Western nation did all it could to make it impossible for him to communicate with you or anyone else. But his ingenuity and hope found a way to send out his words of peace, releasing them like birds and hoping they might reach you to open a wider dialogue with you. This book will be your bridge to many people like Behrouz, and it will equip you to make real contributions to both local and planetary dialogues around the refugee crisis.

International law currently defines a refugee as 'someone who is unable or unwilling to return to their country of origin owing to a well-founded fear of being persecuted for reasons of race, religion, nationality, membership of a particular social group, or political opinion'.[2] Today, 68.5 million people are forcibly displaced around the world – by far the largest number ever. They include:

- *internally displaced persons* who have had to flee to another part of their own country to escape harm or persecution;
- *asylum seekers* who fled to a foreign country to apply for political asylum on the grounds that they would face persecution if sent back to their own country.

If an asylum seeker's application is accepted, they then become legally recognized as a *registered refugee*, entitled to international assistance and protection. But if an asylum seeker's request is refused, they can be deported back to their country of origin. Among the 68.5 million people forcibly displaced around the world at the moment, 25 million have political asylum, 3.5 million are awaiting asylum application responses and 40 million are still seeking resettlement.[3] Wars in the Middle East have opened floodgates of displacement over the past few years. But Latin America is predicted to be facing a refugee crisis comparable to that of the Syrians, with over 5 million displaced in Venezuela, Colombia and Central America.

Two-thirds of all the world's refugees have been displaced for over three years, and half for over ten years. By 2015, 51% of refugees were children. Most were separated from their parents and fleeing with other relatives or friends, or travelling alone. Over half of refugee children are not in school.[4] Unfortunately, the current global figure of 68.5 million displaced is set to balloon when climate change starts making whole regions of the world uninhabitable in the decades ahead. As one United Nations (UN) report puts it:

> The age of environmental migration is upon us, and the world is woefully unprepared for it (…) areas threatened range from Bangladesh and Nigeria to New York City and Washington, DC (…) this is a global problem threatening developed and developing countries alike.[5]

## A Global Surge of Innovation

Even if you have some prior knowledge about refugees or about oral history, this book will show you both through lenses that may be relatively new to you. Despite – or because of – the unprecedented numbers displaced now, there is actually an exciting climate of innovation and lateral thinking around refugee issues.

As Oxford University's Professor Alexander Betts puts it: 'The humanitarian system is at a crossroads. With growing needs and finite resources, creative solutions are urgently needed'.[6] In one of his recent reports, part one is called '*The Rethink*' (with sections on 'Rethinking Ethics', 'Rethinking Assistance' and so on) and part two is called '*The Remake*'.[7] Overall, the message from the world's leading experts, both at design and delivery levels, is that:

- 'The refugee system was created 50 years ago, and is nowhere near fit for purpose in a fast changing, globalized world'.[8]
- Only new relationships and partnerships can tackle the scale and complexity of the problem.
- Every single person in the world – with any skill or idea in any field – is invited to respond to this need with their own creative innovations.
- Only a whole society, 360-degree approach can work, both locally and globally.
- Only deeply participatory approaches will work, i.e. listening to service-users and community members, and involving them in designing services and policies; top-down solutions won't fit.

So the UN – together with all the major agencies designing and delivering refugee services – have put out a formal call to the whole world, inviting everyone to contribute their ideas to a movement called 'Humanitarian Innovation', which they consider to be the only way forward.[9] This book is reaching out to you as part of that call, giving you tools to respond in your own unique way, wherever you are.

Consider, for instance, the creativity that refugees themselves are showing in their use of the simple, free resource that is language. Refugees have realized that replacing one tired, overused word with a fresh one can sometimes unleash huge new resources. They are teaching us that one of the easiest, cheapest and most effective improvements we can make to the refugee crisis is to start by *changing the story*, simply by changing our vocabulary. For instance, there are networks of Syrians online who now refer to themselves not as refugees but as *Syrian expatriates.* (On the spectrum of all English-language terms for those who live in a foreign country, this is the most high-status, while *refugee* is surely the lowest. For instance, 'expatriate' is the word the British have always proudly used to refer to themselves only, when they choose to live abroad.) Meanwhile, some host communities have learned to swap the term *refugee* for *newcomers*. Those resettled in Berlin are often referred to now as *New Berliners*, a term replete with all the resources these new residents can bring to the old city. Refugees receiving asylum from Canada are proudly welcomed by the Canadian government as *New Canadians*. The term inherently clarifies too that the former refugee must now adopt the shared values and responsibilities of Canadian citizenship: they can't import with them a set of incompatible values from their old country. Those have to be traded in, in exchange for their new Canadian identity.

The field of migration studies too has improvised some important new ways of looking at people and place that are not just academic jargon. They include concepts like the 'transnational', the 'translocal', 'localization' and even 'glocalization'. Other new perspectives include the 'No-Borders' movement, 'thinking through oceans', and concepts like the 'Refugee Nation' and the 'Refugee Economy'. We will unpack all these ideas as we move through our chapters. For instance, the 'transnational' is a perspective that ignores national boundaries to trace instead the connections that cross or transcend them, such as travel-routes, export-routes and other lines of international communications and relationships. The 'transnational' is clearly an indispensable perspective when describing the networks, movements and relationships of migrant diasporas, which can stretch right around the globe, well beyond a little country of origin.[10]

The 'translocal' is a subset of the 'transnational' approach.[11] The translocal zooms in on the tight weave of connections that may link up two *localities* that are far apart geographically. An example could be the rural parts of the island of Sicily off southern Italy and the Bronx area of downtown New York where so many Sicilian migrants settled across the twentieth century. Though so far apart both in distance and in landscape style, the two localities are densely bound through links of migration, family relationships, regular journeys in both directions, gifting relationships and exchanges of money, as well as through the resulting ties of language, culture and collective memory. Another example of translocality would be the intense relationship between the tiny village port of Lampadusa in southern Italy and the sub-Saharan African villages, whose youth, seeking a better economic future in Europe, are dumped in their thousands upon Lampadusa by people smugglers.

Another example of a potent reuse of language is the online movement called '*Not just a refugee*'.[12] On a related website, forcibly displaced persons upload their photo and an account of their professional background, offering their skills to the world under the banner '*I'm not a refugee, I'm … a musician*', '*…a lawyer*', '*…a teacher*', '*…a nurse*', '*…an IT analyst*'.[13] And some experts are now referring to the collective 'Refugee Nation': given the current numbers of refugees, it's the equivalent of a medium-sized country scattered across the globe. Taking the concept further, the 'Refugee Economy' is a new term for the combined economic activities of that population. Meanwhile, the composer and Syrian refugee Moutaz Arian has composed a 'National Anthem' for the 'Refugee Nation'. And at the last Olympics, young athletes from across this 'Refugee Nation' processed into the Olympic stadium alongside other nations, carrying the 'Refugee Flag'.[14]

Through this fresh alchemy of words, naming and dialogue, both hosts and refugees are learning new ways of thinking. Some experts are rebooting our concepts of territory too, with approaches such as 'thinking through oceans': this shift of perspective ignores land and its borders to instead view seas like the Mediterranean as virtual countries, with whole populations of refugees travelling their well-worn sea-routes. Unfortunately the Mediterranean – the escape route for countless sea-borne refugees in recent years – has also come to be described as their 'liquid cemetery'.[15] Over 13,000 displaced people died trying to cross the Mediterranean between 2015 and 2018.[16]

These creative shifts in language and perspective are the kind of change being sought now by the Innovation Service of the United Nations High Commissioner for Refugees (UNHCR). They take

> an innovative approach to the growing humanitarian needs of today, and more critically – the future. As the world becomes increasingly complex, (responses to refugees) must become more adaptable and agile. We must adapt to new systems, technologies, and innovations to be fit for purpose, challenging the status quo.

They explain: 'We aim to support a culture of creativity and collaboration ... We don't consider ourselves innovators per se, but rather, the facilitators. We want to help you create an enabling environment for innovation and continuous learning'.[17] The leaders of Oxford University's own 'Humanitarian Innovation Project', in turn, explain that they 'engage with actors and ideas traditionally off-limits to humanitarians: the role of markets, affected communities, the military, and politics. By breaking down conventional boundaries, we aim to highlight untapped opportunities for dialogue and collaboration'.[18]

Across this book, you will see that effective solutions for refugee problems do in fact lie all around us, and are often revealed by looking at things differently. For instance, when we look through the lens of 'a self-reliance model for refugees',[19] we see the 'growing evidence that refugees are economic actors who are able to sustain themselves, and to make socioeconomic contributions to their hosting society'.[20] In fact, it turns out that 'the skills, talents, and aspirations of crisis-affected communities themselves offer a neglected resource'.[21] As we go deeper into this fine-grained detail of the refugee experience, you'll often see popular notions challenged or inverted like this, using an 'asset-based' approach that highlights resourcefulness rather than victimhood. Both professionals and the public are being actively taught to reverse their perspectives now, turning old models upside down and using creative lateral thinking to design new solutions. This shift to 'acknowledging the world that refugees have made, not just the world that has been made for them' is just one example.[22]

We will also reverse some preconceptions that the media tend to present about refugees. They are usually depicted as helpless victims drawing on the resources of others, but those working with refugees in the field often find the opposite now.[23] For instance, the media probably haven't told you about the country whose large intake of refugees has measurably *boosted* its national economy. Or about the places where new refugees are themselves providing paid employment to the host community. In Kyangwali, Uganda, 45% of businesses run by foreign refugees have host-community Ugandans as the majority of their customers. And in a fifth of those refugees' businesses, almost half of the employees are Ugandans.[24] You probably won't have heard in the media either about the school that Zimbabwean refugees set up to teach their own children, which is now serving children from the South African host community too.[25] Or the recording studio that refugees resourcefully put together for themselves from materials left lying around: it's now recording host-community musicians too, enabling them to sell their music locally and online.[26] For this sort of radical innovation, refugees use skills like lateral thinking, foraging, recycling, upcycling, *bricolage*, adaptation, exchange and barter. If penniless refugees stuck in tented camps can do these things, we – with so many more resources available to us – can innovate too.

Just as refugees make unforeseen journeys, I believe this book will take you too on an amazing journey. In the chapters ahead, both among refugees and in host communities, you will meet remarkable people doing ingenious, surprising things. You're probably not used to hearing about the refugee crisis as a positive opportunity but you'll see that in many ways it is one, both for humanity in general and for you.[27] You will emerge from this book fully equipped with all the skills you need to respond to the UN's call for innovative action *wherever you are*. You don't need to move house or give up your day job. You can make a huge contribution just by applying the skills you'll learn in this book to oral history projects that you can do yourself – whether with your own local community around you, or with refugees there, or with communities elsewhere or online. On the topic of refugees, you will reach a new landscape of knowledge, ability and action.

Both the UN and the International Rescue Commission (IRC) – the two leading international organizations for assisting refugees – have declared that the design of all future refugee services must be participatory, using service-users' testimonies from the beginning to design services that are more tailor-made and less wasteful.[28] They believe that this is not yet common enough. As the IRC puts it:

> National consultations have (…) little involvement of refugees and host communities, local civil society organizations, or local government entities (…) Consultations have been ad-hoc and it remains unclear how findings are feeding back (…) and informing decisions about policies and programs that affect refugees… (We) should define a consultative process for regularly engaging refugee and host populations.[29]

And according to Oxford University's Refugee Studies Centre:

> Although 'humanitarian innovation' has been increasingly embraced by the humanitarian world, this kind of 'bottom-up' innovation by crisis-affected communities is (still) often neglected. This oversight disregards the capabilities and adaptive resourcefulness that people and communities affected by conflict and disaster often demonstrate.[30]

So the UN and IRC are spearheading a *Global Compact on Refugees* based on the approaches above.[31] The applied oral history methodology taught in this book embraces this participatory approach that involves *all* stakeholders.

In fact, the expert cited earlier, Professor Betts, is already doing his own cutting-edge oral histories with individual 'refugee innovators' around the world, so as to scale up and apply their insights methodically elsewhere.[32] There are eight main ways in which targeted oral testimonies like this, gathered from service-users, can improve any public policy or service, targeting it to be more fit for purpose and avoid waste. These 'eight gains' from strategically applied oral history are summarized in Figure 1.1 below.

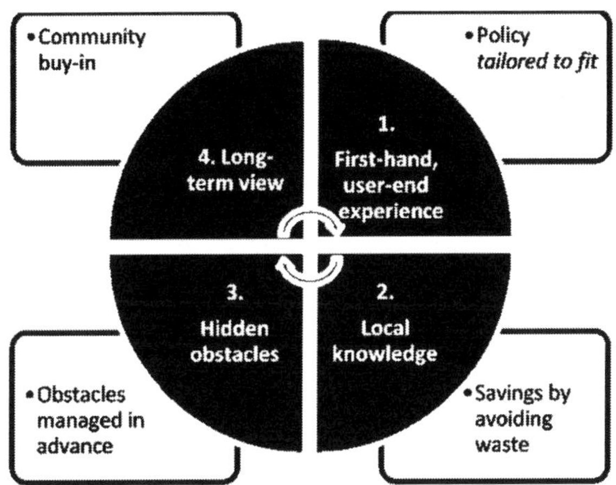


**FIGURE 1.1** The eight gains from using oral history to improve public policies and programs

Specifically in the world of refugee policy and services, it is now clear to all that we must consult service-users about their needs *before* designing any services because:

- the need is so urgent and huge;
- resources for refugee services are stretched;
- most service providers have never been refugees themselves, so they can't know exactly what's needed;
- refugees may stream into one camp from very different backgrounds and cultures, so what's needed by those in one tent may be quite inappropriate for those in the tent next door.

Fortunately, as you will see across this present book, a very wide range of professions are already doing applied oral history with refugees along all the stages of their journeys – in camps and at borders, at reception centers, in asylum detention centers, in resettlement programs and during long-term integration into host communities. In this way, lessons have been learned from failed projects such as Japan's 'Pilot Refugee Resettlement Program' in 2012. Over time, half of the refugees offered asylum there refused to accept it, due to the severe problems encountered by those who had already accepted. As one of the world's wealthiest countries and most financially equal societies, with some of the world's highest levels of trust and social cohesion, where on earth did Japan go wrong?[33] An official review of the failed program says that its failure 'forced all concerned parties to reconsider the past approaches and re-examine hitherto untested assumptions and mindsets'.[34]

In fact, the review found that the problem was that Japan had done zero listening to its incoming refugees beforehand, and had prepared 'one-size-fits-all solutions' for them, assuming that they would all have the same familiar needs that local Japanese citizens do. Unsurprisingly, the review found that

> to minimize the integration problem, the government should (instead) listen to the voices of the refugees, both in the camps and in Japan, to understand their interests, expectations and concerns and social norms, and should encourage them to participate in designing the integration support system.[35]

By contrast with this failed Japanese example, Figure 1.2 below shows you eight different fields whose professionals *are* now doing oral histories as a necessary part of delivering their own work with refugees. It shows how, in each case, the gathering of oral testimony is a fundamental part of 'processing' refugees and providing the services they need. These professionals come from the public sector, nongovernmental agencies and charities large and small. They may be medical or legal staff, community workers, translators, academic researchers or online campaigners and activists.

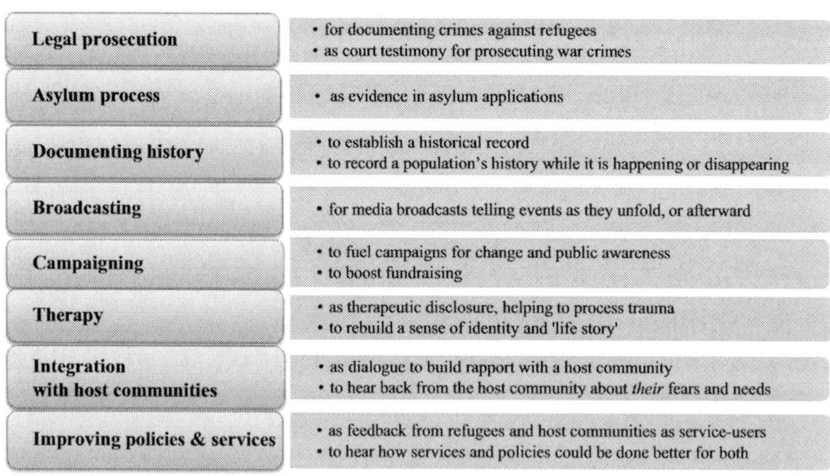

Legal prosecution
• for documenting crimes against refugees
• as court testimony for prosecuting war crimes
Asylum process
• as evidence in asylum applications
Documenting history
• to establish a historical record
• to record a population's history while it is happening or disappearing
Broadcasting
• for media broadcasts telling events as they unfold, or afterward
Campaigning
• to fuel campaigns for change and public awareness
• to boost fundraising
Therapy
• as therapeutic disclosure, helping to process trauma
• to rebuild a sense of identity and 'life story'
Integration with host communities
• as dialogue to build rapport with a host community
• to hear back from the host community about *their* fears and needs
Improving policies & services
• as feedback from refugees and host communities as service-users
• to hear how services and policies could be done better for both


**FIGURE 1.2** Eight fields where applied oral histories are being used to assist refugees and host communities

Their practice shows that oral history is particularly well suited to refugee environments because it:

- is relatively inexpensive;
- can be done in the field, outdoors or in transit;

- can expose suppressed truths of politics, crime and armed conflict;
- can help tailor services to individuals' needs, improving outcomes and reducing waste;
- is person-centered, restoring some dignity to those deprived of a voice;
- can be therapeutic;
- can help build mutual understanding and dialogue with resistant host communities.

## Whole Populations on the Move

We know that there are 68.5 million people forcibly displaced, but who *are* they really? In the media, refugees are often clumped together with economic migrants under the collective title of 'migrants'. Debates rage about the differing rights and merits of these two groups – refugees and economic migrants. Importantly, this book does not address economic migrants: it deals only with those *forcibly displaced* by conflict, persecution or environmental disaster. (Some commentators claim that extreme poverty in undeveloped economies is itself a form of forcible displacement, but that debate lies beyond the scope of this book.) Yet, there is one informative distinction that we can note here between refugees and economic migrants: economic migrants tend to come from a narrower demographic. The majority are young, single, risk-takers (mostly, though not all, male) with few qualifications. Chronically unemployed or underemployed, they are willing to abandon home and risk their lives for what they perceive as the chance to join in with the prosperity of the West.[36]

Refugees, by stark contrast, are a whole population on the move, with the same spread of age-groups, finances, education levels, professions and personalities that any ordinary settled population would have. The only thing refugees have in common with each other is that, unlike economic migrants, they didn't want to leave home in the first place: most had a perfectly good life before local troubles ripped it from them. They are on the road involuntarily, just to stay alive or get out of physical danger. An analogy would be to imagine the whole population of your own local community all having to just get up and leave – the young, the old, the sick, the disabled, the strong, the weak, the highly educated, the unschooled – all carrying whatever they can on their backs.

Once you see refugees as a cross section of a population like this, you see the diverse needs and vulnerabilities that they carry along with them. Newborns, nursing mothers, the elderly, handicapped children, single men in their twenties, professors, cabdrivers, torture survivors – as refugees, they all have to trudge along together. Like the throw of a dice in a board game, these factors strongly influence how well each will succeed at the challenges of making the refugee journey, making a successful asylum application, and settling and integrating into a host community. I feel that a good metaphor for these extreme variables in the refugee journey is the board-game 'Snakes & Ladders' (called 'Chutes & Ladders' in the US). As you advance along the board in that game, random throws of the dice either promote you up ladders towards winning the game, or slide you down on the backs of snakes or on chutes, right back towards where you started. So, let's look more closely at these variables that can have such a 'Snakes & Ladders' effect on outcomes for individual refugees.

For instance, it is well documented that in societies that are experiencing violent conflict, gender and age alone thrust whole sections of the population into specific dangers.[37] Young males are more likely to experience street violence, be conscripted or be forced into armed conflict. Girls and women are more likely to be raped or enslaved. Unaccompanied children are particularly at risk of long-term mental health damage and of being trafficked. So, as you read through the different demographic groups listed below, ask yourself: 'What could be the specific dangers of the refugee journey for *this* particular group?'

- children or teenagers, bereaved or orphaned, travelling alone or with relatives;
- young men alone, or with young male friends;
- young women alone, or with young female friends;
- pregnant women, or mothers with small children and/or babies;
- elderly or disabled people (e.g. the frail, arthritic or diabetic, those in a wheelchair, those with learning disabilities or mental illnesses), being helped along by other refugees;
- an extended family of several generations, from babies to the very elderly.

Now – as if rolling the dice of fortune over these people's heads again – go back over the list and ask yourself, for each demographic group: 'What are the specific needs that they will each have (a) during the escape journey, (b) while awaiting asylum decisions and (c) in order to achieve integration in a host country long-term?'

The proliferating vulnerabilities and needs that you see emerging here come solely from age, gender, reproduction and health. So let's throw the dice again, this time to expose the further dramatic variations among refugees in terms of their education, transferable skills and internationalism, and the effects these will have on their refugee experience. The table below (Figure 1.3) depicts two extremes, but any refugee population will contain many people dotted along the spectrum between these extremes.

Overlaying the extremes listed above, let's look now at the extreme diversity there can be in the personal finances of individual refugees, which will affect how much they can pay their way out of danger and into a new life. The shaded columns on the right in Figure 1.4 show how financial disadvantage can spiral a refugee much further down than simply 'having no money': it can quickly entangle them in illicit debts that lead to beatings, kidnap, enslavement and serious threats to family back home.

Finally, cruel as this game may seem, let's throw the dice one more time over the heads of our refugee population on the move. This time – layered on top of the variables that we've seen – we're now going to spot the *political* vulnerabilities

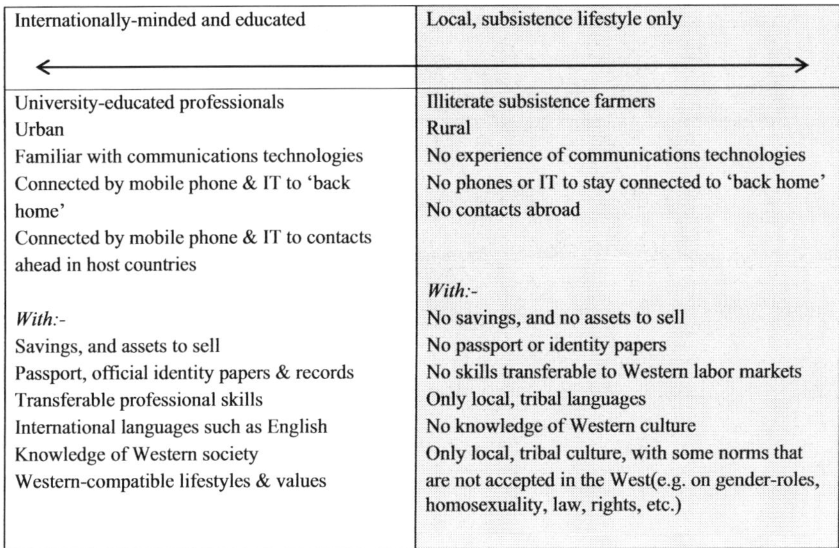

| Internationally-minded and educated ← | Local, subsistence lifestyle only → |
|---|---|
| University-educated professionals<br>Urban<br>Familiar with communications technologies<br>Connected by mobile phone & IT to 'back home'<br>Connected by mobile phone & IT to contacts ahead in host countries<br><br>*With:-*<br>Savings, and assets to sell<br>Passport, official identity papers & records<br>Transferable professional skills<br>International languages such as English<br>Knowledge of Western society<br>Western-compatible lifestyles & values | Illiterate subsistence farmers<br>Rural<br>No experience of communications technologies<br>No phones or IT to stay connected to 'back home'<br>No contacts abroad<br><br>*With:-*<br>No savings, and no assets to sell<br>No passport or identity papers<br>No skills transferable to Western labor markets<br>Only local, tribal languages<br>No knowledge of Western culture<br>Only local, tribal culture, with some norms that are not accepted in the West(e.g. on gender-roles, homosexuality, law, rights, etc.) |

**FIGURE 1.3** Extremes of variation in refugees' education, transferable skills and internationalism

that individual refugees can also have (which may not be visible to you when you meet them). If fleeing a persecutory regime or a civil war, they may have been conscripted, radicalized or brainwashed into unwanted military or paramilitary activity. Today, men from the countries producing the most refugees such as Syria, the Sudan or Eritrea, have very often had to flee precisely to escape this. But those

| Financial advantages ← | | | | Financial disadvantages → | | | | |
|---|---|---|---|---|---|---|---|---|
| Wealthy | Has some savings, and assets to sell | Their family back home can afford long-distance plane flights to get the refugee to safety | Transferable skills for employment in the West | Only local skills back home, and only for subsistence | No assets or possessions, even before fleeing | Big debts to dangerous lenders or traffickers | Refugee kidnapped or enslaved for ransom en route | Family back home threatened by dangerous lenders or traffickers |

**FIGURE 1.4** Spectrum of variations in individual refugees' finances

dynamics behind them still leave them vulnerable now to those who were engaged in the other side of that conflict, who may well be on the refugee road with them or in a host country ahead of them, or – most common of all – threatening their loved ones and associates back home. Or a refugee on the road may still be hounded by religious, party political or tribal allegiances. Civil rights activists, refugees who are or were proponents of free speech, women refusing to obey certain religious strictures, people known to be gay or transgender ... they can all be very vulnerable to specific persecutions by their own home culture or compatriots, which can follow and target them even abroad.

So the many variables that we have seen above – of age, gender, education, internationalism, transferable skills, digital literacy and political background – must be considered about any individual refugee before appropriate services and support can be delivered to them. That is why, at the simplest level, all those working with refugees have to hear and process a refugee's story in an organized way before they can respond and assist them.

## The Unthinkable Costs of Failing, and Why We're All Invited to Help

When glancing ahead to the potential costs of failing to manage the world refugee crisis, we are spoiled for choice. Realistically, the future costs could well include the triumph of far-right politics in the West; civil society structures collapsing, unprepared for the influx of climate refugees; millions of refugee youth growing up feral in inhuman camps, never having known education or a stable society; terrorists recruiting among this new generation born into lifelong displacement and exclusion. For now, let's just take two of these problems to look at here – the rise of the far right and the connection between refugees and terrorism.

A robust literature has demonstrated that turning away from the grievances of host communities and merely dismissing them as racist actually fuels the rise of the far right.[38] That's very much the argument of this present book too, which offers an alternative way forward. As for refugees and terrorism, this topic may look like a minefield that you don't want to step into, strewn with ideological prejudices, media distortions and political correctness. But let's walk in: you may be surprised to find that the facts are actually just logical common sense. The proven data show that yes, there *is* a causal relationship between terrorism and refugees, and this is it:

- Resettlement and integration with decent life chances in a stable society lead to negligible terrorism.[39]
- If generations are left to rot in vast subhuman refugee camps without education, homeland or civil society structures, this is likely lead to unprecedented amounts of future terrorism.[40]

That's not so complicated after all, when you think it through. But unfortunately, the correct steps for avoiding terrorism are exactly the opposite of those advocated by populists, whose strategy is: 'To avoid terrorism, *don't* resettle refugees'. One can perhaps understand the fearful thinking behind that approach, but it is counterproductive and unsustainable. For instance, in the world's largest refugee camp – Dadaab in Eastern Kenya – of the 330,000 Somalis living in the camp, 100,000 were born there and have never known another way of life. Overall, the average refugee is displaced for ten years. But if they've been a refugee for over five years, they can expect on average to end up displaced for 21 years in all.[41] Abandoning refugees for generations in this way is what the head of the International Rescue Commission calls 'sitting on a grenade with the pin pulled out'.[42] He explains:

> strategically, humanitarian crisis is the product of political crisis, but it also is the *cause* of further political instability. And you only have to look at the Middle East today and its consequences way beyond there into Europe to see the danger.[43]

In order to see even more clearly into the causal relationship between terrorism and *non-settled* refugees, consider the five well-documented facts below, which are based on military intelligence and counterterrorist research.[44] You'll notice that they do in fact reflect the actual events and trends that you see unfolding in the news, locally and globally, once the fog of hysteria is stripped away:

1. The number of resettled refugees involved in acts of terrorism in host countries is negligible.
2. The vast majority of terror attacks in the US are by US citizens, mostly white natives from far-right movements.
3. The vast majority of terrorist attacks in Europe are by European citizens, though these are sometimes from a poorly integrated 'second generation' born to refugee parents.
4. So, in Europe there is a small risk of radicalization among the second generation born to migrant or refugee parents, but only when poorly integrated.
5. However, there is an overwhelming, 'time bomb' likelihood of future radicalization among the tens of millions displaced for life in the refugee camps of the Middle East and Africa – especially among children born and raised in subhuman conditions there without any education, homeland or prospects for a meaningful human life.[45]

Figure 1.5 just restates these facts in graph form. Its curve shows that yes, there is an overwhelmingly urgent and common-sense relationship between refugees and terrorism. The data show that if we do the right thing for refugees, they don't turn to terrorism: well-resettled, integrated refugees have too much to lose, in terms of meaningful life chances and a sense of belonging in their host country. But if we choose to isolate them in their homeless millions, their camps will become a terrorist recruiting ground the likes of which the modern world has not yet seen or imagined. Or, as one expert puts it more elegantly, weighing up the pragmatic

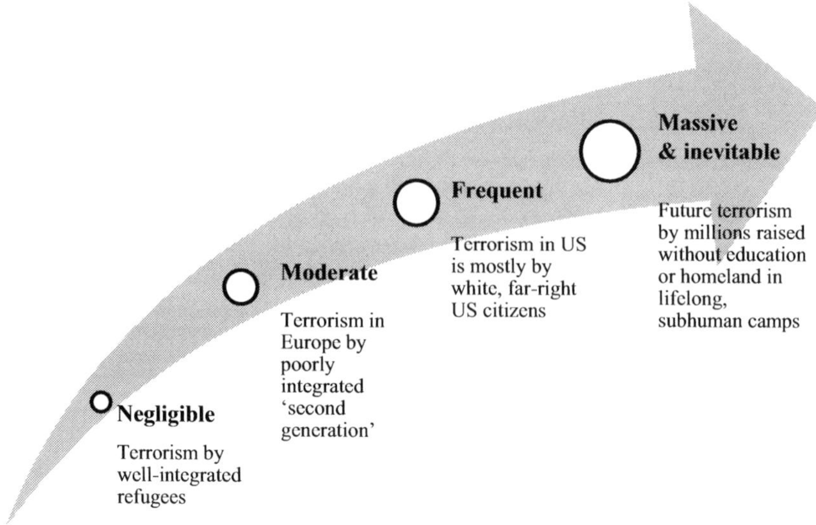
Massive
& inevitable
Future terrorism by millions raised without education or homeland in lifelong, subhuman camps
Frequent
Terrorism in US is mostly by white, far-right US citizens
Moderate
Terrorism in Europe by poorly integrated 'second generation'
Negligible
Terrorism by well-integrated refugees

**FIGURE 1.5** Curve of causal relationship between refugees and terrorism

arguments for and against resettling refugees: 'The small security risks of admission are outweighed by what is gained in promoting global peace and order'.[46]

The reality is that the largest costs of failure to manage refugee situations lie in our future, and they are still preventable. In our concluding chapter, we will look again at these issues of the future. But, by then, you will be equipped with all the tools and information you need to be actively part of the solution, rather than part of the problem. This introductory chapter has given you a glimpse of the prevalence, range and efficacy of applied oral history with refugees, and the surge of further innovations and applications ahead. By the end of this book, you will be qualified to dive in and participate in that work as fully as you wish, from wherever you are.

## References

Betts, Alexander, Bloom, Louise, Kaplan, Josiah and Omata, Naohiko, *Refugee Economies: Rethinking Popular Assumptions*. Oxford: Humanitarian Innovation Project, Oxford University, 2014.

Betts, Alexander, Bloom, Louise and Weaver, Nina, *Refugee Innovation: Humanitarian Innovation that Starts with Communities*. Oxford: Humanitarian Innovation Project, Oxford University, 2015.

Betts, Alexander, Kaplan, Josiah, Bloom, Louise and Omata, Naohiko, *Refugee Economies: Forced Displacement and Development*. Oxford: Oxford University Press, 2016.

Betts, Alexander and Collier, Paul, *Refuge: Transforming a Broken Refugee System*. London: Allen Lane, Penguin, 2017.

Betts, Alexander and Collier, Paul, 'A Self-Reliance Model for Refugees', *The Washington Post*, 18-6-2018 [Available at www.washingtonpost.com/news/theworldpost/wp/2018/06/18/refugee-camp/?noredirect=on&utm_term=.9affd129fe44; accessed on 21-6-2019].

Bloom, Louise, *Bottom-Up Humanitarian Innovation*. Oxford: Refugee Studies Centre, Oxford University, 2015.

Boochani, Behrouz and Sarvestani, Arash Kamali, *Chaukka, Please Tell Us the Time*. Einhoven: Sarvin Film Productions, 2017.

Boochani, Behrouz and Zable, Arnold, *Dialogue with Behrouz Boochani*. Melbourne: *NGV Triennial* digital project, University of Melbourne, 2017 [Available at www.ngv.vic.gov.au/exhibition_post/arnold-zable-dialogue-with-behrouz-boochani, 2017; accessed on 21-6-2019].

Boochani, Bherouz and Tofighian, Omid, *No Friend but the Mountains*. Sydney: Pan Macmillan, 2018.

Clemens, Greiner and Sakdapolrak, Patrick, 'Translocality: Concepts, Applications and Emerging Research Perspectives', *Geography Compass*, 7(5), 2013.

Collier, Paul, *The Bottom Billion: Why the Poorest Countries Are Failing and What Can Be Done about It*. Oxford: Oxford University Press, 2008.

Collier, Paul, *Exodus: How Migration Is Changing Our World*. Oxford: Oxford University Press, 2013.

Collier, Paul, *The Future of Capitalism: Facing the New Anxieties*. London: Penguin, 2018.

Cooke, Rachel, 'David Miliband: "We're Sitting on a Grenade with the Pin Pulled Out"', *The Guardian* online, 12-11-2017 [Available at www.theguardian.com/politics/2017/nov/12/david-miliband-book-rescue-refugees-political-crisis-interview; accessed on 21-6-2019].

Crone, Manni and Falkentoft Felicia, Maja, *Europe's Refugee Crisis and the Threat of Terrorism: An Extraordinary Threat?* Copenhagen: Danish Center for International Studies, 2017.

Curtis, Kimberley, 'The Need for a New International Agreement on Climate Refugees', *UN News & Commentary: Global News Forum*, 24-4-2017 [Available at www.undispatch.com/climate-refugees-explained/; accessed on 21-6-2019].

Dempster, Helen and Hargrave, Karen, 'Understanding Public Attitudes towards Refugees and Migrants', *Working Paper* No. 152, June 2017. London: Overseas Development Institute, 2017.

Donner, William and Rodriguez, Havidran, 'Disaster Risk and Vulnerability: The Role and Impact of Population and Society', *Population Bulletins*. Washington, DC: Population Reference Bureau, 2011.

Gatrell, Peter, 'What's Wrong with History?', *Journal of Refugee Studies*, 30(2): 170–189, 2017.

Hecker, Mark, '137 Shades of Terrorism: French Jihadists before the Courts', *Strategic Focus*, 79, April 2018. Paris: French Institute of International Relations, 2018.

'Humanitarian Innovation Project', website [Available at www.oxhip.org; accessed on 21-6-2019].

International Rescue Commission, *Towards a New Global Compact on Refugees: Early Lessons from East Africa*. New York: IRC, 2017 [Available at www.rescue.org/sites/default/files/document/1961/globalcompactearlylessonsandrecsseptember2017final.pdf; accessed on 21-6-2019].

Joyce, Foni, 'I Am Not Just a Refugee', *Welcome Stories*, Amnesty International website [Available at www.amnesty.org/en/i-welcome-community-2/stories-of-welcome/i-am-not-just-a-refugee; accessed on 21-6-2019].

King, Natasha, *No Borders: The Politics of Immigration Control and Resistance*. Chicago: University of Chicago Press, 2016.

McCoy, John, 'Hope and Hopelessness: Unraveling the Connections between Refugees and Terrorism', *Migration Views*. Edmonton: University of Alberta, 2015 [Available at http://migrationviews.ualberta.ca/john-mccoy-hope-and-hopelessness-unraveling-the-connections-between-refugees-and-terrorism/; accessed on 21-6-2019].

Miliband, David, *Rescue: Refugees and the Political Crisis of Our Time*. New York: Simon & Schuster, 2017.

Omata, Naohiko, 'Who Thrives, Who Struggles? Exploring the Determinants of Economic Success among Refugees', *Oxford University Press Blog*, 2017 [Available at www.rsc.ox.ac.uk/news/who-thrives-who-struggles-exploring-the-determinants-of-economic-success-among-refugees-naohiko-omata; accessed on 21-6-2019].

Pickett, Kate and Wilkinson, Richard, *The Spirit Level: Why Equality Is Better for Everyone*. London: Penguin, 2010.

Schmid, Alex, *Links between Terrorism and Migration: An Exploration*. The Hague: International Center for Counter-Terrorism, 2016.

Scriven, Kim, 'Humanitarian Innovation and the Art of the Possible', *Humanitarian Exchange*, 66, April 2016.

Simon, Scott, 'Helping Refugees Is the Test of Our Times, David Miliband Says', interview on NPR National Public Radio, 11-11- 2017.

Takizawa, Saburo, 'Pilot Refugee Resettlement Program: Japan Experience', *Focus*, 82, Dec 2015. Osaka: Asia-Pacific Human Rights Center, 2015.

Verme, Paolo and Schuettler, Kirsten, *The Impact of Forced Displacement on Host Communities: A Review of the Empirical Literature in Economics*. Washington, DC: World Bank Policy Research, 2019.

UNHCR, *Statistical Yearbook 2016*. Geneva: UNHCR, 2017a.

UNHCR, 'Figures at a Glance'. In *Statistical Yearbook 2016*. Geneva: UNHCR, 2017b [Available at www.unhcr.org/uk/figures-at-a-glance.html; accessed on 21-6-2019].

United Nations, 'Convention Relating to the Status of Refugees', *Treaty Series*, 189, p. 137. Geneva: United Nations, 1951.

United Nations High Commissioner for Refugees (UNHCR) Innovation Service, website [Available at www.unhcr.org/innovation; accessed on 21-6-2019].

## Notes

1 Behrouz Boochani and Arnold Zable, 'Dialogue with Behrouz Boochani', Melbourne: *NGV Triennial* digital project, University of Melbourne, 2017. Urls are given in this chapter's references.

2 United Nations (UN), 'Convention Relating to the Status of Refugees', *Treaty Series*, 189, p. 137. Geneva: United Nations, 1951.

3 United Nations High Commissioner for Refugees (UNHCR), 'Figures at a Glance'. In *Statistical Yearbook 2016*. Geneva: UNHCR, 2017b.

4 UNHCR, *Statistical Yearbook 2016*, 2017a.

5 Kimberley Curtis, 'The Need for a New International Agreement on Climate Refugees', *UN News & Commentary: Global News Forum*, 24-4-2017.

6 Alexander Betts, Louise Bloom and Nina Weaver, *Refugee Innovation: Humanitarian Innovation that Starts with Communities*. Oxford: Humanitarian Innovation Project, Oxford University, 2015.

7 Alexander Betts and Paul Collier, *Refuge: Transforming a Broken Refugee System*. London: Allen Lane, Penguin, 2017.

8 Betts and Collier, *Transforming*, 2017.

9 Kim Scriven, 'Humanitarian Innovation and the Art of the Possible', *Humanitarian Exchange*, 66, April 2016.

10 Paul Collier, *Exodus: How Migration Is Changing Our World*. Oxford: Oxford University Press, 2013.

11 Greiner Clemens and Patrick Sakdapolrak, 'Translocality: Concepts, Applications and Emerging Research Perspectives', *Geography Compass*, 7(5), 2013.
12 Foni Joyce, 'I Am Not Just a refugee', *Welcome Stories*, Amnesty International website.
13 You can see individuals' profiles and photos and contact them directly at http://iamnotarefugee.com.
14 See the clever design work behind the 'Refugee Flag' and hear the 'Refugee Anthem' at www.therefugeenation.com.
15 Peter Gatrell, 'What's Wrong with History?', *Journal of Refugee Studies*, 30(2), 2017.
16 David Miliband, *Rescue: Refugees and the Political Crisis of our Time*. New York: Simon & Schuster, 2017.
17 Humanitarian Innovation Project website home page.
18 Humanitarian Innovation Project website home page.
19 Alexander Betts and Paul Collier, 'A Self-Reliance Model for Refugees', *The Washington Post*, 18-6-2018; Betts and Collier, *Transforming*, 2017.
20 Naohiko Omata, 'Who Thrives, Who Struggles? Exploring the Determinants of Economic Success among Refugees', *Oxford University Press Blog*, 2017.
21 Betts and Collier, *Transforming*, 2017.
22 Gatrell, 'What's Wrong with History?', 2017.
23 Paolo Verme and Kirsten Schuettler, *The Impact of Forced Displacement on Host Communities: A Review of the Empirical Literature in Economics*. Washington, DC: World Bank Policy Research, 2019.
24 Alexander Betts, Louise Bloom, Josiah Kaplan and Naohiko Omata, *Refugee Economies: Rethinking Popular Assumptions*. Oxford: Humanitarian Innovation Project, Oxford University, 2014.
25 Betts, Bloom and Weaver, *Refugee Innovation*, 2015.
26 Betts, Bloom and Weaver, *Refugee Innovation*, 2015.
27 Natasha King, *No Borders: The Politics of Immigration Control and Resistance*. Chicago: University of Chicago Press, 2016.
28 Louise Bloom, *Bottom-Up Humanitarian Innovation*. Oxford: Refugee Studies Centre, Oxford University, 2015.
29 International Rescue Commission, *Towards a New Global Compact on Refugees: Early Lessons from East Africa*. New York: IRC, 2017.
30 Betts, Bloom and Weaver, *Refugee Innovation*, 2015.
31 International Rescue Commission, *Towards a New Global Compact*, 2017.
32 Alexander Betts, Josiah Kaplan, Louise Bloom and Naohiko Omata, *Refugee Economies: Forced Displacement and Development*. Oxford: Oxford University Press, (2016); and Betts, Bloom and Weaver, *Refugee Innovation*, 2015.
33 Kate Pickett and Richard Wilkinson, *The Spirit Level: Why Equality is Better for Everyone*. London: Penguin, 2010.
34 Saburo Takizawa, 'Pilot Refugee Resettlement Program: Japan Experience', *Focus*, 82, Dec 2015. Osaka: Asia-Pacific Human Rights Center, 2015.
35 Saburo Takizawa, 'Pilot Refugee Resettlement Program', 2015.
36 Paul Collier, *The Bottom Billion: Why the Poorest Countries Are Failing and What Can Be Done about It*. Oxford: Oxford University Press, 2008 and Paul Collier, *The Future of Capitalism: Facing the New Anxieties*. London: Penguin, 2018.
37 William Donner and Havidran Rodriguez, 'Disaster Risk and Vulnerability: The Role and Impact of Population and Society', *Population Bulletins*. Washington, DC: Population Reference Bureau, 2011.

38 Helen Dempster and Karen Hargrave, 'Understanding Public Attitudes towards Refugees and Migrants', *Working Paper* No. 152, June 2017. London: Overseas Development Institute, 2017.
39 Alex Schmid, *Links between Terrorism and Migration: An Exploration*. The Hague: International Center for Counter-Terrorism, 2016.
40 David Miliband, *Rescue*, 2017.
41 David Miliband, *Rescue*, 2017.
42 Rachel Cooke, 'David Miliband: "We're Sitting on a Grenade with the Pin Pulled Out"', *The Guardian* online, 12-11-2017.
43 Scott Simon, 'Helping Refugees Is the Test of Our Times, David Miliband Says', interview on NPR National Public Radio, 11-11- 2017.
44 Manni Crone and Maja Falkentoft Felicia, *Europe's Refugee Crisis and the Threat of Terrorism: An Extraordinary Threat?* Copenhagen: Danish Center for International Studies, 2017; and Mark Hecker, '137 Shades of Terrorism: French Jihadists before the Courts', *Strategic Focus*, 79, April 2018. Paris: French Institute of International Relations, 2018.
45 David Miliband, *Rescue*, 2017.
46 John McCoy, 'Hope and Hopelessness: Unraveling the Connections between Refugees and Terrorism', *Migration Views.* Edmonton: University of Alberta, 2015.

# 2

# THE IMPORTANCE OF LISTENING TO HOST COMMUNITIES

## Two Types of Host Communities, and Why We Must Listen to Their Concerns

So which countries and communities are actually hosting refugees? The stark answer – rarely conveyed by the media or politicians – is that 85% of the world's refugees are hosted long-term by the world's poorest countries, who are right now sharing with them the very little that they have. Despite recent hysteria over how many refugees wealthy Europe could afford to absorb, none of the eight countries hosting the most refugees are in the European Union. The reality is that for logistical reasons, 80% of all refugees settle in a country neighboring their own, rather than attempt the long journey to the West. Over half of the world's recent refugees poured out of just three desperate countries: Syria, Afghanistan and Somalia. And as the majority fled to neighboring areas, just eight countries – including some of the world's poorest – now host over half the world's refugees. Those eight are Turkey, Pakistan, Uganda, Lebanon, Iran, Jordan, Ethiopia and Kenya. Our case studies in Chapter 5 will look at applied oral history projects with host communities in several of them.

The figures above show how politics and the media can distort reality, with their bloated rhetoric about refugees flooding the West (often a camouflage for shifting economic policies to the right for reasons that have nothing to do with refugees). Wealthy, developed economies host only 15% of refugees while the world's poorest host 85% so there is a clear inverse relationship between countries' financial *ability* to help, and the numbers of refugees they actually host. The outcome of this is that there are two very different types of 'host communities' across the globe:

1. The poorest communities in the least developed economies, who host the most refugees but have the least resources to improve things, either for themselves or for refugees.

2. Western communities who proportionally host very few refugees, but whose leaders make most of the world's major policy and finance decisions about what is to be done for the world's refugees, now and in the future.

These Western 'host communities' in turn fall into two categories: residents of Western towns and regions that do receive noticeable numbers of refugees, and the majority of Western residents who have never met a refugee in person, as their region receives so few. Clearly, the material contact that these Westerners have with refugees couldn't be more different from that of the dirt-poor host communities crowded around the developing world's vast refugee camps. But, importantly, this book approaches them all as 'host communities', albeit of very different sorts. We argue here that in our rapidly shrinking global village, we are all necessarily 'hosts' to the 68.5 million displaced, whether we push them far away into another country or hold them close in our own. We will also argue that, for political reasons, the only way forward out of the world refugee crisis includes listening to and engaging with the concerns of *all* these different shades of 'host communities'.[1]

In Chapter 5's case studies, you will hear a lot more about the resistance and discontent emerging now from host communities in the poorest countries who were already destitute before vast numbers of refugees arrived to draw further on their impossibly meager resources. It's clear that the dynamic they are enduring is both unfair and dangerous, and needs to be addressed urgently. Chapter 5 will show you a range of case studies where applied oral history is successfully being used on the spot to help tackle this looming problem.

Meanwhile, this book argues that the vocal resistance of Western communities to refugees (even when their region accepts hardly any) is extremely important too, though for quite different reasons. One reason is that opportunist media and politicians are whipping it up into a form of right-wing politics that is becoming increasingly intolerant, towing behind it a far-right ideology that seems to be aspiring to become a mainstream fascism for the twenty-first century.[2] This book will show you how applied oral history can play its part in tackling this alarming drift, thus helping to protect and maintain the civil democracies that have taken centuries to become established in the West.

The other reason why we need to engage with Western populations' resistance to refugees is that, ironically, only those populations can solve the refugee crisis in the long-term. They can do this by choosing politicians who will take the practical, evidence-based actions that will actually calm the world refugee crisis and yield win/win outcomes for both refugees and host communities. Across this book you will see that those win/win solutions do exist, but they require the political will to implement them. As one United Nations High Commissioner for Refugees (UNHCR) director has put it, 'There are no humanitarian solutions to (these) humanitarian problems … The international community must stop using humanitarian action as a fig leaf for political inaction'.[3] In other words, humanitarian aid can only cushion the blows and try to pick up the pieces afterwards – it's not a solution. Only political decisions by governments, working together internationally, can stop the blows coming. So informing and reeducating the Western public on the truths around refugees is an indispensable step, in order for that political will to emerge. This means making clear to Western populations:

- the true facts about refugee numbers, and where they are hosted;
- how some media and politicians misrepresent those facts in order to manipulate the West's fears, emotions and voting patterns;
- the ideological reasons why they do this, and the future consequences of giving in to those ideologies.

Applied oral historians need to get to work listening to the masses who elect Western politicians, because those politicians wield most of the political and economic power on the world stage, and make the biggest decisions. This effectively means that every citizen of every free democracy is individually answering the 'refugee question' every day. The question is: '*Are we willing to share a small sliver of our resources with refugees now, in order to prevent worse outcomes for us all later?*' Citizens answer either by actively voting for politicians who have a specific policy on refugees, or passively accepting politicians whose refugee policies they don't agree with. The fact remains that in the future, when refugee numbers soar worldwide due to climate change (including in parts of developed countries that will become uninhabitable), everyone will be directly affected by the ensuing chaos and conflict if we don't all plan globally now for resourcing the climate refugees of the future near to their former homes.[4]

Also, even in the prosperous West it is unfair, undemocratic and dangerous to simply relegate host communities' concerns as 'anti-immigrant' or racist. The truth is that the resettlement of refugees does involve some sharing of public resources. But, in this book, you'll see innovative projects showing that that doesn't have to mean locals must lose out. Research shows that integrating refugees well can bring added material value to communities in the long run, enriching economies, labor markets and culture.[5] In terms of competition for jobs, it's true that refugees will seek work and further training. But if handled properly in the interests of *both* sides of the community, having more skilled people in work can boost local economies and development, generating yet more jobs. An increasing body of research now shows how refugees can be received in ways that can work well for all, economically and culturally. This means not isolating them, not refusing them work permits and not ignoring the resistance and concerns of locals – mistakes that many hosting governments tend to make at the moment.[6]

In terms of cultural values, it's also a justified concern in the West that some refugees may come from cultures whose values around gender, religion, sexuality or human rights are incompatible with those of the host country. But there are ways to address this. Refugees can be taught that the price of admittance and asylum is that they must observe the law of the land, and that in the West that includes respecting all the rights, freedoms and lifestyles that are protected by law there.[7]

There are important measures and explanations that can reassure host communities on these issues, and they have a right to hear those explanations in full. These issues need to be proactively managed by engaged, competent governments. Without hearing all the facts and necessary information, people cannot be expected to understand these dynamics, nor the solutions to them. (Examples of issues where this kind of mass reeducation and dialogue have been, or are being, successfully implemented include feminism, anti-smoking, HIV/AIDS, climate change, gay rights. Applied oral history has assisted constructively with all those public conversations too.)

Further below you will see that the past few years have seen some insightful oral histories done with anti-migrant communities in the West. But we urgently need many more. So the how-to section in the second half of this book explains how to get involved and contribute.

## The Spectrum of Political Reactions among Host Communities

You have seen above that the landscapes that the forcibly displaced have to make their way across are not just physical territories, but very much political ones too. Many of the features on the refugee landscape – routes, borders, points of admission or deportation – are political phenomena dictated by ideology and policy decisions, rather than by geography. So, before this book advances any further into this landscape of the displaced, we need to take a moment to consider the whole spectrum of political stances that host communities can take on the admittance of refugees. Figure 2.1 shows eight different shades of political ideology that are found across host communities worldwide. It can be useful to think of them as doors that are to various degrees open or shut: reading across the table's columns from left to right, you'll move from the most extreme '*Doors wide open to everyone*' position on the far left, to the '*Doors closed to everyone but ourselves*' position of ethno-nationalists on the far right. You will probably have heard most of these political positions expressed at some point, in some part of the media or in some shade of public opinion around you. And, almost inevitably, you will hold one of these positions yourself too. (And if you feel that you don't ascribe to any of them, that can be problematic as well, as we'll see below.)

Seeing these eight positions laid out across a political spectrum from the far left to the far right reminds you that:

- any given individual, media outlet, organization or nation state *anywhere* is likely to espouse one of these positions;
- the question of how to respond correctly to refugees is highly contested;
- even within households, people hotly debate the positions above, not to mind across whole swathes of the population in any given host country;
- you yourself probably hold one of these positions: it is important to be lucid and honest with yourself about which it is, before engaging with the work taught in this book.

| Political far left ⟵⟶ Political far right | | | | | | | |
|---|---|---|---|---|---|---|---|
| 'There should be **No Borders** for anyone, anywhere' | 'All migrants who can get here can stay, live off our social welfare system and **shouldn't be obliged to integrate'** | 'All migrants who get here can stay – but they must learn our language, earn their living and **must integrate'** | 'Only those **applying for political asylum** can come here' | 'Only those ***already* granted political asylum** can come here' | 'Only legally registered, pre-arranged, employed, tax-paying **economic migrants** can come here – no refugees or asylum-seekers' | **'No economic migrants,** even if legally registered and employed' | **'No immigrants at all,** whether economic or asylum-seeking, legally registered or not' |

**FIGURE 2.1** The spectrum of host communities' political positions on migration

In Chapter 6, on ethics and legalities, we will see that it is often important to keep one's political opinions to oneself while doing this work. But I believe it is also important to be honest with *yourself* internally about your own position on the spectrum above before you start. For instance, if you feel the compassionate urge towards the '*No Borders*' position, letting in all would-be migrants, you also need to think through and plan for what that would involve – namely, a very intense redistribution of resources in developed countries.[8] In order to avoid degrading the host society to become as chaotic as the one refugees were fleeing from, you would have to plan for managing all the effects of a '*No Borders*' influx, in terms of redistributing resources, law and order, the quality of public services when spread so much thinner, care of the collective environment, establishing shared cultural norms and civil society behaviors, and so on.

Economist Professor Paul Collier is one of the world's most authoritative advocates for the global poor: he works on behalf of the world's 'poorest billion', and on how best to redistribute the world's resources more equally to them. But after a lifetime of economic research in aid, development and critiques of capitalism, even he warns that the two extreme positions at either end of Figure 2.1 are equally unhelpful. In books like *Exodus: How Migration Is Changing Our World*, he examines the long-term future of the mass migration of economic migrants from the poorer southern hemisphere to the affluent north. And even though he is 'on the side of' the poor, he warns that *both* ideologies at either end of the spectrum above, if applied in practice, would only bring further problems to humanity overall, not solutions: he describes them as 'headless heart' on the left, and 'heartless head' on the right.[9]

From my own years working for city government, I know that the day-to-day reality of choosing policies and delivering public services imposes hard, complex, hands-on decisions about:

- how to distribute finite public resources in the most fair and effective ways;
- how to balance the competing needs, claims and worldviews of many stakeholders;
- how wide to cast the net of who you should serve, when your resources are finite (your own town, region or country? orphaned children everywhere? all humans equally?).

Once you have genuinely thought through all the real-life implications of each position on the spectrum in Figure 2.1, you may well feel that you just can't weigh up all the pros and cons enough to choose one position. That's fine too. What matters for the applied oral history work undertaken in this book is that you have some insight into the *claims* of each position.

In fact, one's own position may well shift around the spectrum a bit through doing this work. It can give you real-life exposure to – and even some empathy for – the views, needs and experiences of people in ideological positions quite different from your own. For instance, I originally came to this kind of work with an anti-racist, liberal, pro-migration position (not least because I was an economic migrant myself). But I then spent several years doing a job that required me to listen formally and deeply to the testimonies of white, underclass, anti-migrant communities in England. I never got to 'like' their culture or feel an affinity with it, but from hearing their concerns about migration diluting their access to jobs, public services and local culture, I gained some understanding of the reasonable needs and fears that drive some anti-migrant positions. Some of their fears are not unfounded, and have quite rational bases. It's just that much better solutions to those problems exist, rather than the ones served up to them by far-right, isolationist, anti-migrant ideologies that create more problems than they solve. This book provides a methodology for engaging in that conversation which, like all meaningful conversations, has to start with genuine listening.

As this book goes to print, Donald Trump is the US president, Britain is abandoning the European Union and far-right movements are on the rise all over the democratic world. We have seen that it would be genuinely dangerous, as well as unfair, to just bat away the concerns of populist voices in host communities as simply 'anti-migrant'. Instead, this book offers a methodology that can listen to and sift through host community resistance in order to locate the genuine grievances that need to be addressed, and separate them out from any racist elements. Part of our work as applied oral historians can be to intervene in that entanglement and unhook it, showing how reasonable fears and grievances are being hijacked by radicalizing forces. I believe you will be making an important contribution to world peace and equality by engaging in that work.

## Recent Oral Histories with Host Communities

Two very different streams of attention are starting to be given to host community concerns around the world. The primary, official approach is from high-level international aid organizations like the World Bank, the United Nations (UN, the European Union, the UK's Department for International Development and Oxfam. They are becoming aware of, and just beginning to address, the grievances of host communities in undeveloped economies where, as we have seen, some 85% of the world's refugees are hosted. For that purpose, these organizations have started to do some applied oral history listening to those host communities. In Chapter 5's case studies, we will see them doing these oral histories in several different ways so as to investigate (a) exactly what grievances these host communities have, and (b) how best to address them. But, understandably, rather than mainly doing oral histories, the primary action from those aid organizations at the moment is to just get on with trying to provide those host communities with the basic food, water, shelter and safety that they so often lack.

Meanwhile a very different, but potentially equally important, form of listening is being turned towards the grievances of host communities in the developed world. This is because, as we saw above, their opposition to refugees, asylum-seekers and other migrants tends to be driven and exploited by populist and far-right politics that are posing an increasing threat to democratic systems in the West.[10]

To try to respond to those dynamics, some – though as yet not nearly enough – applied oral history is starting to be done with these communities. In fact, claims and complaints around *lack of voice* and *not being heard* are absolutely central to the discontent expressed by these new populist masses. Members universally complain of having for a long time felt that they have not had a voice, have not been heard or listened to, and have felt invisible and ignored while other groups' voices were prioritized (those of the educated middle classes and of minorities).[11] And, remember, this is the domain of oral history par excellence: excluded groups' pleas to be listened to are something that oral history has traditionally been good at responding to in an organized, productive way. Granted, oral history has traditionally been more comfortable responding to that plea from excluded groups on the left. But I hope this book will convince you that it's important now to apply our oral history skills towards similar pleas from communities on the right too, even if some of them might feel less appealing to you. As one anthropologist doing this sort of work has put it, 'I do not know of any anthropology textbook that would imply one needs to like the people one studies'.[12]

And you will be in powerful company. The US Justice Department is not an agency that wastes time or money on frivolous, unnecessary activities. They recently commissioned independent experts to do in-depth oral history interviews with 89 former white supremacists. By achieving a high level of trust, safety and anonymity for the narrators, the resulting report was able to dig deep into profiling the psychological motivations and rewards that drive membership of white supremacist groups. Called *Addicted to Hate: Identity Residual among Former White Supremacists*, this important applied oral history report supplied the US Justice Department with guidelines towards preventing this sort of radicalization in the future.[13] In our Chapter 4 case studies, we will see another example where applied oral history is being used by specialized police as the core tool of a national anti-terrorism strategy.

Meanwhile the more public-facing oral history that has been done recently with the West's increasingly vocal populists has produced a swathe of mainstream, investigative books by concerned thinkers. These are by journalists, sociologists and politicians who have travelled through the West's white, populist communities and interviewed them in depth, trying to understand their perspective and meet it in a constructive way.[14] For instance, one did oral histories with 100 Trump voters, to try to understand why they voted for Trump despite believing, as they put it, that he 'could destroy the whole world'.[15] A range of authors from across the political spectrum have in this way produced works that you may find informative, even if you don't agree with the ideology of some of them. (It's worth noting the ideological position of the author before you read any of these works.)

For instance, these interviewers have included leftists sitting down to listen in depth to anti-migrant Westerners, in an effort to reduce the chasm that has opened up between these working people and the left-wing labor movements that used to represent them a few decades ago. Lauded examples that we will return to among our host case studies in Chapter 5 are *Strangers in Their Own Land: Anger and Mourning on the American Right* by US sociologist Arlie Russell Hochschild and *The Politics of Resentment: Rural Consciousness in Wisconsin and the Rise of Scott Walker* by Katherine Cramer – the result of almost a decade of listening closely to political attitudes among those who are now Trump voters.[16] Another example was the television documentary series *Travels in Trumpland* by left-wing British politician Ed Balls, who spent time listening to voters in Trump's heartland, trying to understand their motivations.

Other leftists have looked back, using interviews to try to trace where progressive and left-wing movements went wrong and lost the allegiance of the white working classes in developed economies.[17] An example is Jeff Sparrow in Australia who wrote *Trigger Warnings: Political Correctness and the Rise of the Right*. Another is North American oral historian and labor activist Stephen High, with his profound listening to the losses and disillusionments of those workers in books like *The Deindustrialized World: Confronting Ruination in Postindustrial Places*. Justin Gest has also listened to and published about what he calls *The New Minority: White Working-Class Politics in an Age of Immigration and Inequality*.

Meanwhile, centrist and moderate right-wingers concerned about their constituents' drift towards the far right, have also been listening critically to populist voters.[18] Examples include *The Road to Somewhere: The Populist Revolt and the Future of Politics* by David Goodhart or the slightly more controversial *Whiteshift: Populism, Immigration and the Future of White Majorities* by Eric Kauffman. Centrist think tanks like the American Council on Foreign Relations have looked on with anxious interest, broadcasting public debates on 'The Rise of Global Populism'.[19] And the International Strategy and Diplomacy wing of Britain's top political science school, the London School of Economics and Political Science, has issued a *Strategic Update* on 'Understanding the Rise of Global Populism'.[20]

Aside from the populist oral testimonies that the diverse authors above have gathered from ordinary people, it is important to be aware too of core far-right thinkers who give voice to and promote the key narratives that have been taken up by 'their' people and movement. An example of one of these seed ideas or motifs of the new far right is the concept of *The Great Replacement*, the title of a book by Frenchman Renaud Camus in 2012.[21] It crossed into the German and Dutch languages as a conspiracy theory among far-right European groups. The 'Great Replacement' theory is the belief that white, working-class Europeans are being deliberately 'reverse-colonized' by migrants of color who will outnumber and displant them. Subscribers believe this is a strategy designed and implemented by the West's liberal elites. This is one reason for their recent rejection of liberal political leaders in favor of populist nonprofessionals like Donald Trump or Volodymyr Zelenskiy. Zelenskiy is a comedian who was recently elected as President of Ukraine, having previously acted the role in a television series.

Aided by the internet, seed ideas like the 'Great Replacement' have travelled like a meme or a virus across the language barriers of developed economies in recent years. By 2017 the originally French concept had become the rallying cry of American neo-Nazis shouting '*You will not replace us!*' at their demonstration that turned murderous in Charlottesville, Virginia. Since then, by travelling inside the white supremacist culture, journalist Glenna Gordon produced the important oral history project *American Women of the Far Right*. For a year, in 2017, she moved carefully through the far-right networks of the US, interviewing in depth two dozen women who hold leadership and campaigning roles in 'The Movement', as they call it. As Gordon wittily puts it:

> It is a universal truth that women's work is seldom recognized. But failing to acknowledge women's part in sustaining white supremacy is not just sexist; it's a dangerous mistake. For every media report about a white male terrorist who is portrayed as a 'lone wolf' or a 'madman', there are untold stories about the women who provide support for, nurture, and connect these groups and individuals.[22]

Intelligence agencies have long known that women play fundamental, willing and active roles in sustaining extremist networks, from the white supremacy movement to Islamic Jihadism. As one female counter-terrorism expert has put it: 'In reality, when it comes to joining violent extremist causes, women are susceptible to the very same processes as men: narratives, ideology, grievances, and various push and pull factors'.[23]

Finally, a moving crop of first-person life stories has been published by a range of what you might call ambivalent 'innocents' who were born and raised into alienated, sub-working class, white cultures but escaped them by accessing a wider education. A famous recent example in the US is *Hillbilly Elegy: A Memoir of a Family and Culture in Crisis* by J.D. Vance, who tries to reveal and explain the frustrations of his loved ones who are still sunk within that deprived culture.

And such a voice from Europe is the more controversial young French memoirist Édouard Louis. His books, *The End of Eddy*, *History of Violence* and *Who Killed My Father?*, give truly harrowing life-story accounts of growing up in the deindustrialized, white, underclass subculture in France. Voices like his are complicating our traditional, politically correct ideas about which group has been treated as the 'outsider', left behind and excluded. Compared to any other social class, minority or incomer in their country, Louis' homebred underclass would argue that they feel crushingly oppressed and excluded. The voice of Renaud Camus, writing *The Great Replacement* in French in 2012, had shouted out violently in protest against the influx and rise of other groups such as feminists and ethnic minorities. But the voice of Édouard Louis is a non-simplistic counterpoint, conveying his community's anguish without directing his anger against other minorities. (Essentially, his anger flies above race, gender and sexual orientation to accuse the economic inequalities that he sees as being imposed by the political ruling classes.)

The voices of Vance and Louis are not *oral* history. They didn't wait to be interviewed by oral historians – they found their way to being self-articulated voices in the life-story or memoirist tradition. But I recommend that you keep their voices in mind if you do go interviewing Western host communities who are resistant to refugees. Your narrators may be feeling similar things, without having the education, self-reflection or eloquence of a Vance or a Louis to articulate them.

## How This Book Enables You to Engage with Host Communities

A great deal of oral history has been done with refugees, and relatively little with host communities. This book aims to show you that doing more applied oral history with hosts (as well as with refugees) is an unavoidable step for resolving the refugee crisis into the future. So, as well as equipping you to work with refugees, this book's oral history methodology can also be used to engage with all the different levels of host community mentioned in this chapter. The method can be used by:

- professionals delivering services to refugees in camps or processing centers in developing countries, who have to mediate with host communities who feel their own limited resources are threatened;
- anyone doing applied oral history with a Western host community where comparatively small numbers of refugees have been resettled;
- anyone doing applied oral history on the subject of refugees with any Western community, even if there are no refugees in their region at the moment.

With all these different kinds of 'host communities', you can use this method to:

- engage hosts to understand refugees' issues more accurately (and vice versa, if you work with refugees too);
- affect public opinion;

- affect the refugee policies demanded by voters in host communities;
- help ensure that host communities' reasonable concerns are heard and addressed;
- help ease the reception and integration of refugees in host communities, as a win/win that gives better outcomes for both sides.

Our next chapter will give a brief survey of the century-old tradition of oral histories with refugees. It doesn't address host community oral histories because, by comparison, they are only beginning to be done. But Chapter 5's case studies will bring you as many oral histories with host communities as Chapter 4 does with refugees. The majority will be with host communities in developing countries, as they host most of the world's refugees. We include just a few case studies with host communities in the West, as not many of those have been done yet. But I believe they will be inspiring enough to make you want to do some.

As you know, the second half of the book is then a step-by-step manual equipping you to do oral history projects of your own with either refugee or host communities. Some of that practical guidance is generic, applying to oral history fieldwork with either community. And some sections address needs, risks, requirements or opportunities that are specific to working either with refugees or with hosts.

## References

Altman, Sam, '100 Trump Voters Explain Why They Voted for Him Even though They Think He "Could Destroy the Whole World"', *Business Insider* online, 23-2-2017 [Available at http://uk.businessinsider.com/sam-altman-interview-trump-supporters-2017-2; accessed on 21-6-2019].

Anderson, Carol, *White Rage: The Unspoken Truth of Our Racial Divide*. New York: Bloomsbury, 2016.

Balls, Ed, *Travels in Trumpland*. London: BBC TV, 2018.

Balz, Dan and Rucker, Philip, 'An Oral History of 2016: How Donald Trump Won: The Insiders Tell Their Story', *The Washington Post* online, 9-11-2016 [Available at www.washingtonpost.com/graphics/politics/2016-election/how-donald-trump-won-the-inside-story/; accessed on 21-6-2019].

Betts, Alexander, Kaplan, Josiah and Omata, Naohiko, *Refugee Economies: Rethinking Popular Assumptions*. Oxford: Humanitarian Innovation Project, Oxford University, 2014.

Betts, Alexander, Kaplan, Josiah, Bloom, Louise and Omata, Naohiko, *Refugee Economies: Forced Displacement and Development*. Oxford: Oxford University Press, 2016.

Camus, Renaud, *You Will Not Replace Us!* Plieux: Chez l'Auteur, 2018.

Collier, Paul, *The Bottom Billion: Why the Poorest Countries Are Failing and What Can Be Done about It*. Oxford: Oxford University Press, 2008.

Collier, Paul, *Exodus: How Migration Is Changing Our World*. Oxford: Oxford University Press, 2013.

Collier, Paul, *The Future of Capitalism: Facing the New Anxieties*. London: Penguin, 2018.

Council on Foreign Relations, 'The Rise of Global Populism', a debate by Berman, Sheri, Gest, Justin and Luce, Edward, online, 30-10-2018 [Available at www.realclearpolitics.com/video/2018/10/30/council_on_foreign_relations_panel_the_rise_of_global_populism.html; accessed on 21-6-2019].

Cox, Michael, 'Understanding the Rise of Global Populism', LSE Ideas, *Strategic Updates*. London: London School of Economics and Political Science, 2018.

Cramer, Katherine, *The Politics of Resentment: Rural Consciousness in Wisconsin and the Rise of Scott Walker*. Chicago: University of Chicago Press, 2016.

Dempster, Helen and Hargrave, Karen, *Understanding Public Attitudes towards Refugees and Migrants*. London: Overseas Development Institute, 2017.

Gest, Justin, *The New Minority: White Working-Class Politics in an Age of Immigration and Inequality*. Oxford: Oxford University Press, 2016.

Goodhart, David, *The Road to Somewhere: The Populist Revolt and the Future of Politics*. London: Hurst, 2017.

Gordon, Glenna, 'American Women of the Far Right', *New York Review of Books* online, 13-12-2018 [Available at www.nybooks.com/daily/2018/12/13/american-women-of-the-far-right; accessed on 21-6-2019].

High, Steven, MacKinnon, Lachlan and Perchard, Andrew, editors, *The Deindustrialized World: Confronting Ruination in Postindustrial Places*. Vancouver: University of British Columbia Press, 2018.

Isenberg, Nancy, *White Trash: The 400-Year Untold History of Class in America*. New York: Viking, 2016.

Jones, Reece, *Violent Borders: Refugees and the Right to Move*. London: Verso, 2017.

Kauffman, Eric, *Whiteshift: Populism, Immigration and the Future of White Majorities*. London: Allen Lane, 2018.

King, Natasha, *No Borders: The Politics of Immigration Control and Resistance*. London: Zed Books, 2016.

Kuhn, David Paul, *The Neglected Voter: White Men and the Democratic Dilemma*. New York: St. Martin's Press, 2007.

Louis, Édouard, *The End of Eddy*, translated by Michael Lucey. London: Harvill Secker, 2017.

Louis, Édouard, *History of Violence*, translated by Lorin Stein. New York: Farrar, Straus and Giroux, 2018.

Louis, Édouard, *Who Killed My Father?*, translated by Lorin Stein. London: Harvill Secker, 2019.

Malik, Nikita, 'Why Do We Underestimate the Role of Women in Terrorist Organizations?', *Forbes* online, 26-9-2018 [Available at www.forbes.com/sites/nikitamalik/2018/09/26/why-do-we-underestimate-the-role-of-women-in-terrorist-organizations; accessed on 21-6-2019].

Miller, Todd, *Storming the Wall: Climate Change, Migration and Homeland Security*. San Francisco: City Lights, 2017.

Pasieka, Agnieskza, 'Anthropology of the Far Right: What if We like the "Unlikable" Others?', *Anthropology Today*, 35(1), Feb 2019.

Russell Hochschild, Arlie, *Strangers in Their Own Land: Anger and Mourning on the American Right*. New York: The New Press, 2016.

Schmid, Alex, *Links between Terrorism and Migration: An Exploration*. The Hague: International Center for Counter-Terrorism, 2016.

Simi, Pete, Blee, Kathleen, DeMichele, Matthew and Windisch, Steven, 'Addicted to Hate: Identity Residual among Former White Supremacists', *American Sociological Review*, 8(6): 1167–1187, 2017.

Sparrow, Jeff, *Trigger Warnings: Political Correctness and the Rise of the Right*. Victoria: Scribe, 2018.

Tan, Vivian, 'Ogata Calls for Stronger Political Will to Solve Refugee Crises', *News* UNHCR online, 25-5-2005 [Available at www.unhcr.org/uk/news/

latest/2005/5/4297406a2/ogata-calls-stronger-political-solve-refugee-crises.html; accessed on 21-6-2019].

Vance, J.D., *Hillbilly Elegy: A Memoir of a Family and Culture in Crisis*. New York: HarperCollins, 2016.

## Notes

1 Helen Dempster and Karen Hargrave, *Understanding Public Attitudes towards Refugees and Migrants*. London: Overseas Development Institute, 2017.

2 Katherine Cramer examines this phenomenon, as do many other publications cited in this chapter's references. Katherine Cramer, *The Politics of Resentment: Rural Consciousness in Wisconsin and the Rise of Scott Walker.* Chicago: University of Chicago Press, 2016.

3 Vivian Tan, 'Ogata Calls for Stronger Political Will to Solve Refugee Crises', *News* UNHCR online, 25-5-2005. Urls are given in this chapter's references.

4 Todd Miller, *Storming the Wall: Climate Change, Migration and Homeland Security*. San Francisco: City Lights, 2017.

5 Alexander Betts, Josiah Kaplan, Louise Bloom and Naohiko Omata, *Refugee Economies: Forced Displacement and Development*. Oxford: Oxford University Press, 2016.

6 Alexander Betts, Josiah Kaplan and Naohiko Omata, *Refugee Economies: Rethinking Popular Assumptions.* Oxford: Humanitarian Innovation Project, Oxford University, 2014.

7 Alex Schmid, *Links between Terrorism and Migration: An Exploration*. The Hague: International Center for Counter-Terrorism, 2016.

8 Reece Jones, *Violent Borders: Refugees and the Right to Move*. London: Verso, 2017; Natasha King, *No Borders: The Politics of Immigration Control and Resistance*. London: Zed Books, 2016.

9 Paul Collier, *The Bottom Billion: Why the Poorest Countries Are Failing and What Can Be Done About It*. Oxford: Oxford University Press, 2008.

10 This is examined by Eric Kauffman, as well as by other titles in this chapter's references. Eric Kauffman, *Whiteshift: Populism, Immigration and the Future of White Majorities.* London: Allen Lane, 2018.

11 Nancy Isenberg, *White Trash: The 400-Year Untold History of Class in America*. New York: Viking, 2016; David Paul Kuhn, *The Neglected Voter: White Men and the Democratic Dilemma*. New York: St. Martin's Press, 2007.

12 Agnieskza Pasieka, 'Anthropology of the Far Right: What If We Like the "Unlikable" Others?', *Anthropology Today*, 35(1), Feb 2019.

13 Pete Simi, Kathleen Blee, Matthew DeMichele and Steven Windisch, 'Addicted to Hate: Identity Residual among Former White Supremacists', *American Sociological Review*, 82(6), 2017.

14 Dan Balz and Philip Rucker, 'An Oral History of 2016 -: How Donald Trump Won: The Insiders Tell Their Story', *The Washington Post* online, 9-11-2016.

15 Altman, Sam, '100 Trump Voters Explain Why They Voted for Him Even though They Think He "Could Destroy the Whole World"', *Business Insider* online, 23-2-2017.

16 Citations for all works named in this section are given among this chapter's references.

17 Paul Collier, *The Future of Capitalism: Facing the New Anxieties*. London: Penguin, 2018.

18 Carol Anderson, *White Rage: The Unspoken Truth of Our Racial Divide*. New York: Bloomsbury, 2016.

19 Council on Foreign Relations, 'The Rise of Global Populism', a debate by Sheri Berman, Justin Gest and Edward Luce, online 30-10-2018.

20 Cox, Michael, 'Understanding the Rise of Global Populism', LSE Ideas, *Strategic Updates*. London: London School of Economics and Political Science, 2018.

21 Renaud Camus, *Le Grand Remplacement*, Plieux: Chez l'Auteur, 2012; Renaud Camus, *You Will Not Replace Us!* Plieux: Chez l'Auteur, 2018.

22 Glenna Gordon, 'American Women of the Far Right', *New York Review of Books* online, 13-12-2018.

23 Nikita Malik, 'Why Do We Underestimate the Role of Women in Terrorist Organizations?', *Forbes* online, 26-9-2018.

# 3

# THE TRADITION OF ORAL HISTORY WITH REFUGEES, AND HOW IT'S RADICALLY CHANGING

> There was a woman with an infant in her arms who was killed as she touched the flag of truce, and the women and children were strewn all along the circular village until they were shot. Right near the flag of truce, a mother was shot down with her infant. The child, not knowing that its mother was dead, was still nursing and that especially was a very sad sight. The women, as they were fleeing with their babies, were killed together – shot right through – and the women who were very heavy with child were also killed.
>
> All the Indians fled in three directions. After most all of them had been killed, a cry was made (by the US Army) that all those who were not killed or wounded should come forth and they would be safe. Little boys who were not wounded came out of their places of refuge, and as soon as they came in sight a number of soldiers surrounded them and butchered them there.

This is an oral history of the massacre of Native American refugees at Wounded Knee in 1839. It was told by a Lakota man named American Horse at the court of the Commissioner of Indian Affairs in Washington, and typed by the court stenographer as he spoke. This opening example, an eyewitness oral history from the 'Trail of Tears', is challenging to read.[1] But it's here to show you that refugee oral history *really* matters, and that it's been having an impact in court and on policy for a long time already. In this chapter, you'll see that noble tradition undergoing a surge of new creativity and applications now. We'll overview the evolution of oral history as a tool for working with refugees, from traditional to more recent approaches. We'll explore the important methodological differences between oral histories with refugees, and other types of interviews with them. And you'll see the new techniques that are publicizing and communicating the content of cutting-edge refugee testimonies today – from those produced by refugee children through therapeutic play, to lavish feature films and high-tech digital mapping of refugees' accounts of their journeys across continents.

## A Century of Tradition, and Changing Fast

First, let's overview the grand sweep of the tradition as it's been practiced for more than a century. Figure 3.1 gives us a bird's eye view of how, since the nineteenth century, oral history has responded to the experience of 'refugeedom', as if running alongside it, trying to keep up with its twists and turns.[2] You'll see that right from its beginnings in the nineteenth century, oral history with refugees was often already 'applied'. In the example that opened this chapter, it was used in a nineteenth-century court to help decide legal judgments and reparations. So 'applied' oral history with refugees is also a long and respected tradition, not some new or untested invention.

| Era studied | *Sample oral histories from major refugee groups* | Done by whom, when, using what method? |
|---|---|---|
| Late C19 | **Native Americans displaced by the American Indian Wars** | |
| | *Family Stories from the Trail of Tears* by George Foreman, 1937 [1] | By ethnographers visiting Indian Reservations; traditional oral histories with survivors many years later |
| Early C20 | **2 million Russian Jews displaced by pogroms, 1880-1920** | |
| | *A Whole Empire Walking - Refugees in Russia during World War I* by Peter Gatrell, 1999 | By an academic historian in long retrospect; using library research and oral histories with long-settled descendants |
| 1940s | **60 million people displaced by World War 2** | |
| | *Shoah Foundation*: 115,000 hours of oral history videos online, started in 1994 | Often done in long retrospect, with elderly survivors recalling childhood memories; innovates with artificial intelligence, projecting holograms that the audience can 'converse' with |
| | **15 million displaced by partition of India & Pakistan, 1947** | |
| | *The 1947 Partition Archive*: over 4,300 interviews with survivors of Pakistan's Partition | By oral historians and volunteers; partly crowdfunded; done in long retrospect; begun in 2010, published in 2017 and only in part, due to political sensitivities |
| 1970s | **2 million displaced by Cambodian Khmer Rouge & US-Vietnam war, 1970-75** | |
| | *'Survivors of Genocide – Cambodian Genocide'* by Baylor University's Institute for Oral History | By academics; oral history videos done in long retrospect in 2015, with elders long resettled in the US |
| 1990s | ***A trend: Oral historians interviewing refugee groups long settled in host societies*** | |
| | *'Polish Migration to Britain - War, Exile and Mental Health'* by Michelle Winslow, 1999 | Done in retrospect by academics and oral historians, with resettled refugees and their descendants |
| 2000s | ***A trend: Methodological questioning on how best to do oral history with migrants & their sub-groups*** | |
| | *Oral History with Migrants*, special issue of *Oral History Society* journal, 2008 | Methodological reflections on how to do oral history with migrants & specific demographics among them, e.g. women |
| 2010s | ***A trend: Oral history with climate refugees to improve policies around climate-change*** | |
| | *Moving Voices – The Voices of People who Move in the Context of Climate-Change* by Randall, Salsbury & White, 2014 | By refugee policy professionals, to help design global, future-oriented policy strategies around climate change |
| | **5.4 million Palestinians still displaced** | |
| | *'Speaking back to a world of checkpoints - Oral history as a decolonizing tool in the study of Palestinian refugees'* by Mette Lundsfryd, 2017 | Interviews with Palestinian refugees about borders (being enclosed by them/banned from them/crossing them, etc.); part of awareness-raising on behalf of the Palestinian cause |
| | **Biggest world refugee crisis to date, with human smuggling & trafficking as a major business** | |
| | *Cast Away - Stories of Survival from Europe's Refugee Crisis* by Charlotte McDonald-Gibson, 2016 | Done with refugees en route, in dangerous settings as they migrate illegally |
| | *Exodus – Our Journey to Europe* by BBC TV, 2016 | Uses lightweight, cheap recording technologies to capture live, first-person footage amidst trauma |
| 2016 | **13.5 million Syrians forcibly displaced** | |
| | The *Syrian Oral History Project* by International Coalition of Sites of Conscience, 2016 | By a worldwide network of 'places of memory', against 'the pressure to forget… in order to ensure a more just and humane future' [2] |
| 2018 | **5 million displaced in Latin America** | |
| | *'The Politics of Resettlement: Expectations and Unfulfilled Promises in Chile and Brazil'* by Marcia Espinoza, 2018 | Interviews with long-term Colombian refugees, on their disappointment with their resettlement situation in neighboring countries |

**FIGURE 3.1** The tradition of refugee oral history, and its evolving methods

In Figure 3.1, the left columns briefly summarize over a century of major refugee populations: Native Americans displaced in the nineteenth century; Jews fleeing the 1940's Holocaust; the expulsion of five million Palestinians left stateless to this day; 13 million Syrians and five million Latin Americans displaced in recent years. Refugee history is indeed a growing 'Trail of Tears'. The table gives you an example of a famous oral history project about each era, and the column on the right shows the different methodologies used to produce them. The table also highlights some major trends in the way oral history has approached refugees in recent decades.

In terms of methodologies used, you will see that some of the oral histories cited, like the Native American one, were recorded verbatim from an eyewitness. Others – like Peter Gatrell's 1999 study of Russian refugees displaced almost a century before his time – were done in distant retrospect, more than a lifetime after the events occurred, by piecing together written archives, old recordings and interviews with descendants.[3] Some of the projects in this table had massive funding, like Steven Spielberg's Shoah Foundation whose oral history videos would take 13 years to watch in full. Others, like those produced by refugee children through play and games, cost almost nothing to produce. First, read down through the table, which will bring you right up to the present day. Then we'll examine the table's overview, before looking ahead to the remarkable bursts of innovation that are working with refugee oral histories today.

## The World's Political Responses to Refugee Populations

Politically, it had been hoped that World War II would be 'the war to end all wars'.[6] Unfortunately, local conflicts continued to proliferate across the 1950s and 1960s, causing mass displacement of civilians. But journalists increasingly travelled abroad to those conflict zones, and their frontline reports drew new attention onto the plight of civilians caught up in armed conflicts.[7] Under this global scrutiny, 1951 and 1967 saw new international legislation governing the rights and settlement of refugees.[8] And Refugee Studies emerged as a formal discipline – one that used oral history as a tool from the beginning. Across the next two decades, the combined efforts of policy professionals, academics, international lawyers and governments caused policies on assisting refugees to become more standardized internationally. This was real progress – an example of the more global approaches to governance and rights that were able to emerge in the second half of the twentieth century.[9]

Before the Middle Eastern refugee crisis of 2015, the only other really big obstacle to progress on refugees had been the 70-year impasse around the fate of 5.4 million Palestinian refugees displaced by Israel's occupation of their territory.[10] 75% of the world's Palestinians have been displaced for decades, and about 33% of all those in the world who have refugee status are Palestinians, a fact rarely mentioned in Western media.[11] In 2005 the UN confirmed that 'by far the most protracted and largest of all refugee problems in the world today is that of the Palestine refugees, whose plight dates back 57 years'.[12] Although the occupation of Palestinian territory is illegal under international law, most governments fail to challenge Israel about it.[13] Nonetheless, a law book published by Cambridge University Press in 2018 reaffirmed again that, legally, there is 'an overwhelming (and rare) international legal consensus that the territories are occupied, that the law of belligerent occupation applies, and that the settlements are illegal and indeed constitute a grave breach of the Geneva Convention IV'.[14] Already, back in 1990, the *American Journal of International Law* had confirmed that 'the view that the fourth Geneva Convention is applicable, and should be applied, in all the territories occupied by Israel in 1967 has been very widely held internationally. Indeed, a remarkable degree of unanimity prevails on this matter.'[15]

In 2018, the United Nations Assembly formally voted again

> to continue to exert all efforts to promote the realization of the inalienable rights of the Palestinian people, including their right to self-determination, to support the achievement without delay of an end to the Israeli occupation that began in 1967, and of the two-State solution on the basis of the pre-1967 borders.[16]

Since 1949, a distinct branch of the United Nations (UN) has existed to assist Palestinian refugees, separate from the United Nations High Commissioner for Refugees (UNHCR) that serves all other refugees.[17] The United Nations Relief and Works Agency for Palestine Refugees (UNRWA) was created in 1949 as a temporary agency to assist Palestinians who had just been expelled from their homeland. It was never expected that their statelessness could last so long. But as the UN puts it, 'in the absence of a solution to the Palestine refugee problem, the General Assembly has repeatedly renewed UNRWA's mandate' to this day.[18]

It is no coincidence that the world's two longest displaced refugee populations – the Palestinians and the Tibetans – were displaced with relative impunity by two of the world's most influential governments.[19] But in the past few years, solutions to refugee crises have stalled in other ways too. One roadblock emerged in 2015 when civil wars in the Middle East and Africa produced the largest numbers ever displaced on the planet.[20] In fact, local civil wars have turned out to be the biggest obstacle to modern peace. Often a legacy left behind by colonial occupiers, civil wars tend to be the hardest to resolve, and are the greatest producers of refugees today. As one expert puts it, 'wars within states tend to last longer than wars between them'. These civil wars have 'tended to last three times longer in the second half of the twentieth century than in the first half – and are much more prone to recur than any others'.[21]

In 2015, with the unprecedented influx of refugees escaping Middle Eastern conflicts, even the close-knit states of the European Union began to disagree about shared policies on, and responsibilities for, refugees. The topic has since proved a rich breeding ground for populist politics. As this book goes to print in 2019, whole populations of those war-torn refugees are still making multistage journeys across multiple countries, living for years at a time in vast camps, urban and rural.[22]

Meanwhile, a triple refugee crisis has unfolded across Latin America in the past few years, driven by a mix of extreme violence and economic collapse in Venezuela, Colombia and Central America. (42 of the world's 50 most violent cities are in Latin America.) And the continent's refugee crisis is predicted to worsen in the year ahead, with the UN estimating that over five million Latin Americans will be displaced by 2020.[23] Ironically, Venezuela – now exporting millions of starving refugees of its own – was in the twentieth century a welcoming flagship destination for refugees.[24] One of the first countries to support the International Refugee Organization (precursor of the UNHCR), Venezuela was 'a magnet for migrants and a poster child for successful integration', welcoming tens of thousands of European refugees after World War I.[25] In fact, Latin America has a history of openness and integration towards refugees, and has done its best to absorb its own internally displaced people in recent years as well. But with resources cracking and populist politicians stoking resistance, its current refugee crisis is threatening to destabilize the region.

With murder rates in Central America among the region's highest ever, the number fleeing northward for their lives has increased ten times over in the past five years. As one report puts it, 'the combination of weak state institutions, corruption, organised crime, extreme social inequality and violence is an explosive cocktail'.[26] It has given rise to the phenomenon of the human 'caravan', where displaced populations now self-organize to march en masse towards borders that they aspire to cross without permission. Providing mutual assistance and some 'safety in numbers', these marches are highly mediatized spectacles, providing rich fodder for both the pro- and anti-migration media. In November 2018, the largest to date, organized by '*Pueblo Sin Fronteras*' ('Village Without Borders'), swelled to about 5,000, marching ten abreast and stretching for almost a mile. It was an iconic sight that we can expect to see much more of in the future, when the numbers of climate change refugees surge around the world.[27] Meanwhile, under the populist policies of President Donald Trump, the US continues to tighten its asylum and immigration conditions against them.

But, as one commentator warned ominously, 'should Venezuela's neighbors buckle under the pressure, vulnerable Venezuelans will have no choice but to potentially travel across Central America, Mexico, and onto the United States in search of safety'.[28] And, in fact, we see that desperate people will travel much farther than that. In a single month in mid-2019, over 500 fleeing Africans – mainly from the war-torn Democratic Republic of Congo and Angola – decided not to attempt the usual Mediterranean crossing to Europe which was by then becoming even more heavily policed and dangerous. Instead, they carved out a new refugee escape route all the way to the US, to request asylum there. They made an illegal journey of over 8,000 miles to South America, then up through Central America and Mexico, and on to their destination over the US border in Texas.[29]

## Who Is Interviewing Refugees, and How?

We saw in the previous chapter that a wide spectrum of different professions are sweeping in to provide a broad range of services to these unprecedented masses of refugees around the world. Just to help them do their jobs, many of those professionals are now seeking the applied oral history skills taught in this book. Oral history is booming as a tool that can capture and publicize refugee experiences and needs on the road.

But before we, as oral historians, ever meet refugees, they are already being processed along a conveyor belt of other professional interviewers. Border police, immigration officials, lawyers, doctors, social workers, camp administrators, psychologists, journalists, anthropologists – they all have their own interview methods that are central to their work with refugees. Although they supplement with other methods, these professionals must begin their contact with refugees by interviewing them, in order to start establishing things such as:

- the facts of a refugee's identity, origins and 'backstory', to help decide what level of assistance they have a legal right to;
- an individual refugee's level of resources (e.g. their current income and assets; their education and skills; their ability to join the host-country's labor market, etc.);
- a refugee's level of need (e.g. any medical conditions or disabilities; any vulnerabilities such as experience of torture or history of mental illness, etc.).

Those professionals need to question (and even cross-examine) a refugee to verify his or her individual circumstances and origins. By contrast, our applied oral history questioning has a wider lens, eliciting refugees' end-user experience, insights and embedded knowledge about how the whole process of settling and integrating refugees could be done better.

But as well as differences in content and purpose, there are also crucial methodological differences between oral history interviews and those done by other professionals. In my opinion, no other discipline deploys all four of the *Golden Pillars* that guarantee the integrity of the oral history method. As shown in Figure 3.2, these pillars are:

1. genuine power-sharing in the interview process;
2. transparent publishing and public archiving of all transcripts;
3. a thorough framework of ethical protections for narrators at all stages;
4. some ownership of the finished products and positive outcomes for narrators.

Among the other professions doing interviews – from police, lawyers and journalists to doctors, social workers and anthropologists – some do maintain *some* of these *Four Golden Pillars* (for instance, by doing interviews that are empathic, are for the public good rather than for profit, and are published). But no other technique of qualitative interviewing maintains all four, which are all fundamental to oral history. For instance, doctors' interviews do not power-share to the extent that oral historians' interviews do. And both journalists and anthropologists interview for their own purposes, which are often not fully disclosed to their narrators. These types of interviewers later draw up their own theories and conclusions from their background interviews (often unattributed) to publish in their own name as part of their own career path, without transparently publishing or archiving the original interviews that they feel they used as a springboard for their conclusions. This is quite unlike the oral history method, where ownership, attribution, transparency and control of the material are much more rigorous.

These *Four Golden Pillars* or quality standards are maintained across all properly done oral histories today. But apart from maintaining these core ethical standards, you'll see that oral history projects with refugees can vary enormously in other ways. To help you navigate through the diversity of oral histories being done with refugees now, Figure 3.3 lists ten criteria that will help you to categorize and situate them. These are common-sense questions of the sort that you might instinctively ask about any cultural product or event you come across in everyday life, from a television advertisement to a street demonstration: 'Who has organized and funded this? What's their identity and background? What's their intended purpose or message?'

By posing the ten basic questions listed in Figure 3.3, you can neatly map out the roles and identities, scale and purpose of any given refugee oral history. (These

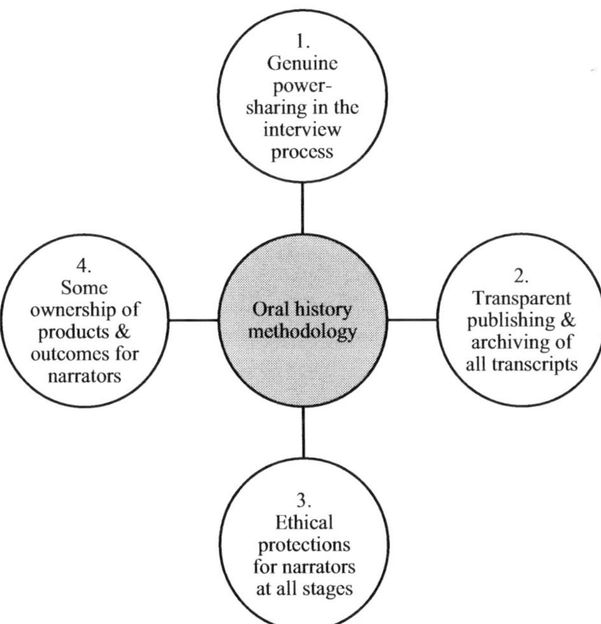


**FIGURE 3.2** The *Four Golden Pillars* of the oral history method[30]

| ← | → |
|---|---|
| ***Time*** – How close to the event was the interview done? | |
| On the spot, as it happened, or shortly afterward | Retrospectively, long after the events that are being described |
| ***Place*** – Where was the interview done? | |
| In the field or 'on the go', amidst the trauma of flight | In a 'safe' and 'neutral' setting, far removed from danger and conflict |
| ***Voice*** – Who is narrating? | |
| First-hand account | Second-, third- or even fourth-hand account, e.g. as passed down through a family |
| ***Identity*** – Who is interviewing? | |
| Someone connected to the refugee population, or themselves a refugee | An outsider in relation to this refugee population |
| ***Status*** – Who is funding and approving? | |
| Done independently or informally, with little or no funding | A well-funded project by an official authority or institution |
| ***Scale*** – How many interviews? | |
| Half a dozen local interviews, or a once-off interview with a single narrator | A major national or international project with hundreds or even thousands of interviews |
| ***Medium*** – Old or new methods, elaborate or simple? | |
| Multi-media, digital & online; high-tech film or 'low-tech' mobile phone footage | Interviews typed on paper in an archive |
| ***Purpose*** – Intended audience and outcomes | |
| As a campaigning tool, for action against an ongoing injustice | As 'pure history', preserved for the record |
| ***Impact*** – Effect of the interview on you as audience | |
| Highly impactful; makes you want to take some action as a result | Low impact; doesn't feel particularly relevant to you, nor make you feel you want to '*do*' anything about it |
| ***Training*** – Done by trained oral historians or not? | |
| By people new to oral history | By trained, qualified oral historians |

**FIGURE 3.3** *Ten Variables* in the methodology of refugee oral histories

questions can also be usefully applied to any type of oral history but they are especially important around refugee oral histories, where variables like the *Time*, the *Voice*, the *Purpose* and the *Impact* of the project can produce dramatically different results.)

Note that none of these *Ten Variables* is a value judgment on the quality or importance of a given oral history project or interview. For instance, don't assume that well-funded projects done by highly qualified oral historians for prestigious institutions are always the best. Some of the most widely broadcast and politically influential refugee oral histories have been recorded by utterly *unfunded* refugees on their own mobile phone while narrowly escaping drowning at sea.[31] So the *Ten Variables* below each have their own merits. But to orient yourself among the shifting sands of today's refugee oral histories, it is important to be aware of these methodological differences, and the impacts they can have. The near-drowning example above is an extreme one: remember that for each question in Figure 3.3, any given project may also lie somewhere along the middle of the spectrum, not necessarily at either end. And, obviously, any given project's answers to the ten questions is likely to 'zigzag' down between the two columns, rather than fitting neatly into one column all the way down.

## Publicizing Refugee Oral Histories through the Arts

The number of oral histories with refugees is mushrooming, and they are being captured in all the ways listed in Figure 3.3. As refugee voices have multiplied, so too have the ways of hearing and communicating them, leaking out into the media, the blogosphere, technology and the arts.[32] This explosion of creative expression, pulling in so many 'civilians' previously uninvolved with refugees, is happening because:

- the sheer number of refugees in the world has soared in recent years;
- vivid media coverage has made it a problem that people globally are aware of;
- it's an emotive, heartrending plight that many in society feel called to respond to, as it could happen to anyone;
- once resettled, refugees may live around us in our own societies;
- even if no refugees live near us, our fellow citizens often have strong views on the subject;
- debates over refugees have become something of a political 'football'.

These factors have resulted in a plethora of artistic adaptations of refugees' oral histories. For instance, theatre groups of settled or asylum-seeking refugees are turning their own oral histories into improvised plays that they perform in public street-spaces. This can be therapeutic for refugees, helping them to express traumatic experiences in cathartic, productive ways. It also empowers the host community to witness things from the refugees' perspective.

This kind of theatre takes refugees' oral testimonies into theatre workshops, transforming them into scripts to be performed for audiences as a play. It is known either as 'testimonial theatre' (which mainly uses oral histories) or 'verbatim theatre (which uses oral histories only, nothing else). As one commentator has put it,

> over the past two decades verbatim theatre has come to occupy a central place on the British stage, and is seen as one of the most incisive forms of political theatre. It has moved from the fringes to the mainstream, with some of the highest profile theatres staging verbatim plays.[33]

The work may be a collaboration between theatre professionals in the host community and incoming refugees who are new to theatre. But some is created and performed entirely by refugees, trained up by fellow refugees who were theatre professionals back home. Such plays may be performed in closed workshops, or may be performed semi-improvised by refugees in the street to catch the interest of passersby in the host community.

Some are taken on formal tours as part of the official repertoire in the city theatres of the host community. For instance, *REACT* (‘*Refugee Engagement and Integration through Community Theatre*’) is a partnership between theatre groups around Europe – ‘a community theatre program for refugees to share their stories with host communities’.[34] Some of its theatre troupes have specialized in particular demographics, for example such as creating plays from the oral histories of refugee women in asylum detention centers, helping them to rebuild the sense of self that they lost first through the Rwandan genocide and then through detention in Britain.[35] Women refugees’ oral histories have also been turned into a cutting-edge play performed by refugee actors for theatre audiences in the British host community. The play, called *Rule 35*, is named after a British law that prohibits particularly vulnerable individuals like torture survivors from being incarcerated in harsh detention centers that can further damage their mental and physical health. Performed by refugee women detainees whose oral histories produced the script, it exposes the British government’s failure to apply its own rule. One host community reviewer described it as ‘vital subject matter, in an extremely powerful format and performance. I am in awe of the refugee women bringing this performance to people – committing to educate others when they have experienced this trauma themselves.’[36] In fact, this sort of refugee theatre is being used all over the world to help reach out and build bridges of understanding and dialogue with host communities. As one academic impact study put it, refugee theatre gives refugees the chance to be ‘seen to be doing something positive within the wider community, to be contributing to, and benefiting, community life … It is hard to hate someone who has made you laugh, or whose story has brought you to tears’.[37]

As you will see in the many examples below, graphic novels, cartoons and puppet shows have followed suit. As relatively inexpensive media that can be produced in private, they allow individuals – whether refugees or artists in the host community – the space to retell their own and others’ stories with some distance and hindsight. These malleable, playful media also allow haunting, traumatic emotions to be engaged with and shared in ways that are touching or even entertaining, without being overwhelming for either the narrator or the audience.

It’s not only the modes of expression for refugee testimonies that are rapidly transforming, but also the refugee demographics who are doing the telling. Increasingly, oral testimonies by refugee children are emerging in formats from games to animation films that the children help to make. Adolescent refugee girls from home cultures where they had no public voices at all are now using multimedia to express their aspirations and demand their human rights. An example is teenager Rahaf Mohammed al-Qunun, who posted her own testimonies on social media to escape her family’s repressive approach in Saudi Arabia, and as a result was granted asylum by Canada in 2019.[38] Meanwhile, refugee oral histories are also being used therapeutically by psychologists and psychiatrists, to help rebuild broken life narratives and nurture recovery from deep traumas such as torture.[39] This is highly specialized work that we will look at more closely in the next chapter.

Among the arts, film is always a powerful, high-status medium, though expensive to produce to a high standard and broadcast widely. But refugees' stories have gradually climbed the 'status ladder' of the arts, to be depicted now in lavishly produced feature films. One of the most daring collaborations was the sophisticated, award-winning BBC film *Exodus: Our Journey to Europe*, whose Syrian refugee star, Ahmad al-Rashid, kindly offered advice for this present book. The film – hypnotically watchable and artistically elegant – was co-produced with refugees using mobile phone footage self-filmed by them during their dangerous escape journeys. Another example is *Human Flow*, the evocative feature film made by the world-famous Chinese artist and refugee, Ai Weiwei. Filmed across one year and 23 countries, it captures 'both the staggering scale of the refugee crisis and its profoundly personal human impact'.[40]

Figure 3.4 shows how refugee oral histories are being told and retold through a huge range of creative media. Further below we will look at an example from each of these art forms. If you have any interest in the arts yourself, even as a hobby, why not use this kaleidoscope of examples to trigger ideas for artworks you could make yourself, or enable others to make, using refugee oral histories or testimonies as your source material?

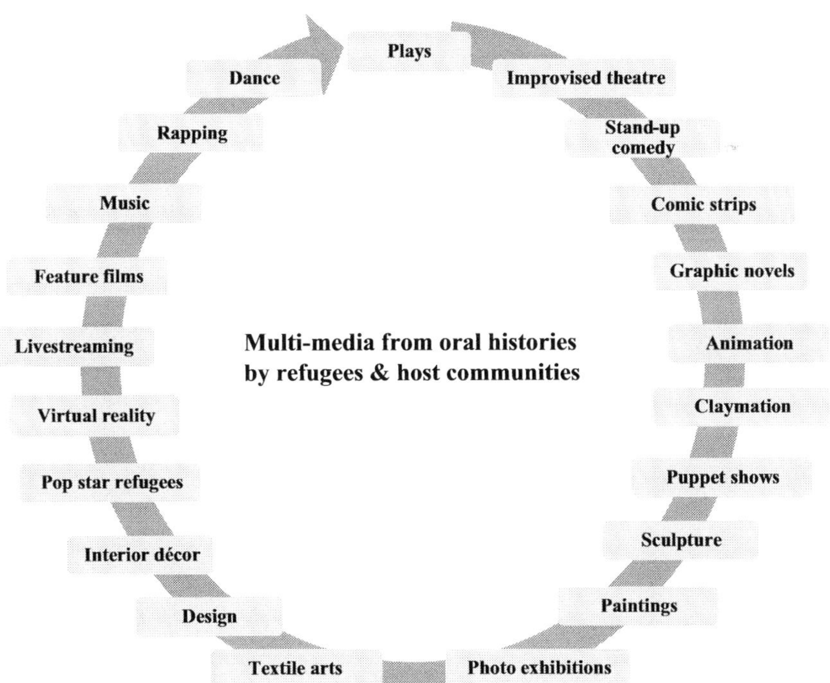


**FIGURE 3.4** Arts and multimedia publicizing refugee oral histories

As we go on now to survey the wheel of creative expressions in Figure 3.4, it's worth noting:

- how these arts present and re-express refugee oral histories in *very* diverse ways, yet without losing the integrity or authenticity of the original accounts;
- that they come from extremely diverse locations and refugee demographics – from every continent, and from refugee children, teens, women and men from dozens of nationalities and backgrounds;
- that they make creative play with the very notion of *voice*.

In these artworks, refugee voices initially speak and host communities listen. But host artists and audiences also respond and react, creating a spiral of mutual self-expression. Who is expressing themselves here, and to whom? In the examples below, you will see that the boundaries become creatively blurred into rich call-and-response dialogues between refugees and host communities.

### *Plays: with Somali Women Refugees in the UK*

In what's called 'Playback Theatre', actors perform or 'play back' the oral histories that refugees have entrusted to them. Professor Nira Yuval-Davis has done this with Somali women refugees to help them reconstruct their sense of identity.[41]

### *Improvised Theatre: with Middle Eastern Refugee Actors in Berlin, Germany*

The Exil Ensemble – all refugee actors from Middle Eastern countries – perform their play *Winter Journey*: it enacts real-life bus journeys that they made through Germany's winter landscapes and shows how *they*, the refugees, perceive this alien place and their encounters with its natives.[42]

### *Stand-Up Comedy: by a Vietnamese Refugee Who Is a Popular Professional Comedian in Sydney, Australia*

Anh Do, already a famous comedian in Australia, went on tour with his sellout stand-up show *The Happiest Refugee: Live*, adapted from his own life history and his feature film of the same name.[43]

### *Comic Strips: with a Young Eritrean Refugee Woman in the UK*

*Journey: Helen's Story* is a nonfiction comic strip telling the oral history of one young refugee, as she confided it to the organization Women for Refugee Women. It is published as part of *ILLEGAL*, the next art form on our list.

## *Graphic Novels: Telling the Story of a Refugee Child's Journey across Africa to Europe*

*ILLEGAL: One Boy's Epic Journey of Hope and Survival* is a graphic novel for children by a world-famous team of comic writers, based on refugee children's real-life oral histories.[44]

## *Animation: with Child Refugees in the UK*

On its website the British Refugee Council hosts three beautifully drawn animated films that tell the stories of refugee children in their own words. You can view them at www.refugeecouncil.org.uk/animation.

## *Claymation: with 13 Refugee Pupils from Seven Countries, all Resettled in Australia*

*Ali and the Long Journey to Australia* is a charming 'claymation' film using little hand-formed clay figures who act out the story. The refugee children drew on their own life stories to compile the plot of 10-year-old Ali's search for safety.[45]

## *Puppet shows: with Syrian Refugee Children in the Camps in Lebanon*

Syrian refugee and former teacher Jassem uses puppets to bring his country's rich oral history heritage to life for Syrian child refugees in the camps in Lebanon, many of whom have no memory of home. (Lebanon shelters almost a million registered refugees from Syria's conflict, more than half of them children.[46])

## *Sculpture: by Refugee Children in the Camps of South Africa*

'The World in a Suitcase' is a formal art-therapy process, facilitated by psychologists, where refugee children first take their own personal oral history and then design, adapt and decorate their own portable suitcases to express and carry that story. An impact assessment report found that 'the process measurably improved the children's mood, motivation and organizational skills'.[47]

## *Paintings: with Syrian Child Refugees in Beirut, Lebanon*

Syrian child refugees first recalled their own life histories. They then turned these into poems, which also expressed their greatest wishes or longings. Lebanese artists interpreted each poem, depicting each one back as a painting. The children co-presented the resulting art exhibition, entitled *Longing*.[48]

### Photo Exhibitions: by Refugee Children in Camps in Namibia, Africa

The UNHCR's online photo exhibition *Do You See What I See?* got refugee children in the camps photographing their own lives and environment, so as to 'see refugee life through the voices and visions of children, who are experts on their own lives'.[49]

### Textile Arts: by Palestinian Women Refugees in the United Arab Emirates

Palestinian refugee craftswomen were invited to take their own oral histories and express these life stories and feelings through textiles. They created the exhibition *Standing Tall*, a parade of beautiful, totemic figures the size of real women, made from handwoven textiles and embroidery.[50]

### Design: by Refugees with Asylum in Amsterdam, Holland

'Makers Unite' – an incredibly creative network of refugees – make new designer objects from the discarded orange and black lifejackets of seafaring refugees! Supported by IKEA, they sell online their genuinely elegant range of bags, laptop bags and iPad pouches, as well as little freestanding flagpoles that will sit on your desk and fly the international 'Refugee Flag' designed by the collective – an orange flag with a black stripe that honours the memory of seafaring refugees and others. (You can browse their beautiful products at www.makersunite.net.)

### Interior Décor Installation: with a Syrian Refugee Family, by the Red Cross and IKEA in Oslo, Norway

IKEA Norway visited and did an oral history interview in situ with a family of Syrian refugees internally displaced in Syria, surviving inside the bare shell of a bombed-out building. Back home in Oslo, IKEA painstakingly reconstructed an exact replica of the 25-metre-square interior that the family were surviving in. It was presented as an awareness-raising installation alongside IKEA's usual furniture showrooms in Oslo. 40,000 people visited the installation, whose fundraising netted £19 million for Syrian humanitarian relief.[51]

### A Pop Star's Refugee Oral History: with Rita Ora, one of Britain's Leading Pop Stars

The *Traces Project* interviews a range of famous artists in the UK who all previously arrived in the country as refugees. Placed along an online chronological timeline showing their dates of arrival, the interviews include the testimony of pop star Rita Ora from *The Voice* television show. She arrived in the UK as a young child refugee from Kosovo.[52]

### *Virtual Reality Holograms: with Jewish Refugees Who Escaped the Nazis*

The Shoah Foundation in New York runs *Dimensions in Testimony*, a display of interactive, life-like holograms who tell the oral histories of Holocaust survivors but can also converse with the audience, answering individual questions on the spot.[53]

### *Livestreaming: Refugee Journeys Livestreamed by an IT Company in Helsinki, Finland*

Data company Lucify use data gathered by the UNHCR to constantly broadcast online a moving pictogram showing the 'live' traffic flows of refugees whose testimonies show they are currently moving to specific European countries.[54]

### *Film: with a Teenage Girl Refugee in El Salvador, Central America*

*Los Comandos* is a prizewinning film that uses one girl's oral history to show how gangs' gun violence obliged her to flee alone, becoming part of the unaccompanied minors refugee crisis.[55]

### *Music Classes: by a Congolese Refugee Seeking Asylum in Nairobi, Kenya*

Using borrowed and rented instruments, refugee Eric Museveni created a music school that now teaches 40 refugees plus three Kenyans from the host community.[56]

### *Rapping: by a Teenage Syrian Refugee in Greece, with a YouTube Celebrity in Bangalore, India*

Indian YouTube star Wilbur Sargunaraj's rap video 'Migrants' features teenage Syrian refugee rapper Tamman in situ in Greece: they sing and rap together in a rhyming fundraising song that tells the story of being a refugee. It is melodic, catchy and humorous.[57]

### *Dance: with Refugees in Camps in the Democratic Republic of Congo*

Funded by the UNHCR with the NGO 'African Artists for Development', dance company Kongo Drama delivered a program called 'Refugees on the Move' in a camp of more than 16,000 refugees. Refugees and host communities were facilitated to express their frustrations by choreographing and dancing out their own life stories. The project measurably reduced violence within the camps and boosted dialogue between refugees and host community neighbors.[58]

## The Tech Industry's Innovations with Refugees' Oral Histories

If the arts world has been so proactive in engaging with refugee oral histories, the technology community hasn't been left behind either. With witty slogans like '*Let's Tech the Borders Down*', they too are increasingly involved with refugees' life stories. Some affluent, global-minded young tech entrepreneurs are taking on the challenge of the refugee crisis, much as Bill Gates did with the problem of world poverty at the turn of the millennium, using the first wave of tech wealth. For instance the online network *Startups Without Borders* describe themselves as 'the ecosystem for migrant and refugee entrepreneurs'.[59] And *Techfugees* is a community of over 18,000 tech innovators around the world who are now tackling refugee issues through their own projects, inventors' competitions, social media and events. Over 500 attended their recent Global Summit on all the potential uses of technology to help forcibly displaced people.[60]

Industry magazine *TechCrunch* ran a recent feature on '25 of the most innovative new projects using tech to help refugees'.[61] They include various technologies that use refugees' oral testimonies to channel practical help back to them. For instance, in Montreal, refugee youth learned employable digital skills while telling their own stories online about the difficulties of integrating.[62] Meanwhile, in the space of 24 hours, the Twitter hashtag *#SaveRahaf* raised 27,000 followers for the oppressed Saudi teenage girl whom we mentioned earlier, who had temporarily escaped from her family's compound and was pleading for international help online. It was bloggers' retweeting of her testimony that enabled her to be rescued by the UNHCR, and to go on to receive asylum in Canada.

In the next chapter you'll see another example of IT in action for refugees, where a technology professor first amassed refugees' accounts of their journey routes, and then created an online resource giving practical, logistical help to the subsequent refugees who would follow along those routes. That work is part of a new, interdisciplinary academic field called Digital Migration Studies, which examines migration through the lens of IT. One of their research articles explains how IT has transformed migration processes, and migration has in turn reshaped the use of IT: 'Top-down management of migration flows and border control is increasingly dependent on digital technologies and datafication, while from the bottom-up migrants use smart phones and apps to access information, maintain transnational relations, establish local connections and send remittances.'[63]

Meanwhile, a casual social encounter led Danish IT technicians David and Christopher Mikkelsenng to hear firsthand the oral testimony of one Afghan refugee who described the pain of losing touch with his loved ones during his escape journey. The brothers decided to help him find his family. But they also did a lot more. From that experience, they learned that one of the most acute distresses for refugees is when loved ones get separated and lose contact in the course of refugee journeys. This causes a triangular anguish of disconnect between those still in transit, loved ones settled ahead of them in host countries and those left behind at home. So the brothers set up a website and phone hub where refugees can provide details about the person they have lost contact with, and can easily search for each other on there.[64] Today, with over a million registered users, *Refunite* is the world's largest missing persons' platform for refugees and displaced populations.[65] As the hub grew in effectiveness, tech and phone companies came on board to sponsor it. *Refunite* has now reconnected over 600,000 refugees with lost loved ones. This is an example of something really practical and helpful that members of a host community were able to do, after first listening to refugees' oral accounts of what was distressing them most.

For instance, five-year-old Rahma had gotten separated and left behind when her family fled Somalia for a refugee camp in Kenya. But with neighbors' help she survived, and 22 years later she herself fled to a Kenyan refugee camp. Hearing about the *Refunite* database, she used her mobile phone to search it for her father and brother, with whom she had had no contact in 22 years. Finding several people with her brother's name and age, she texted them all. Within five hours, she had an answer back from her brother! Long settled with political asylum in the US, her brother and father had registered a search for Rahma on *Refunite* a year earlier. As *Refunite* put it: 'Within 24 hours, she was speaking on the phone with her father, brother, and three sisters. Given 22 years of silence and uncertainty, her father could not believe she was still alive.'[66]

In fact, many refugee oral history projects have now discovered that the need to stay connected online and by mobile phone is central to the refugee journey.[67] Without hearing this directly from them, we might have assumed that Wi-Fi connections were the least of people's worries when running for their lives – but we'd have been wrong. When refugees are ripped from their home environment and forced to flee elsewhere, they are projected into a world of solely *virtual* connections. In fact, recent oral histories done by the official refugee agencies have discovered that 'mobile phone and internet access are as critical to refugees' safety and security as food, shelter and water'.[68] In fact, refugee oral histories on the subject have shown interviewers that mobile phones and Wi-Fi are their only means of:

- getting information on where and how to travel: transport options; border routes they can pass through; bus, ferry or train times; contacts with people smugglers; weather conditions en route; political or military conflicts erupting en route, etc.;
- staying in touch with those they have left back home, for mutual reassurance that both parties are safe, and to receive or send funds if that's an option;
- knowing what to do when they arrive in a host country: getting information on its refugee processes, legal rights and police procedures; making applications for aid, asylum, healthcare and housing; finding schooling for children and language classes for all ages; accessing services and opportunities to find work or training.

Now we see why the UN has found that 'a third of refugees' disposable income is often spent on staying connected'.[69] It's clear that the potential for wealthy tech companies to help is almost limitless. Simply providing mobile phone and wifi coverage to refugee camps and centers wouldn't make much of a dent in their vast profits. And many networks of IT professionals are already helping, as we have just seen.

Meanwhile, out on the frontline of refugees' actual journeys, personal technologies worn on the body are now enabling first-person oral testimonies to be videoed and broadcast from extreme, life-threatening situations. Online footage, social media and mobile phone videos produce a sort of amateur reportage that is supplementing the work of mainstream news companies. But, unfortunately, in this post-truth era of fake news, even 'social media becomes weaponized', as explained by war journalist Lyse Doucet in her BBC film *Syria: The World's War*. She has explained how in recent years in conflict zones, social media and amateur reportage

> increasingly became a battleground, each side accusing the other of falsifying evidence and presenting their own version of the truth. Footage taken by activists is now manipulated and used as evidence by conspiracy theorists and those who seek to discredit the mainstream media.[70]

As we saw earlier, this is why the *Four Golden Pillars* of the oral history method have become increasingly valuable. Being accessible, affordable and adaptable, oral history is being sought out now as a reliable, reputable methodology that can be deployed by any professional or volunteer for the public good. In Chapter 6 we will carefully explore the ethical and legal underpinnings of doing oral history with refugees or host communities. But first, Chapters 4 and 5 will show you a panoramic range of successful case studies with them from around the world.

## References

ACTA Community Theatre, 'Refugee Engagement and Integration through Community Theatre', Brussels: Creative Europe, Refugee Integration Projects, European Union, 2016 [Available at www.creativeeuropeuk.eu/funded-projects/refugee-engagement-and-integration-through-community-theatre-react; accessed on 21-6-2019].

Alfakih, Fidaa and Kabbara, Khaled, 'Puppet Show Teaches Syrian Refugee Kids Their Heritage', UNHCR website, 22-8-2018 [Available at www.unhcr.org/news/stories/2018/8/5b7d304a4/puppet-show-teaches-syrian-refugee-kids-heritage.html; accessed on 21-6-2019].

Annas et al., *Ali and the Long Journey to Australia: Noble Park Primary School & TRUST Project*. Tampere, Finland: University of Tampere, 2017 [Available at www.theguardian.com/world/2018/jun/19/refugee-childrens-story-turned-into-a-heartwarming-claymation-video2017; accessed on 21-6-2019].

Armitage, David, *Civil Wars: A History in Ideas*. New Haven: Yale University Press, 2017.

Bahar, Dany, 'Why It Matters that We Call Fleeing Venezuelans Refugees, Not Migrants', *Foreign Affairs* online, 23-10-2018 [Available at www.foreignaffairs.com/articles/venezuela/2018-10-23/latin-america-facing-refugee-crisis; accessed on 21-6-2019].

Bannon, Brendan, *Do You See What I See? Photographic Collections for UNHCR*, on Flickr website [Available at www.flickr.com/photos/unhcr/collections/72157617167524699/2018; accessed on 21-6-2019].

BBC News Online, 'Rahaf al-Qunun: Saudi Teen Refugee Arrives in Canada', online, 12-1-2019 [Available at www.bbc.co.uk/news/world-us-canada-46851723; accessed on 21-6-2019].

BBC2 TV, *Exodus: Our Journey to Europe*. London: BBC, 2016.

Ben Naftali, Orna, Sfard, Michael and Viterbo, Hedi, *The ABC of the OPT: A Legal Lexicon of the Israeli Control over the Occupied Palestinian Territory*. Cambridge: Cambridge University Press, 2018.

Boyd, Doug and Larson, Mary, editors, *Oral History and Digital Humanities: Voice, Access and Engagement*. New York: Palgrave Macmillan, 2014.

Cantrell, Tom 'Verbatim Theatre', *Drama Online* website [Available at www.dramaonlinelibrary.com/genres/verbatim-theatre-iid-2551; accessed on 21-6-2019].

Clacherty, Glynis, 'The World in a Suitcase: Psychosocial Support Using Artwork with Refugee Children in South Africa', *Participatory Learning and Action*, 54:121–127, April 2006.

*Climate Migration* and *Climate Outreach* websites [Available at http://climatemigration.org.uk/testimonies-climate-migration/and https://climateoutreach.org/purpose; both accessed on 21-6-2019].

Colfer, Eoin, Donkin, Andrew and Rigano, Giovanni, *Illegal: One Boy's Epic Journey of Hope and Survival*. London: Hodder, 2017.

Commissioner of Indian Affairs, *Report of the Commissioner of Indian Affairs for 1891*. Washington, DC, 1891. Vol. 1, pp. 179–181 [Available at www.pbs.org/weta/thewest/resources/archives/eight/wklakota.htm; accessed on 21-6-2019].

Community Arts Northwest website, 'Rule 35: A New Provocative Show about the British Detention System', 2015 [Available at http://can.uk.com/2015/02/05/rule-35-new-provocative-show-british-detention-system-sat-28-march-z-arts and http://can.uk.com/current-artistic-programme/exodus/refugee-womens-theatre-programme/rule-35; both accessed on 21-6-2019].

Dekker, Rianne, Engbersen, Godfried, Klaver, Jeanine and Vonk, Hanna, 'Smart Refugees: How Syrian Asylum Migrants Use Social Media Information in Migration Decision-Making', *Social Media & Society*, 4(1), Jan-March 2018, online, 20-3-2018.

Dekker, Stefanie, 'Haneen: Exhibition of Syrian Children's Longings in War', *Al-Jazeera* online, 23-2-2018 [Available at www.aljazeera.com/news/2018/02/haneen-exhibition-syrian-childrens-longings-war-180223151650843.html; accessed on 21-6-2019].

Deng, Boer, 'Africans Trek to Texas as Med Grows Too Dangerous', *The Times*, 15-6-2019.

Department of Sound Records, Imperial War Museum, *Britain and the Refugee Crisis, 1933–1947*. London: Imperial War Museum, 1982.

Do, Ahn, *The Happiest Refugee*. Crow's Nest, Australia: Allen & Unwin, 2011.

Doucet, Lyse and Roudin, Michael, *Syria: The World's War*. London: BBC TV, 2018.

Dunsky, Marda, *Pens and Swords: How the American Mainstream Media Report the Israeli–Palestinian Conflict*. New York: Columbia University Press, 2008.

Espinoza, Marcia Vera, 'The Politics of Resettlement: Expectations and Unfulfilled Promises in Chile and Brazil'. In *Refugee Resettlement: Power, Politics, and Humanitarian Governance* (pp. 223–243), edited by Adele Garnier, Liliana Jubilut and Kristin Bergtora Sandvik. New York: Berghahn, 2018.

Findley, Paul, *They Dare to Speak Out: People and Institutions Confront Israel's Lobby*. Chicago : Chicago Review Press, 2003.

Foreman, Grant, editor, 'Family Stories from the Trail of Tears: Life and Experience of a Cherokee Woman'. In *Indian-Pioneer History Collection*. Little Rock : American Native Press Archives, 1937 [Available at https://ualrexhibits.org/tribalwriters/artifacts/Family-Stories-Trail-of-Tears.html#LifeAndExperience; accessed on 21-6-2019].

France 24 TV, The Observers, 'No, Journalists Did Not Stage These Images to Draw Sympathy for Migrants', online, 27-8-2018 [Available at https://observers.france24.com/en/20180827-debunked-media-stage-video-migrants; accessed on 21-6-2019].

Gatrell, Peter, *A Whole Empire Walking: Refugees in Russia during World War I*. Bloomington : Indiana University Press, 1999.

Gatrell, Peter, *The Making of the Modern Refugee*. Oxford: Oxford University Press, 2013.

Gatten, Emma, 'Social Media Has Become Weaponized: Lyse Doucet Reflects on Seven Years of War in Syria', *The Telegraph* online, 3-5-2018 [Available at www.telegraph.co.uk/news/2018/05/03/social-media-has-become-weaponised-lyse-doucet-reflects-seven; accessed on 21-6-2019].

Gedan, Benjamin and Saldias, Nicolas, 'Latin America Has an Open-Door Policy for Venezuelan Refugees: But How Long Will It Last?', *Foreign Policy* online, 23-8-2018 [Available at https://foreignpolicy.com/2018/08/23/latin-america-has-an-open-door-policy-for-venezuelan-refugees; accessed on 21-6-2019].

Goldman, A.J.,. 'In Germany's Theaters, Stories of Exiles and Refugees', *New York Times* online, 4-1-2018 [Available at www.nytimes.com/2018/01/04/theater/winterreise-gorki-amerika-deutesches-theater-drums-in-the-night-munich.html; accessed on 21-6-2019].

*GSMA* website, 'Refugees and Connectivity', 2017 [Available at www.gsma.com/refugee-connectivity/refunite; accessed on 21-6-2019].

Haft, Helen, 'Telling Memories: Jewish Émigrés from the Former Soviet Union Tell Inconsistent Stories. What Does This Say about the Nature of Memory?', *Aeon* online, 9-2-2017 [Available at https://aeon.co/essays/what-the-oral-histories-of-russian-jews-reveal-about-memory; accessed on 21-6-2019].

Hoke, Mateo and Malek, Cate, *Palestine Speaks: Narratives of Life under Occupation*. London: Voice of Witness Series, Verso Books, 2015.

*Human Flow* film website, 'About', [Available at www.humanflow.com/synopsis; accessed on 21-6-2019].

Institute for Oral History, *Survivors of Genocide: Cambodian Genocide*. Waco : Baylor University, 2016 [Available at www.baylor.edu/oralhistory/index.php?id=941060; accessed on 21-6-2019].

International Coalition of Sites of Conscience website, 'About Us', [Available at www.sitesofconscience.org/en/who-we-are/about-us; accessed on 21-6-2019].

Khalaf, Hala, 'The Palestinian Women Refugees Using Arabian Motifs and Poetry to Create Art', *The National* United Arab Emirates online, 15-10-2018 [Available at www.thenational.ae/lifestyle/the-palestinian-women-refugees-using-arabian-motifs-and-poetry-to-create-art-1.780842; accessed on 21-6-2019].

Kushner, Tony and Knox, Katherine, *Refugees in an Age of Genocide: Global, National and Local Perspectives during the Twentieth Century*. London: Psychology Press, 1999.

Koen Leurs and Madhuri Prabhakar, 'Doing Digital Migration Studies: Methodological Considerations for an Emerging Research Focus'. In *Qualitative Research in European Migration Studies* (pp. 247–266), *IMISCOE Research Series*, edited by Ricard Zapata-Barrero and Evran Yalaz. New York: Springer, Cham.

Levin, Amy, *Global Mobilities: Refugees, Exiles and Immigrants in Museums and Archives*. Abingdon: Routledge, 2016.

*Los Comandos*, website [Available at http://loscomandos.film; accessed on 21-6-2019].

*Lucify*, website [Available at www.lucify.com/the-flow-towards-europe; accessed on 21-6-2019].

Lundsfryd, Mette Edith, 'Speaking Back to a World of Checkpoints: Oral History as a Decolonizing Tool in the Study of Palestinian Refugees', *Middle East Journal of Refugee Studies*, 2(1): 74–95, 2017.

Masalha, Nur, editor, *Catastrophe Remembered: Palestine, Israel and the Internal Refugees, Essays in Memory of Edward W. Said*. Chicago : University of Chicago Press, 2005.

McDonald-Gibson, Charlotte, *Cast Away: Stories of Survival from Europe's Refugee Crisis*. London: Portobello Books, 2016.

McKernan, Bethan, 'Ikea Builds Syrian Home Replica in Store to Show Horrors of War', *The Independent* online, 10-11-2016 [Available at www.independent.co.uk/news/world/middle-east/ikea-builds-syrian-home-replica-in-store-to-show-horrors-of-war-a7409896.html; accessed on 21-6-2019].

'Migrants', rap song video on YouTube [Available at www.youtube.com/watch?v=JO62aYPgO9s; accessed on 21-6-2019].

*Migration, themed edition of Oral History: Review of the Oral History Society*, 27(1)), 1999.

Miller, Liz, Luchs, Michele and Dyer Jalea, Gracia, *Mapping Memories: Experiences of Refugee Youth*. Montreal: Concordia University, 2012.

Mollica, Richard, *Healing Invisible Wounds: Paths to Hope and Recovery in a Violent World*. Nashville:Vanderbilt University Press, 2009.

Ndubi, Modesta, 'Congolese Asylum Seeker in Kenya Changing Lives through a Music School, despite Odds', UNHCR online, 25-10-2017 [Available at www.unhcr.org/ke/12535-congolese-asylum-seeker-kenya-changing-lives-music-school-despite-odds.html; accessed on 21-6-2019].

Nilsson, Marco and Badran, Danny, 'Conflicts and Relative Deprivation in Ein El Hilweh: Palestinian Refugees in the Shadow of the Syrian Civil War', *Journal of Refugee Studies*, 15-2-2019. Oxford: Oxford University Press 2019.

Prine Pauls, Elizabeth, 'Trail of Tears: Facts, Maps and Significance'. In *Encyclopedia Britannica*, 2008. [Available at www.britannica.com/event/Trail-of-Tears; accessed on 21-6-2019; ].

Randall, Alex, Salsbury, Jo and White, Zach, *Moving Stories: The Voices of People Who Move in the Context of Environmental Change*. Oxford: Climate Outreach, 2014.

*Refunite* website, 'Stories of Change', 2018 [Available at https://refunite.org/reconnection-stories/reunited-mother-community-leader-network-young-kenyan-wants-become-refunite-leader and https://refunite.org/testimonial/reconnected-after-22-years-of-separation; accessed on 21-6-2019].

Rempel, Terry, 'Who are Palestinian Refugees?', *Forced Migration Review*, 26: 5–7, Aug 2006.

Roberts, Adam, 'Prolonged Military Occupation: The Israeli-Occupied Territories since 1967', *American Journal of International Law*, 84(1): 44–103, 1990.

Shoah Foundation, Institute for Visual History and Education, University of South California [Available at https://sfi.usc.edu/collections/holocaust/ndt; accessed on 21-6-2019].

Skretteberg, Richard, '2019 Will Be Another Year of Crises', Oslo: Norwegian Refugee Council website, 2019 [Available at www.nrc.no/shorthand/fr/2019-will-be-another-year-of-crises/index.html; accessed on 21-6-2019].

*Startups Without Borders*, website [Available at https://startupswb.com; accessed on 21-6-2019].

*TechCrunch* website, 'Here Are 25 of the Most Innovative New Projects Using Tech to Help Refugees and NGOs', 2018 [Available at https://techcrunch.com/2018/10/27/here-are-25-of-the-most-innovative-new-projects-using-tech-to-help-refugees-and-ngos/?guccounter=1; accessed on 21-6-2019].

*Techfugees*, website [Available at https://techfugees.com; accessed on 21-6-2019].

*The 1947 Partition Archive* Berkeley : Pakistani American Culture Center, 2017 [Available at www.1947partitionarchive.org; accessed on 21-6-2019].

Thrall, Nathan, 'The 6-Day War at 50: The Past 50 Years of Israeli Occupation. And the Next', *New York Times* online, 2-6-2017 [Available at www.nytimes.com/2017/06/02/opinion/sunday/the-past-50-years-of-israeli-occupation-and-the-next.html; accessed on 21-6-2019].

*Traces Project*, website [Available at www.tracesproject.org/rita-ora; accessed on 21-6-2019].

Trincia, Chiara, 'The Worst Refugee Crisis in Latin American History Is within Our Reach', *VNY, La Voce di New York* online, 11-1-2019 [Available at www.lavocedinewyork.com/en/news/2019/01/11/the-worst-refugee-crisis-in-latin-american-history-is-within-our-reach/; accessed on 21-6-2019].

Turner, Vania and Kirchhof, Andreas, 'Congo Dance Project Helps Refugees Take Steps towards Rebuilding Lives', UNHCR online, 12-3-2018 [Available at www.unhcr.org/news/stories/2018/3/5aa666c14/congo-dance-project-helps-refugees-steps-towards-rebuilding-lives.html; accessed on 21-6-2019].

UN, *Official Records of the General Assembly*. Seventy-Third Session, Supplement No. 35, A/73/35. New York: UN General Assembly, 2018, p. 2.

UN International Organization for Migration (IOM), *Migration Trends in the Americas: Bolivarian Republic of Venezuela*. Costa Rica: UN-IOM, 2018.

UNHCR, *The State of the World's Refugees, 2000: Fifty Years of Humanitarian Action*. Oxford: Oxford University Press, 2000.

UNHCR, *The State of the World's Refugees*. UNHCR: Geneva, 2006.

UNHCR, 1951 *Convention Relating to the Status of Refugees* and 1967 *Protocol Relating to the Status of Refugees*. Geneva: UNHCR, 2010.

UNHCR, *Connecting Refugees: How Internet and Mobile Connectivity Can Improve Refugee Well-Being and Transform Humanitarian Action*. Geneva: UNHCR, 2016.

UNWRA website, 'Who We Are', [Available at www.unrwa.org/who-we-are; accessed on 21-6-2019].

Winslow, Michelle, 'Polish Migration to Britain: War, Exile and Mental Health', *Oral History*, 27(1): 57–64, 1999.

Yuval-Davis, Nira and Kaptani, Erena, 'Participatory Theatre as a Research Methodology: Identity, Performance and Social Action among Refugees', *Sociological Research Online*, 13(5): 2, 2008.

Yuval-Davis, Nira and Kaptani, Erena, 'Performing Identities: Participatory Theatre among Refugees'. In *Theorizing Identities and Social Action*, edited by Margaret Wetherell. London: Palgrave Macmillan, 2009.

## Notes

1 The US government expelled 100,000 Native Americans from their homelands, on an enforced march that stretched 5,045 miles westward in all; 15,000 died along the way (Elizabeth Prine Pauls, 'Trail of Tears: Facts, Maps and Significance'. In *Encyclopedia Brittannica*, 2008).

2 The term was coined by Peter Gatrell while documenting how the history and concept of refugees have evolved, both legally and in the popular mind (Peter Gatrell, *The Making of the Modern Refugee*. Oxford: Oxford University Press, 2013).

3 Helen Haft, 'Telling Memories: Jewish Émigrés from the Former Soviet Union Tell Inconsistent Stories. What Does This Say about the Nature of Memory?', *Aeon* online, 9-2-2017.

4 Citations for works cited in this table are given in this chapter's references.

5 'About Us', website of International Coalition of Sites of Conscience. All urls are given in this chapter's references.

6 Department of Sound Records, Imperial War Museum, *Britain and the Refugee Crisis, 1933–1947*. London: Imperial War Museum, 1982.

7 Tony Kushner and Katherine Knox, *Refugees in an Age of Genocide: Global, National and Local Perspectives during the Twentieth Century*. London: Psychology Press, 1999.

8 UNHCR, 1951 *Convention Relating to the Status of Refugees* and 1967 *Protocol Relating to the Status of Refugees.* Geneva: UHCR, 2010.
9 Amy Levin, *Global Mobilities: Refugees, Exiles and Immigrants in Museums and Archives.* Abingdon: Routledge, 2016.
10 Nur Masalha, editor, *Catastrophe Remembered: Palestine, Israel and the Internal Refugees, Essays in Memory of Edward W. Said.* Chicago : University of Chicago Press, 2005.
11 Marda Dunsky, *Pens and Swords: How the American Mainstream Media Report the Israeli–Palestinian Conflict.* New York: Columbia University Press, 2008; and Paul Findley's *They Dare to Speak Out: People and Institutions Confront Israel's Lobby.* Chicago: Chicago Review Press, 2003.
12 UNHCR, *The State of the World's Refugees.* Geneva: UHCR, 2006.
13 Nathan Thrall, 'The 6-Day War at 50: The Past 50 Years of Israeli Occupation. And the Next', *New York Times* online, 2-6-2017.
14 Orna Ben Naftali, Michael Sfard and Hedi Viterbo, *The ABC of the OPT: A Legal Lexicon of the Israeli Control over the Occupied Palestinian Territory.* Cambridge: Cambridge University Press, 2018.
15 Adam Roberts, 'Prolonged Military Occupation: The Israeli-Occupied Territories Since 1967', *American Journal of International Law,* 84(1): 44–103, 1990.
16 UN, *Official Records of the General Assembly,* Seventy-Third Session, Supplement No. 35, A/73/35. New York: UN General Assembly, 2018.
17 Terry Rempel, 'Who are Palestinian Refugees?', *Forced Migration Review,* 26: 5–7, Aug 2006.
18 UNWRA website, 'Who We Are'.
19 Mateo Hoke and Cate Malek, *Palestine Speaks: Narratives of Life under Occupation.* London: Voice of Witness Series, Verso Books, 2015.
20 Marco Nilsson and Danny Badran, 'Conflicts and Relative Deprivation in Ein El Hilweh: Palestinian Refugees in the Shadow of the Syrian Civil War', *Journal of Refugee Studies,* 15-2-2019. Oxford: Oxford University Press 2019.
21 David Armitage, *Civil Wars: A History in Ideas.* New Haven: Yale University Press, 2017.
22 UNHCR, *The State of the World's Refugees, 2000: Fifty Years of Humanitarian Action.* Oxford: Oxford University Press, 2000.
23 UN International Organization for Migration (IOM), *Migration Trends in the Americas: Bolivarian Republic of Venezuela.* Costa Rica: UN-IOM, 2018.
24 Benjamin Gedan and Nicolas Saldias, 'Latin America Has an Open-Door Policy for Venezuelan Refugees: But How Long Will It Last?', *Foreign Policy* online, 23-8-2018.
25 Dany Bahar, 'Why It Matters that We Call Fleeing Venezuelans Refugees, Not Migrants', *Foreign Affairs* online, 23-10-2018.
26 Richard Skretteberg, '2019 Will Be Another Year of Crises', Oslo: Norwegian Refugee Council website, 2019.
27 *Climate Migration* and *Climate Outreach* websites.
28 Chiara Trincia, 'The Worst Refugee Crisis in Latin American History Is within Our Reach', *VNY, La Voce di New York* online, 11-1-2019.
29 Boer Deng, 'Africans Trek to Texas as Med Grows Too Dangerous', *The Times,* 15-6-2019.
30 Thanks to Routledge for permission to reproduce this diagram and concept from my *Practicing Oral History to Improve Public Policies and Programs.* Abingdon: Routledge, 2018.
31 France 24 TV, The Observers, 'No, Journalists Did Not Stage These Images to Draw Sympathy for Migrants' online, 27-8-2018.
32 Doug Boyd and Mary Larson, editors, *Oral History and Digital Humanities: Voice, Access and Engagement.* New York: Palgrave Macmillan, 2014.
33 Tom Cantrell, 'Verbatim Theatre', *Drama Online* website.

34 ACTA Community Theatre, 'Refugee Engagement and Integration through Community Theatre'. Brussels: Creative Europe, Refugee Integration Projects, European Union, 2016.
35 Nira Yuval-Davis and Erena Kaptani, 'Performing Identities: Participatory Theatre among Refugees'. In *Theorizing Identities and Social Action*, edited by Margaret Wetherell et al. London: Palgrave Macmillan, 2009; Nira Yuval-Davis and Erena Kaptani, 'Participatory Theatre as a Research Methodology: Identity, Performance and Social Action among Refugees', *Sociological Research Online*, 13(5): 2, 2008..
36 'Rule 35: A New Provocative Show about the British Detention System', Community Arts Northwest website, 2015.
37 ACTA Community Theatre, 'Refugee Engagement', 2016.
38 BBC News Online, 'Rahaf al-Qunun: Saudi Teen Refugee Arrives in Canada', online, 12-1-2019.
39 Richard Mollica, *Healing Invisible Wounds: Paths to Hope and Recovery in a Violent World*. Nashville: Vanderbilt University Press, 2009.
40 *Human Flow* film website, 'About'.
41 Yuval-Davis and Kaptani, 'Performing Identities', 2009.
42 A.J. Goldman, 'In Germany's Theaters, Stories of Exiles and Refugees', *New York Times* online, 4-1-2018.
43 Anh Do, *The Happiest Refugee*. Crow's Nest, Australia: Allen & Unwin, 2011.
44 Eoin Colfer, Andrew Donkin and Giovanni Rigano, *Illegal: One Boy's Epic Journey of Hope and Survival*. London: Hodder, 2017.
45 Annas et al, *Ali and the Long Journey to Australia: Noble Park Primary School & TRUST Project*. Tampere, Finland: University of Tampere, 2017.
46 Fidaa Alfakih and Khaled Kabbara, 'Puppet Show Teaches Syrian Refugee Kids their Heritage', UNHCR website, 22-8-2018.
47 Glynis Clacherty, 'The World in a Suitcase: Psychosocial Support Using Artwork with Refugee Children in South Africa', *Participatory Learning and Action*, 54, April 2006.
48 Stefanie Dekker, 'Haneen: Exhibition of Syrian Children's Longings in War', *Al-Jazeera* online, 23-2-2018.
49 Brendan Bannon, *Do You See What I See? Photographic Collections for UNHCR*, on Flickr website.
50 Hala Khalaf, 'The Palestinian Women Refugees Using Arabian Motifs and Poetry to Create Art', *The National* United Arab Emirates online, 15-10-2018.
51 Bethan McKernan, 'Ikea Builds Syrian Home Replica in Store to Show Horrors of War', *The Independent* online, 10-11-2016.
52 *Traces Project* website.
53 Shoah Foundation website.
54 *Lucify* website.
55 *Los Comandos* website.
56 Modesta Ndubi, 'Congolese Asylum Seeker in Kenya Changing Lives through a Music School, despite Odds', UNHCR online, 25-10-2017.
57 'Migrants', rap song video on YouTube website.
58 Vania Turner and Andreas Kirchhof, 'Congo Dance Project Helps Refugees Take Steps towards Rebuilding Lives', UNHCR online, 12-3-2018.
59 *Startups Without Borders* website.
60 *Techfugees* website.
61 *TechCrunch* website, 'Here Are 25 of the Most Innovative New Projects Using Tech to Help Refugees and NGOs', 2018.

62 Liz Miller, Michele Luchs and Gracia Dyer Jalea, *Mapping Memories: Experiences of Refugee Youth*. Montreal: Concordia University, 2012.
63 Koen Leurs and Madhuri Prabhakar, 'Doing Digital Migration Studies: Methodological Considerations for an Emerging Research Focus'. In *Qualitative Research in European Migration Studies, IMISCOE Research Series*, edited by Ricard Zapata-Barrero and Evran Yalaz. New York: Springer, Cham.
64 *GSMA* website, 'Refugees and Connectivity', 2017.
65 Some of these individual 'Stories of Change' are told on the *Refunite* website.
66 *Refunite* website.
67 UNHCR, *Connecting Refugees: How Internet and Mobile Connectivity Can Improve Refugee Well-Being and Transform Humanitarian Action*. Geneva: UNHCR, 2016.
68 Rianne Dekker, Godfried Engbersen, Jeanine Klaver and Hanna Vonk, 'Smart Refugees: How Syrian Asylum Migrants Use Social Media Information in Migration Decision-Making', *Social Media & Society*, Jan-March 2018.
69 UNHCR, *Connecting Refugees*, 2016.
70 Emma Gatten, 'Social Media Has Become Weaponized: Lyse Doucet Reflects on Seven Years of War in Syria', *The Telegraph* online, 3-5-2018.

# 4

# CASE STUDIES OF ORAL HISTORIES WITH REFUGEES

## Transforming Lives and Outcomes

This chapter surveys the very diverse ways in which oral histories with refugees are already improving outcomes. It will give you a clear overview of how oral histories can help across the many different stages of the refugee journey. Our first case study will be with a war refugee who, by the time she got to tell her story, really had nothing left to lose. As she later described in her book, 'The slave market (…) was like the scene of an explosion … "They are virgins, right?" they asked a guard, who nodded and said, "Of course!" like a shopkeeper taking pride in his product.'[1] However, through the power of her oral testimony in front of the United Nations Assembly, she subsequently found that 'My story, told honestly … is the best weapon I have against terrorism, and I plan on using it until those terrorists are put on trial'.[2]

In her case, you will find it fairly obvious to see how oral histories can help at many levels – as legal testimony, as a historical record, as therapy, to assist with public awareness raising and campaigning. But in some of our other case studies you will see that it took lateral thinking to improve outcomes using oral history. Both the creativity and the effectiveness of all these projects are truly heartening, and will hopefully get your thoughts going about projects you could do yourself. In all, across these case studies, you will see two main groups doing oral history projects, namely:

1. Various professionals already working with refugees through public services, policy or charities, who are adopting and applying the oral history method in order to do their own jobs better.
2. Diverse people across host societies (from artists and librarians to computer programmers) who have felt moved to do their own oral histories with or about refugees, and to apply them back into their own sectors in useful ways (through exhibitions, broadcasts, provision of useful services, etc.).

Note that many of these projects came from a 'light-bulb moment' where someone in the host community saw something they themselves could do to capture and apply oral histories about refugees in a really useful new way. Some were just watching the refugee crisis unfold on television, or they happened to meet a refugee in the streets around them. But you'll see that they went on to capture and communicate refugee oral histories through media as diverse as theatre, online information hubs, traditional storytelling, business programs at top universities and role-play games where everyday racism gets to laugh at itself. Overall, the projects in these case studies enabled:

1. host communities to hear what refugees have gone through, developing empathy and solidarity towards them;
2. refugees to communicate the positive skills, qualifications and assets that they have to offer to the host society;
3. people of good will on both sides to make contact, developing productive friendships, networks and exchanges.

But this book is also about staying alert to the negative consequences that result when only refugees are listened to, while the concerns of the vulnerable in host communities go unheard – genuine concerns about increased competition for limited resources like jobs, benefits, housing and public services. So Chapter 5 will bring you case studies of oral history projects that do listen to host communities. You will also see there how two-way, *mutual* oral histories can facilitate dialogue between refugees and host communities. In fact, we will see how this type of applied oral history is likely to proliferate in the future as an important tool for resolving conflicts and building integration.[3]

## Oral Histories with Refugees

Each of the following case studies focuses on a different stage of the long refugee journey. They start with the dangers back home that obliged refugees to flee. Then they listen to oral histories all the way through into the second and third generations long after resettlement. Figure 4.1 on page 62 summarizes them all, encompassing their different methods, purposes, audiences and origins. You may want to glance ahead to it as you read through the projects.

### *1. Before Escape from the Conflict Zone: Using Victims' Oral Histories to Prosecute for War Crimes*

War refugee Nadia Murad was one of thousands of young women from the Yazidi community of Kurds in Iraq who were kidnapped and held by ISIS as sex slaves. After she escaped, Nadia managed to make her way to the United Nations Assembly where – visibly shaking – she told them about being raped and beaten at length by ISIS militants. Her case is actually quite a formal and traditional application of oral

| Stage of journey | Oral history project & purpose | By whom | Final product | Refugee group & location |
|---|---|---|---|---|
| **1. Before escape from conflict-zone** | Amal Clooney's recording of Yazidi women's testimonies : to prosecute for war-crimes against refugee women enslaved by ISIS | International human rights lawyers | Legal testimonies to use in court prosecution | Yazidi women raped and enslaved by ISIS – Geneva & Iraq |
| **2. During the escape journey** | *'Mapping Refugee Media Journeys: Smartphones and Social Media Networks'* : to make refugee journeys safer by providing online info-packs en route | UK's Open University, with French media companies | Online travel information that makes refugees' journeys safer and easier | All refugees travelling along those routes –UK & along Europe's refugee-routes |
| **3. In refugee camps** | With refugee women on how they need reproductive health services to be delivered : to improve targeting, uptake & efficiency of under - used services | Women's Refugee Commission & other health agencies | Improved uptake of contraceptive and menstrual hygiene services in refugee camps | Adolescent girls and women of child-bearing age –Djibouti, Myanmar & Lebanon |
| **4. In asylum-detention centers** | Berouz Boochani's testimonies smuggled out of Manus Island prison : to reveal to the world an abuse of detained refugees | Kurdish refugee journalist unlawfully imprisoned in Australia | International awareness, plus a prize-winning book and film | Imprisoned refugees –Australia |
| **5. Newly settled** | 'Mapping Memories: Participatory Media, Place-based Stories and Refugee Youth' : to assist integration, give refugee youth new skills andeducate host communities | Social science academics & multi-media tutors | Online videos, an exhibition and learning materials used by schools and local politicians | Resettled refugee youth –Canada |
| **6. Longer-term settled** | 'Trauma Story Assessment and Therapy'Harvard Program in Refugee Trauma : a psychiatric treatment method for refugees who are torture-survivors | A clinical psychiatrist | Successful treatment protocol delivered in 30 languages to over 10,000 refugees worldwide | Refugee survivors of torture and trauma –worldwide |
| **7. Long-term settled or second-generation** | *Prevent* counter-terrorism program : to rehabilitate radicalized youth among resettled refugees and their second generation | Police & social workers within the host community | Specialized rehabilitation program centered around videoed oral histories | Resettled and second-generation being groomed by radicalizers –UK |

**FIGURE 4.1** Case studies of oral history projects with refugees

history – an application as old as the law courts and the very concepts of justice and retribution. Led by the glamorous barrister Amal Clooney, this project reaches back into the war zone. It is meticulously gathering oral testimonies from some of the 6,000 Yazidi women abducted by ISIS as sex slaves, in order to prosecute ISIS war criminals in an international court of law.[4] As *The Economist* explains:

> Clooney's first priority is to gather as much evidence as possible before it is lost. Some of this she does herself, painstakingly recording interviews with

> survivors ('the most harrowing witness statements I've ever taken', she says). At the same time, she is pressing the UN Security Council to order a formal investigation on the ground.[5]

There are agonizing complexities around the gathering of oral evidence in this case. Strict taboos in the Yazidi culture require unmarried women to be virgins, making it almost impossible for survivors to acknowledge what has been done to them. But one victim decided that she had lost so much already, she would overturn all that in front of the world's cameras. In front of the United Nations (UN), in her memoir for the general public and in formal oral testimonies recorded by Clooney, young Nadia Murad is shattering those taboos to tell of her rape and enslavement by ISIS.

This project is a collaboration between two women from very different worlds with oral testimonies acting as a bridge between them, with the shared aim of challenging the misogynistic savagery of ISIS. Nadia Murad is iconic as the victim who has nothing left but the voice to tell her story. From the bottom up, she has told truth to power, winning the 2018 Nobel Peace Prize in the process. That prize is not awarded lightly: it declares to the world the fundamental power of oral history to help build peace and justice in the decades ahead.

Alongside these efforts of Murad and Clooney, the novel *The Beekeeper of Sinjar* by Iraqi writer-in-exile Dunya Mikhail publicizes related oral histories in an artistic medium.[6] It tells the true story of another Yazidi hero who survived the horror of ISIS. Beekeeper Abdullah Shrem repeatedly risked his life to rescue as many of the Yazidi women as he could. He also secretly gathered their oral accounts and relayed them out by phone to an Iraqi writer who has asylum in the US, Dunya Mikhail. Receiving the testimonies piece by piece, Mikhail assembled them into the true-story novel *The Beekeeper of Sinjar*. The novel also includes the beekeeper's own testimony. He explains how during his work with bees, 'the movements of the queen bee, her superior flying abilities compared to the males, amazed me [and] made me profoundly appreciate all the women in my life, because her loss would completely destroy the colony'. He describes how, as a result, his rescue network 'worked like a beehive, with extreme care and well-planned initiatives'.[7] They had to be as highly organized as the ISIS slave market was. As one study notes,

> the women's accounts provide material details of the strong infrastructure that was put in place: fleets of buses onto which women were loaded and transported; warehouses (often repurposed schools) where victims were held; facilities where women were viewed and traded.[8]

These two related case studies are outstanding examples of one terrible set of oral histories being put to use successfully in several domains at once – in criminal justice and in novelistic and feminist settings that also draw on ecological metaphors from the natural world.

## *2. During the Escape Journey: Using Oral Accounts to Design Safer Journeys for Refugees Coming Behind*

Our next example is very different. It's a completely new application of oral testimony, but equally inspiring and practical. In the last chapter, we saw how artists have used livestreamed digital mapping of refugees' escape routes to great effect in feature films like the BBC's *Exodus: Our Journey to Europe* or *Human Flow* by the Chinese refugee artist Ai Weiwei. But one academic who had worked on *Exodus* wondered what more she could do to help. Poring over the testimonies that refugees had given about the routes of their escape journeys, Marie Gillespie of Britain's Open University noticed patterns: points where well-used routes split or converged; popular halting spots; known danger zones and obstacles along the way. This was information that refugee travellers needed at every turn. So she used thousands of individual travel accounts to produce interactive, digital maps of these routes and their features.[9] The maps showed where refugee populations most often came from, by what routes, with what stopovers, where they were going next and where they were ultimately headed. Then she backfilled into these online maps all the practical, logistical information that would help make these routes safer and easier for the next refugees who would travel them. Transport links, departure times, weather patterns, services available, emergency response numbers, forms that would have to be filled in at certain points... The project gathered all these and made them available as online resource packs for refugees to access as they travelled the routes on the ground in real time.[10]

The fact is that along all the routes, many people and organizations, both local and online, had been willing to help, but the 'missing link' was how to connect them up with actual refugees travelling the road, as Gillespie did.[11] Some of the resources they made available along the online maps are now quite elaborate. They include a 'Crisis Info Hub' sponsored by Google, a 'Welcome 2 Europe' network of activists willing to befriend and help along the routes, and a network called 'Village of All-Together' that provides real-life local contacts. Gillespie's chapter 'From Paris to Cherbourg: Aspirations, Expectations and Realities' addresses the well-worn route that has brought thousands of refugees to the improvised camps that I myself visited in northern France, where they seek illegal passage as stowaways on the ferries to England.[12] As well as giving practical help along this route, the report also uses refugee testimonies to expose – crucially – the false hopes and misconceptions that lead many refugees there, only to have their dreams dashed on arrival at the reality of what came to be known as 'The Jungle' outdoor migrant camp on the north French coast.

## *3. In Refugee Camps: Applying Women's Intimate Oral Histories to Improve 'Taboo' Medical Services*

This case study is very different again. It's a classic example of the participatory, user-involvement approach to providing public services – here, contraceptive and reproductive health services for refugee women in the camps. The importance of these services can hardly be overstated: it's crucial that refugee women avoid unwanted pregnancies along these dangerous, precarious routes. But this is an example where a needed service can only be provided successfully by first listening in depth to *exactly what* the recipient needs and *the way* they need to access it. Otherwise, precious resources are wasted on services that go unused while the need – to prevent unwanted pregnancies during the refugee journey – continues unmet.

This time, a sensitive application of oral history meant the need did not go unmet, and resources could be tailored for maximum uptake and efficiency. Basically, UN health workers were trained to do oral interviews with refugee women of childbearing age inside the camps, to find out why they had low uptake of contraceptive services, and whether they wanted them in the first place. It was no small achievement to broach this very private, sensitive subject in such a difficult, dangerous and diverse environment. Refugee women from various nations and ethnicities are hedged about by different cultural taboos and norms on the subject. But it emerged that yes, they did badly need and want contraception but they needed it delivered in specific ways that they explained to the researchers, so as to fit in with their cultures' taboos and requirements.[13] Health workers later built on this success by doing further oral histories with refugee women inside the camps on their needs around menstruation, an even more taboo subject. Again, testimonies were gathered in such a culturally sensitive way that they did go on to inform and improve necessary services for menstruating women. As the official report put it, 'the most essential component (in providing women's services) remains continuous consultation with adolescent girls and women'.[14]

## *4. In Asylum Detention Centers: Smuggled Oral Histories Exposing Illegal Incarceration*

While fleeing for his life from Iraq, Kurdish journalist Behrouz Boochani had no idea that he would soon become a world icon, and for a terrible reason. (His testimony opened this book for us in Chapter 1.) Behrouz didn't know that the 'refugeedom' he was escaping into would be almost worse than the regime he was escaping from. That it would mean years of incarceration in an island prison camp as a prisoner not of some tyrannical warlord, but of a modern nation in the 'free world'. Under international law, Boochani's application to Australia for political asylum should have been granted. Instead, he was locked up indefinitely in primitive, isolated conditions on the now infamous Manus Island out in the Pacific Ocean. As part of the Australian government's bid to deter future asylum seekers, these refugee captives were subjected to harsh treatment and illegal conditions.[15] But what was most painful to Boochani, as a writer, was that they were also deprived of access to negotiation or a voice. Forbidden even pen and paper, he ingeniously recorded and stored on his mobile phone his own real-time testimonies of what was happening inside this island prison cut off from the world. Amazingly, he managed to use his phone to smuggle out those snippets of oral testimony (mostly through the messaging service WhatsApp) to fellow journalists around the world who were able to stitch them back together and publish them. They were broadcast online over several years, turning the still-incarcerated Boochani into the voice of incarcerated refugees worldwide. They have now been published as his book, *No Friend but the Mountains*. The book reveals how the brutality of the prison environment – described by one Australian law professor as 'almost beyond belief' – allegedly claimed the lives of two of Boochani's fellow refugees while he was there.[16]

Boochani's self-produced, telephoned history of life behind bars has been compared to the great prison literature produced by the first-person testimonies of famous prisoners of the past like Oscar Wilde and Antonio Gramsci. But the innovation is that thanks to today's communications technology – though deprived of pen and paper – he managed to conceal and accumulate his accounts on a mobile phone, and smuggle them out through social media to a world beyond that *is listening*. His prizewinning book has been hailed as 'a book about, among other things, the power of writing' and 'a text self-consciously positioned within a broader literature of incarceration'.[17] While still stuck on Manus Island, Behrouz spoke via video links to cultural and academic events where he was a (virtual) guest of honour, such as at the Melbourne Writers' Festival or at gatherings at the University of Technology in Sydney. Humanizing us all, his achievement is on a global scale, as an unlawfully incarcerated refugee whose hosts seemed intent on destroying his will, his voice and his communication skills.

## *5. Newly Settled: Multimedia Oral Histories as Tools for Integration*

Many refugees do languish long-term in camps and detention centers, but a small minority are granted asylum and can then get on with trying to integrate into a new culture. Below are just a few examples of how oral history methodologies can help. In Montreal, a project called 'Mapping Memories: Participatory Media, Place-Based Stories and Refugee Youth' taught resettled refugee teenagers to produce their own oral histories expressing their experiences of their new home, along with their thoughts of their old home.[18] As part of the process, the teenagers learned and applied new multimedia skills in photography, videorecording, graphic design and web publishing. Their oral histories were then circulated online and in the region as educational resources for schools, community centers, politicians, the media and the public. We have seen that all over the world, youth and child refugees are becoming major actors and political voices, using innovative methods to translate their oral testimonies into media such as games, drawings, cartoons, puppet theatre and graphic novels.

Meanwhile, in Australia, one researcher did detailed oral histories with newly settled Somali refugees, in order to hear and trace the ways they used their own oral history traditions to help them accommodate to this new life in exile.[19] Did the refugees use their Somali narrative traditions to build a new sense of self? Were the storytelling traditions of the home country adapted to apply to the new crisis setting? How did those traditions help them create new links in this alien environment? The study took a dual-facing 'backwards and forwards' approach, to find out how a refugee community proactively used an old resource from the home culture (oral storytelling) to help with a very new crisis in a totally unfamiliar place. It found that their oral history traditions were indeed 'an important form of agency, counterbalancing narratives of oppressed refugees'. The interviewers discovered that 'despite experiencing the intense social disruption of civil war, idyllic stories of past family and community life *are* told, providing a contrast to disconnection, individualism and risk in Australia, as well as a thread back to a mythical Somalia'.[20] This type of approach to refugees' own oral histories is part of the '*Not Just Victims*' approach, which recognizes refugees' own proactive choices, resources, activities and contributions, rather than just viewing them as passive victims consuming only resources that are provided by others. (Note that the term 'refugee' is in itself grammatically passive, meaning one *receiving* refuge.)

Once resettled, the search for work, training and further education helps determine how successful a refugee's integration will or won't be.[21] Through careful listening to refugees' needs in this domain, people in the host community can always help. In 2015, Eymeric Guinet and Theo Scubla were two French students doing master's degrees at one of the world's top business schools in Paris. They were moved by hearing accounts of talented university students elsewhere becoming refugees. And they decided to do something about it. Theo explained in an interview

> There were just two of us, but we couldn't sit back and let refugees' talents go to waste ... We wanted to give life back to their hopes and dreams, and make a link-up between the host society and the new arrivals.[22]

Gathering all the contacts they had between them, the two students designed a system, called *Wintegreat*, whereby France's top universities now receive appropriately screened refugees for an intensive three-month reorientation program. First, oral interviews listen in depth to the refugee's mix of talents, abilities, previous qualifications and future aspirations. The scheme then finds them a university place or job opportunity that carries them forward on that path. It also provides courses in French and English language and in cultural integration for 'Life in France'. The scheme is delivered by a team of 21 volunteers in their twenties who themselves work or study at the network of sponsoring universities. By 2019, 764 refugees had been trained, and 73% settled in employment or further education three months later.[23]

Meanwhile, in Berlin, *Refugee Voices Tours* is a project with work-hungry refugees, creating meaningful, innovative work for them in the tourist industry. Newly settled refugees give a guided oral history of Berlin's sights to both German and foreign tourists visiting the city. Syrian refugees with asylum in Berlin are leading these guided tours of the city's famous sights, which they've studied in depth. Like any other tour guide, they recount the oral history of Berlin at sites such as the Nazis' torture-prison from World War II, the 'Checkpoint Charlie' barrier that divided East Berlin from West Berlin, and residential zones that were bombed to the ground during the war.[24] But they then add a layer of 'extra value' by also telling the oral histories of the Syrian equivalents: the Syrian regime's torture chambers, the walls dividing Syrian cities now and their bombed-out suburbs. These empathic, 'double-vision' Berlin tours by Syrian expatriates are appreciated by foreigners, German tourists and native Berliners alike.[25] The tours use all of our experiences of home, territory and belonging to make us feel we are all fundamentally one, rather than using them to push us apart.

## *6. Longer-Term Settled: Oral Histories to Treat Torture Survivors: Dr Richard Mollica's 'Trauma Story Therapy'*

Before Dr Richard Mollica, the conventional wisdom among psychiatrists was that torture victims were untreatable. But during 30 years of clinical practice listening in person to the oral histories of refugee patients, Dr Mollica, a professor of psychiatry at Harvard Medical School, discovered that *the way* a trauma survivor tells their story affects their recovery. Working in part as what he now calls a 'storytelling coach', he gradually developed a tried and tested clinical framework that facilitates refugees to tell their trauma narratives in ways that are clinically healing. Called 'Trauma Story Assessment and Therapy', his clinical oral histories have five carefully managed, successive components: the factual; the emotional; the cultural; celebration of survival skills and resiliency; and the listener–storyteller relationship.[26]

With the success of this clinical oral history method, Mollica has become a world leader in the mental treatment and rehabilitation of traumatized people and their communities. His center – the Harvard Program in Refugee Trauma – has treated over 10,000 survivors of extreme violence worldwide. Their clinical framework, considered the gold standard in the field, has been delivered locally in the field in over 30 different languages. It has also helped to move mental health issues nearer to the center of the national recovery process in post-conflict societies.[27]

If only for our own protection, it is imperative that these mental health injuries resulting from trauma, loss, torture and displacement receive a clinical treatment that is as effective as possible. To leave such mental harms and syndromes untreated amidst a resettled refugee population would be to invite further medical and antisocial problems that can eventually fester into acts of terrorism.[28]

## *7. Long-Term Settled and Second Generation: Oral Histories that Prevent Radicalization*

Called *Prevent*, this nationwide program in Britain is, like the one above, a very specialized and formal application of oral history. It is aimed at tackling radicalization and preventing homegrown terrorism. (Studies show that recent acts of terrorism in Europe have mostly been by second-generation migrants, a subset of whom come from refugee backgrounds.[29]) For this program, specialist social workers use community outreach, networking and criminal intelligence from the local community to locate and befriend individuals who are at risk of, or in the process of being, radicalized. Successive, in-depth interviews with these individuals end up serving four functions. First, they enable the person to explore and express the grievances and thought processes that nudged them towards radicalization in the first place. Second, these testimonies help police psychologists to understand exactly *how* vulnerable people are targeted and methodically groomed by terrorist radicalizers. Third, their own oral accounts help the person to stand back and witness, in retrospect, how their vulnerabilities were methodically stalked and exploited by these radicalizers. Finally – and this is the core of the program – these videoed oral histories are then used (with the narrator's permission and cooperation) as a powerful tool to help steer other people back from radicalization.[30]

This highly skilled and sensitive application of oral histories can only succeed through a deep and culturally sensitive partnership between resettled refugee communities, the social services provided to them, and the specialized police and health workers who work with them to prevent radicalization. Through trial and error over the years, the UK's *Prevent* program has now gone through several phases and revisions that have improved it a great deal through end-user feedback. Crucially, it is now being applied in equal measure against the right-wing radicalization that is spreading like a virus – especially online – through many white host communities in the UK, as well as elsewhere in the West. The *Prevent* program's oral history videos have become a powerful tool for exposing how vulnerable people are groomed by radicalizers, and for reversing the radicalization process. As one leader of terrorist group Al-Qaeda has candidly put it: 'More than half of this battle is taking place in the battlefield of the media. We are in a media battle, in a race for the hearts and minds of our ummah'.[31]

Before we move on to the next chapter's case studies with host communities, Figure 4.1 summarizes for you the main oral history projects with refugees that we've just examined.

## References


BBC2 TV, *Exodus: Our Journey to Europe*. London: BBC, 2016.

Blackes, Laura et al., 'Terrorism or Insanity: Attack Underscores Need to Address Refugees' Mental Health', translated by Christopher Sultan, *Der Spiegel*, Issue 32, 10-8-2017.

Blanch, Andrea, *Transcending Violence: Emerging Models for Trauma Healing in Refugee Communities*. Victoria, Australia: National Center on Trauma-Informed Care, 2008.

Boochani, Behrouz, *No Friend but the Mountains*. Sydney: Pan Macmillan, 2018.

Byrne, Liam, *Black Flag Down: Counter-Extremism, Defeating ISIS and Winning the Battle of Ideas*. London: Biteback Publishing, 2016.

Crone, Manni and Maja, Falkentoft Felicia, *Europe's Refugee Crisis and the Threat of Terrorism: An Extraordinary Threat?* Copenhagen: Danish Center for International Studies, 2017.

Dekker, Rianne, Engbersen, Godfried, Klaver, Jeanine and Vonk, Hanna, 'Smart Refugees: How Syrian Asylum Migrants Use Social Media Information in Migration Decision-Making', *Social Media + Society*, Jan-March, 2018, 1–11.

Doherty, Ben, 'UN Body Condemns Australia for Illegal Detentions of Asylum Seekers and Refugees', *The Guardian*, 7-7-2018.

Gillespie, Marie, Ampofo, Lawrence, Cheesman, Margaret, Faith, Becky, Iliadou, Evgenia, Issa, Ali, Osseiran, Souad and Skleparis, Dimitris, *Mapping Refugee Media Journeys: Smartphones and Social Media Networks*. Paris: Open University/France Médias Monde, 2016 [Available at: www.open.ac.uk/ccig/research/projects/mapping-refugee-media-journeys#;accessedon 21-6-2019].

Gillespie, Marie, Osseiran, Souad and Cheesman, Margie, 'Syrian Refugees and the Digital Passage to Europe: Smartphone Infrastructures and Affordances', *Social Media + Society*, Jan-March, 2018.

Guest, Robert, 'Nadia Murad's Fight to Bring Islamic State to Justice', *The Economist* online, Feb/March 2017 [Available at www.1843magazine.com/features/two-women-one-cause; accessed on 21-6-2019].

*Human Flow* film website, 'About', [Available at www.humanflow.com/synopsis; accessed on 21-6-2019].

*In Dialogue.EU* website, 'In Dialogue with the Other: Best Cross-Cultural Practices of Refugee Integration', 2016 [Available at www.in-dialogue.eu/; accessed on 21-6-2019].

Larsson, Naomi, 'Breaking Down the New Berlin Wall: Refugee Guides Show Their Side of City', *The Guardian* online, 21-12-2017 [Available at www.theguardian.com/cities/2017/dec/21/refugee-migrants-berlin-walking-tours-neukolln-sonnenallee; the *Refugee Voices Tours* website is available at refugeevoicestours.org; both accessed on 21-6-2019].

Marfleet, Philip, 'Refugees and History: Why We Must Address the Past', *Refugee Survey Quarterly*, 26(3): 136–148, 2007.

Masmoudi, Ikram 'Gender Violence and the Spirit of the Feminine: Two Accounts of the Yazidi Tragedy', *International Journal of Contemporary Iraqi Studies*, 12(1): 7–21(15), 2018.

Mikhail, Dunya, *The Beekeeper of Sinjar*, translated by Max Weiss. London: Serpent's Tail, 2018.

Miller, Liz, Luchs, Michele and Dyer Jalea, Gracia, *Mapping Memories: Experiences of Refugee Youth*. Montreal: Concordia University, 2012 [Available at www.mappingmemories.ca; accessed on 21-6-2019].

Mollica, Richard, *Healing Invisible Wounds: Paths to Hope and Recovery in a Violent World*. Nashville: Vanderbilt University Press, 2009.

Mollica, Richard, *Trauma Story Assessment and Therapy: Journal for Field and Clinic*. Cambridge, MA: Harvard Program in Refugee Trauma, 2012.

Murad, Nadia, 'I Was an Isis Sex Slave: I Tell My Story because It Is the Best Weapon I Have', *The Guardian*, 6-10-2018 [Available at www.theguardian.com/commentisfree/2018/oct/06/nadia-murad-isis-sex-slave-nobel-peace-prize; accessed on 21-6-2019].

Murad, Nadia and Krajeski, Jenna, *The Last Girl: My Story of Captivity, and My Fight against the Islamic State*. London: Penguin Random House, 2017.

Ramsden, Robyn and Ridge, Damien, '"It Was the Most Beautiful Country I Have Ever Seen": The Role of Somali Narratives in Adapting to a New Country', *Journal of Refugee Studies*, 26(2): 226–246, 2013.

Reilly, Alex, 'Behrouz Boochani's Unsparing Look at the Brutality of Manus Island'. *The Conversation*, 27-8- 2018 [Available at https://theconversation.com/book-review-behrouz-boochanis-unsparing-look-at-the-brutality-of-manus-island-101520; accessed on 21-6-2019].

Schmitt, Margaret et al., 'Understanding the Menstrual Hygiene Management Challenges Facing Displaced Girls and Women: Findings from Qualitative Assessments in Myanmar and Lebanon', *Conflict and Health*, 11(19), 2017.

Sparrow, Jeff, 'A Place of Punishment: *No Friend but the Mountains* by Behrouz Boochani', *Sydney Review of Books*, 21-9-2018 [Available at https://sydneyreviewofbooks.com/a-place-of-punishment-no-friend-but-the-mountains-by-behrouz-boochani/; accessed on 21-6-2019].

Tegegne Tesfaw, Woinshet, *Determinants of Family Planning Practice among Ethiopian Women Refugees Living in Kakuma Camp, Kenya*. Nairobi: University of Nairobi School of Public Health, 2016.

UK Government, 'Let's Talk about It: Working Together to Prevent Terrorism', website [Available at www.ltai.info/what-is-prevent; accessed on 21-6-2019].

UNHCR, *Connecting Refugees: How Internet and Mobile Connectivity Can Improve Refugee Wellbeing and Transform Humanitarian Action*. Geneva: UNHCR, 2016.

UNHCR, *Turn the Tide: Refugee Education in Crisis*. Geneva: UNCHR, 2017.

UNHCR & Women's Refugee Commission, *Baseline Study: Documenting Knowledge, Attitudes and Behaviours of Somali Refugees and the Status of Family Planning Services in UNHCR's Ali Addeh Refugee Camp, Djibouti*. Geneva: UNHCR, 2011. *Wintegreat* website [Available at www.wintegreat.org; accessed on 21-6-2019].

UNHCR website, 'Wintegreat: Les Grandes Écoles et Universités en France au Service des Réfugiés', 13-9-2017 [Available at www.unhcr.org/fr-fr/news/stories/2017/9/598db9c84/wintegreat-les-grandes-ecoles-et-universites-en-france-au-service-des-refugies.html; accessed on 21-6-2019].

## Notes

1 Nadia Murad with Jenna Krajeski, *The Last Girl: My Story of Captivity, and My Fight against the Islamic State*. London: Penguin Random House, 2017.

2 Nadia Murad, 'I Was an Isis Sex Slave: I Tell my Story because It Is the Best Weapon I Have', *The Guardian*, 6-10-2018; urls are given in this chapter's references.

3 *In Dialogue.EU website*, 'In Dialogue with the Other: Best Cross-Cultural Practices of Refugee Integration', 2016.

4 It is estimated that 3,000 Yazidi women and children remained enslaved by ISIS as this book went to press in 2019.

5 Robert Guest, 'Nadia Murad's Fight to Bring Islamic State to Justice', *The Economist* online, Feb/March 2017. Urls are given in this chapter's references.

6 Dunya, Mikhail, *The Beekeeper of Sinjar*, translated by Max Weiss. London: Serpent's Tail, 2018.

7 Dunya, *The Beekeeper*, 2018.

8 Ikram Masmoudi, 'Gender Violence and the Spirit of the Feminine: Two Accounts of the Yazidi Tragedy', *International Journal of Contemporary Iraqi Studies*, 12(1), 2018.

9 Marie Gillespie et al., *Mapping Refugee Media Journeys: Smartphones and Social Media Networks*. Paris: Open University/France Médias Monde, 2016.

10 Marie Gillespie, Souad Osseiran and Margie Cheesman, 'Syrian Refugees and the Digital Passage to Europe: Smartphone Infrastructures and Affordances', *Social Media + Society*, Jan-March, 2018; Rianne Dekker, Godfried Engbersen, Jeanine Klaver and Hanna Vonk, 'Smart Refugees: How Syrian Asylum Migrants Use Social Media Information in Migration Decision-Making', *Social Media + Society*, Jan-March, 2018, 1–11.

11 UNHCR, *Connecting Refugees: How Internet and Mobile Connectivity Can Improve Refugee Wellbeing and Transform Humanitarian Action*. Geneva: UNHCR, 2016.

12 Marie Gillespie et al., *Mapping Refugee Media Journeys, 2016*.

13 Woinshet Tegegne Tesfaw, *Determinants of Family Planning Practice among Ethiopian Women Refugees Living in Kakuma Camp, Kenya*. Nairobi: University of Nairobi School of Public Health, 2016.

14 Margaret Schmitt et al., 'Understanding the Menstrual Hygiene Management Challenges Facing Displaced Girls and Women: Findings from Qualitative Assessments in Myanmar and Lebanon', *Conflict and Health*, 11(19), 2017.

15 Ben Doherty, 'UN Body Condemns Australia for Illegal Detentions of Asylum Seekers and Refugees', *The Guardian*, 7-7-2018.

16 Alex Reilly, 'Behrouz Boochani's Unsparing Look at the Brutality of Manus Island', *The Conversation*, 27-8-2018.

17 Jeff Sparrow, 'A Place of Punishment: *No Friend but the Mountains* by Behrouz Boochani', *Sydney Review of Books*, 21-9-2018.

18 Liz Miller, Michele Luchs and Gracia Dyer Jalea, *Mapping Memories: Experiences of Refugee Youth*. Montreal: Concordia University, 2012.

19 Robyn Ramsden and Damien Ridge, '"It Was the Most Beautiful Country I Have Ever Seen": The Role of Somali Narratives in Adapting to a New Country', *Journal of Refugee Studies*, 26(2), 2013.

20 Ramsden and Ridge, 'It Was the Most Beautiful Country', 2013.

21 UNHCR, *Turn the Tide: Refugee Education in Crisis*. Geneva: UNCHR, 2017.

22 Translation by Marella Hoffman of 'Nous voulions redonner vie à leurs projets, créer du lien entre la société d'accueil et les nouveaux arrivants'. 'Wintegreat: Les Grandes Écoles et Universités en France au Service des Réfugiés', UNHCR website, 13-9-2017.

23 *Wintegreat* website home page.

24 Philip Marfleet, 'Refugees and History: Why We Must Address the Past', *Refugee Survey Quarterly*, 26(3): 136–148, 2007.

25 Naomi Larsson, 'Breaking Down the New Berlin Wall: Refugee Guides Show Their Side of City', *The Guardian* online, 21-12-2017.

26 Richard Mollica, *Trauma Story Assessment and Therapy: Journal for Field and Clinic*. Cambridge, MA: Harvard Program in Refugee Trauma, 2012; Richard Mollica, *Healing Invisible Wounds: Paths to Hope and Recovery in a Violent World*. Nashville: Vanderbilt University Press, 2009.

27 .Andrea, Blanch, *Transcending Violence: Emerging Models for Trauma Healing in Refugee Communities*. Victoria, Australia: National Center on Trauma-Informed Care, 2008.

28 Laura Blackes et al., 'Terrorism or Insanity: Attack Underscores Need to Address Refugees' Mental Health', translated by Christopher Sultan, *Der Spiegel*, Issue 32, 10-8-2017.

29 Manni Crone and Maja Falkentoft Felicia, *Europe's Refugee Crisis and the Threat of Terrorism: An Extraordinary Threat?* Copenhagen: Danish Center for International Studies, 2017.

30 UK Government, *Let's Talk about It: Working Together to Prevent Terrorism* website.

31 'Ummah' is Arabic for 'community'. West Point Combatting Terrorism Center, *The Group that Calls Itself a State*, quoting from Ayman al-Zawahiri; quoted in Liam Byrne's *Black Flag Down: Counter-Extremism, Defeating ISIS and Winning the Battle of Ideas*. London: Biteback Publishing, 2016.

# 5

# CASE STUDIES OF ORAL HISTORIES WITH HOST COMMUNITIES

## Letting Discontent Be Heard

Ruth, an African refugee with asylum in Cambridge, UK, told me in an interview:

> You know many people say that when you die you can go to heaven. Well I tell you, I *have* died and *I am in heaven!* Because life here in Cambridge is heaven and you all don't even realise it. That is why I wanted to tell my story – to help Cambridge people to realise that that you are all living in heaven!
>
> I will tell you why it is heaven here. Because here you '*Buy one, Get one free*'! [doubles over with laughter for a long time]. Just imagine that. For instance, I work as a cleaner. And here in Cambridge if you get a job as a cleaner and you work hard, you can pay your rent and pay for food and clothing and medicines and the bus, and then you can send money home to your family as well to support them! In my country in Africa nowadays, no matter how hard or how long you work you cannot pay for these things – there is no way. It is heaven here in Cambridge because everything is so unbelievably *cheap* compared to in my country!
>
> For example, see this nice warm fleece jacket that I'm wearing? It was £4.99 at the supermarket and it was '*Buy one, Get one free*'! It's unbelievable. Brand new. Can you *imagine* it? [laughs and laughs] In my country there is no way nowadays that any sort of worker can afford to buy a jacket like this, even if he works so hard all week long. Here it's just a small part of your salary – *plus you buy one, get one free*! In the supermarket you just walk in, you get some tins of tomatoes for a few pence and it's '*Buy one, Get one free*'! It's unbelievable. It's like they are giving it all away. In my country no-one can afford a tin of tomatoes anymore, no matter how long they work. A tin of tomatoes has become like a dream. So we are all living in heaven here in Cambridge.

> Where I come from, the people, they are dying – actually dying every day, lots and lots of them. Here in Cambridge, elderly people have a pension to live on and nice accommodation and all the food and medicine they need. The government gives them all this if they don't have the money for it themselves. *They even go free on the bus!* [laughs a lot]. But back home where I come from – if you came there with me this minute – you would see our elderly people just lying on the ground inside the door of a hut or a concrete room, just lying on the bare ground with nothing – nothing – just waiting to die. They have no way of getting any food, clothes, medicines, nothing.[1]

The day I recorded Ruth's oral history, I understood just how effective refugee oral histories can be at reeducating us as hosts, overturning our preconceived ideas and reflecting our own environment back to us in a completely new light. Going out to meet her that morning – a refugee from a starving nation – the last thing in the world I expected her to say was that in Cambridge (one of the most expensive cities in the world's fourth richest economy) she found things laughably *cheap*. In the first five minutes, her fresh gaze taught me so much about my own local environment and its unexpected relationship to the wider world.

This is why, at the World Humanitarian Summit in 2016, it was established that in providing refugee aid to poor and developing economies, there needs to be much more focus on *the local*.[2] In refugee-hosting settings, attending to 'the local' means taking account of the place and the people who already live there, before refugees arrived. What was the local setting and community like, for better and for worse, before the refugee crisis that now requires aid? What were the needs and issues in the host community beforehand? What have been the impacts of the refugee crisis on host communities? How is the current refugee aid addressing or neglecting those issues? How much are host communities bearing the burden of helping refugees, and how much are they being supported themselves? This agenda, known as the 'localization of aid', has shifted the primary focus away from talking about 'international actors' (United Nations (UN) agencies, donor countries, international charities and so on) and onto talking about 'local actors'. And the aim is to develop partnerships with local communities that go deeper than just 'subcontracting local actors to work on international programs'.[3]

## Oral Histories with Host Communities

Several of the case studies below show how agencies are using applied oral history to advance this new approach. But to emphasize to you that this kind of work is *only beginning*, our first case study is a large, well-funded, cutting-edge project of this sort that hasn't yet completed its interviews. For our final case study, we'll look at a hands-on project that I did myself with a resistant host community in the Western city where I live: I hope it will encourage you to just take up these tools and push on with doing such a project of your own, wherever you are.

These seven case studies all did oral histories to gather the testimonies of aggrieved host communities. But as you read them, notice the quite different ways that each project planned from the outset to reach and use its findings. For instance, the first case study uses oral histories to get beyond stereotypes about what host community narrators feel they 'should' be saying, so as to uncover what they really think and feel about the refugee/host situation. The second uses applied oral history as a tool for mediation between refugee and host communities. A related project used oral history as 'detective work', to locate specific problems and tap into the host community's local knowledge for practical solutions. The third case study uses oral histories to review and explore what went wrong in a failed refugee resettlement program. This one focuses not on material issues but on the quality of the *relationship* between the incoming refugees and the host community agencies and officials responsible for resettling them. Interestingly, the project found that the core problem in this case was around communication and emotions (mutual distrust, misunderstandings and misplaced expectations), rather than around a lack of material resources.

The fourth case study uses oral histories to uncover the individual coping strategies improvised by the poorest members of the community that, proportionately, hosts the most refugees in the world – Lebanon. The fifth uses oral histories to capture the motivation of refugees in Colombia who themselves choose to act as hosts for further waves of refugees, voluntarily sharing with them the very little that they have to survive on themselves. The sixth examines two detailed oral history projects done by sociologists in the US within the populist, anti-migrant movement that elected Donald Trump as president. And the seventh uses oral histories to tackle prejudice head-on in a white UK community that was resistant to refugees and asylum seekers.

Hopefully, all these examples will inspire you to start defining some specific aims, methods and intended outcomes for such a project of your own. For that purpose, a short exercise after each case study will invite you to pause and imagine how you and others could do similar projects. We saw at the start of this book that the UN and its partner agencies have put out a global call to every citizen to think up, propose and launch initiatives like these. You will see that once such projects are set up and start to gain momentum, bigger agencies and businesses often step in to scale them up and fund them.

## *1. New Ways of Listening to Host Communities*

Using trained local interviewers, the *Refugee Hosts Project* is doing over 450 oral interviews with nine host communities across Lebanon, Jordan and Turkey – some of the world's most intensive 'refugee-hosting spaces'. The project, called 'Examining Local Community Experiences of and Responses to Displacement from Syria', aims to explore the hidden depths of how these host communities have experienced and responded to their influxes of Syrian refugees. The interviews will examine host communities' 'experiences of providing, seeking, receiving and being excluded from different forms of support'. They fundamentally ask 'who feels supported, and who feels neglected here?' The selection of narrators and the interview questions have also been designed to trace 'the influences of gender, political opinion, ethnicity and religious identity on these processes'.[4]

This project has several nuances worth noting as they help us understand issues around listening to host communities, and they may also help you to see what themes you might like to explore in an oral history project of your own with hosts. First, this project's language, concepts, relationships and methods are specifically designed to get behind the veil of what narrators feel they 'should' be saying, to find out what they really think and do, behind the roles and masks attributed to them within the public discourse around humanitarian aid. The project acknowledges that people often feel an 'obligation to fit the humanitarian narrative' (e.g. of being a generous host or a grateful refugee), which it considers to 'have long acted as a barrier' to real dialogue, often concealing hidden resources, attitudes and activities that could in fact be useful ways forward.[5]

Another twist in this project is that as well as interviewing 450 members of host communities, the project will also separately interview 100 staff of local, national and international refugee aid organizations in these localities. How do *they* feel the local host communities have responded to the influx of Syrian refugees? An interesting triangulation is being set up and explored here. Enabling agency professionals to describe host community attitudes could challenge any insincerity in the hosts' interviews. (Perhaps they will depict themselves as ideal, tolerant hosts, whereas agency staff can reveal that they are not?) But, in fact, a primary purpose of these agency interviews is to assess the *quality* of the relationships and rapport that the refugee aid agencies have with host communities. As the project puts it, these interviews 'will help identify the extent of national and international support for local community responses': in other words, how much are the agencies actually supporting the host communities?

In fact, in all refugee aid settings this relationship has turned out to be crucial and delicate. Unfortunately, both refugees and host communities often end up dramatically mistrusting the very aid agencies that are supposedly there to help (or at least, to help the refugees).[6] A case study further below gives a hands-on example of such a failure in relationships. When you think about it, this is an understandable risk: amidst disaster, both refugees and hosts inevitably *wish for* so much more than the meager assistance that agencies are currently able to provide. Disagreements arise too about *how* these very limited resources should be distributed. Finally, remember that from the refugees' point of view, aid agencies are basically part of and an expression of the 'host community', in that they are responsible for distributing whatever hosting resources are available and they manage the hosting environment where refugees are accommodated.

Yet another way that this project digs beneath stereotypical roles is by facilitating host community members to explore *writing* their own life stories and experiences, as well as narrating them orally in interviews. As the project puts it, these creative writing workshops facilitate host communities to both 'document' and 'resist' *their own* experiences of and responses to the refugee influx around them.[7] The act of writing gives both hosts and refugees a certain distance and 'permission' to express themselves differently. The project then also facilitates narrators to see how their stories connect – in themes, tone and motifs – with the stories of others in the present, in the distant past, in literature and in history. The host community are thus encouraged to connect their own experience with wider universal themes of displacement, welcoming and integration, and so to feel less alone and ignored with those experiences. Finally, the project will disseminate these connected stories to a wide range of audiences in the Middle East and the UK, to 'challenge the image of the individual suffering refugee' and reveal instead the creative, connective resilience in the web of hosts and refugees co-creating their lives together.

**What you could do.** You could, for instance, borrow from this case study the themes of *hosting and welcoming* on the one hand, and *fleeing and seeking integration* on the other. You could float those themes throughout your own project, weaving them into your interview questions as a recurring motif. Whether your project is with a host community only, or with refugees as well, the project could help both sides to reflect on and feel connected to both themes – both the noble, universal tradition of hospitality and giving refuge, and the emotions and realities of having to flee and request that shelter. These are universal experiences that anyone can relate to, at least by imagination and empathy. And even the most settled host communities usually have flight and migration behind them somewhere in their history. Encouraging both sides to reflect on both themes, and to tell their culture's traditions and experience of both themes, can break them out of their fixed, polarized positions into a wider, richer, more equal and universal dialogue.

## 2. When Host Communities Are as Poor as Refugees

We know that some of the resistance to refugees in the West comes from genuine fear that host communities will suffer as jobs, benefits, housing and public services get spread more thinly due to the needs of refugees. But in the least developed economies – which host the majority of the world's refugees – that fear can be much more explosive.[8] In parts of Africa, host communities are already at least as poor as the masses of refugees pouring in to live in their cities and nearby camps. Access to very limited resources like clean water, tillable land, food supplies, healthcare and policing can be desperately overstretched. These host communities' anxieties and conflicts over sharing extremely limited resources can be very real and urgent.[9]

For instance, several hundred thousand Burundi refugees fled armed conflict in the Democratic Republic of Congo to move into northwestern Tanzania in refugee camps run by the UN. But many in the host community – already among the world's poorest – came to feel that the refugees were better provided for in the camps than the locals had ever been by their own government! As desperation grew among the host community over the strain on their already scarce survival resources, two NGOs working in the refugee camps organized a formal process of conflict resolution. It was based entirely on listening to oral testimonies of *all* the stakeholders – not just the refugees – as they stated their concerns.[10]

Those formally listened to included, on the one hand, village leaders, community representatives and politicians from the host communities and, on the other, refugee representatives, refugee camp managers and staff from aid agencies and the UN. As one impact study put it, 'these meetings not only allowed for discussion about problems or conflicts between the refugees and local communities, but also promoted working together to come up with solutions'.[11] Participants stated that the overall relationship between the refugees and the locals improved as a result of the extensive, organized, mutual listening implemented in this conflict resolution process. Mutual listening to testimonies helped to resolve specific conflicts between host and refugee communities, but it also helped to build new social relationships between the two groups.

This was a farseeing, applied oral history project that deliberately addressed the needs and concerns of hosts as well as refugees, as the only way to reduce tensions between host and refugee populations in the poorest environments going forward. The stark reality is that with the coming surge of refugees due to climate change, this technique of deep listening to the roundtable concerns of *both* host communities and refugee groups will have to become the norm.

A different example was in the Diffa region, one of the humanitarian hot spots of the Lake Chad refugee crisis in Africa. More than 133,000 refugees and displaced persons are crowded into the county's four camps. But the needs of the local Mabanese host community, numbering only 36,000, had not been considered when the refugees poured in, 'leaving these already vulnerable communities quickly outnumbered by the new arrivals'.[12]

A cleverly designed project of applied oral history was aimed at locating the *specific root causes* of tensions and disputes between refugees from the area's Gendrassa camp and the surrounding host community villages. Before this, no listening at all had been done on the needs of Diffa's beleaguered host population. But across a single month in late 2015, the United Nations High Commissioner for Refugees (UNHCR) and local agencies did no fewer than 366 'Key Informant Interviews' with host community members at over 130 spots around the locality.[13] Narrators were carefully selected across ages and demographics to ensure there were representative interviews with three categories – women, male elders and male youth. The project also did group oral histories with this host community in workshops that built up 'participatory maps' of how the group perceived their landscape, its traditional boundaries and its hot spots for disputes and conflict with the refugees.

The findings from this thoughtfully planned and rapidly delivered project were indeed, as had been hoped, very specific and pragmatic. As well as detailing the problems and their order of priority, the interviews also proposed specific 'fixes' that could realistically be delivered to resolve them. For instance, it turned out that, unlike in many refugee-hosting areas, access to water wasn't a problem here because since the refugees had arrived, the aid agencies were providing public taps and hand pumps for *both* refugees and hosts. However, it emerged that a lack of legal documentation was in fact as much of a problem for locals as it always is for refugees: the locals themselves had never had identity papers before, and in the new, more official environment this was now restricting *their* movement and access to services as much as those of refugees.

But the core problem came as a further surprise. It turned out to be the single biggest cause of conflict between the two populations, yet one that could be easily remedied: it was the lack of sufficiently clear demarcation boundaries around the refugee camps. Refugees and host communities were getting deeper into conflict over disputed ownership and use of these tracts of land. Host community narrators told interviewers that the creation of visible, agreed boundaries was indispensable for the two communities 'to coexist peacefully in the available space'. The UN report records (translated into the UN's jargon unfortunately, not in the narrators' own words!) that the host narrators also requested that

> once boundaries have been physically demarcated, information campaigns should be used to sensitize both communities to their location, as well as the reasons for their existence. It will be essential for aid actors to raise awareness around these boundaries and what the implications and risks of crossing these would be.[14]

The report concluded that

> whereas it is commonly perceived that displaced populations are more vulnerable than host communities, (this project's) findings disclose that host populations face similar protection concerns. Physical and psychological violations were reported by host communities at the same rate as by Internally Displaced Persons at refugee sites and camps.[15]

As another report had previously put it, 'there is wide recognition of these tensions amongst humanitarian agencies, though it is also widely noted that these problems are ineffectively addressed and under-researched'.[16] This book provides a methodology to help remedy that.

**What you could do**. If you are a professional working with an agency or charity delivering services to refugees anywhere in the world, you could do this kind of project with the surrounding host community. Your findings could help improve the efficiency and acceptance of any public services that you deliver. But if, like most people, you're not delivering specialized services to refugee settlements, you could instead just go and do the necessary listening to whatever 'host' community is around you – whether that's middle-class Westerners who can influence politicians, or a disenfranchised local underclass in the West who are resistant to the very idea of refugee resettlement, even if no refugees are near them.

## *3. What Went Wrong? Interviewing Host Agencies about a Failed Refugee Program*

South American countries have traditionally been receptive to doing their best to resettle refugees. But in 2012, two host communities there decided to learn from the mistakes of one failed resettlement program, before proceeding with any more. An applied oral history project was commissioned to examine what had gone wrong with the process of resettling Palestinian refugees in Chile and Brazil.[17]

In 2007 and 2008, each had accepted for resettlement more than 100 Palestinian refugees, who had previously been surviving for years in refugee camps in the Jordan desert along the border between Iraq and Syria. The resettlement program raised a lot of positive interest among the South American host communities, as well as significant funding. A network of civil society organizations and local municipalities had mobilized to support it.

However, just a few years later, these Palestinian refugees were openly unhappy with their resettlement in Chile and Brazil. There had been a considerable breakdown in relations between them and the agencies responsible for hosting and supporting them. More than 70% of the Palestinian refugees interviewed in Brazil said that the country had not met their expectations, and over 50% of those interviewed in Chile said the same. But when the refugees had complained or raised the issue of 'unfulfilled promises', officials tended implicitly or explicitly to view them as 'ungrateful' and as having an unhelpful 'refugee mentality' from years of having been assisted in refugee camps elsewhere.[18] The authorities wisely decided to organize for an independent listener to come in and hear both sides' experiences in depth so as to learn what had gone wrong, in preparation for the many further resettlements of Middle Eastern refugees that were planned for the years ahead.

To find out exactly what had gone wrong, the project did a total of 80 in-depth interviews with both 'sides' – with the refugees and with the municipal, national and UN staff responsible for their resettlement. The core finding from the interviews was that the tensions between the two sides arose essentially out of 'unfulfilled expectations' on both sides, most crucially around each side's understanding of the notion of '*self-sufficiency*' among resettled refugees. Through the interviews, it became clear that the host society staff administering the resettlement programs in both Brazil and Chile had a set of expectations towards the refugees, from whom they expected a lot of this 'self-sufficiency'. The officials' interpretation of this was that the refugees should quickly develop the ability to sustain themselves economically. But the refugees had understood this term 'self-sufficiency' very differently, taking it to mean that their basic economic needs would be *looked after*, plus they would have a lot of freedom and a high degree of choice and control over their own resettlement process, none of which turned out to be the case.

Fortunately, these two South American governments took a learning approach to this experience, and went on to develop a program of improved responses for the new refugees about to arrive, based on specific recommendations from this project's oral history interviews. The new measures included much more comprehensive information provided to refugees in their own language before they accepted resettlement; better language teaching in the countries offering resettlement; and quicker, smoother legal processes for access to citizenship and passports.

A really important body of such work is emerging around the world – and very much more of it needs to be done – to study the expectations of refugees and host communities towards each other. For instance, host societies may unwittingly have projected to future refugees some very unrealistic scenarios about the lifestyles that refugees can expect to achieve once resettled there. The disappointment can be bitter, and can end up fostering generations of alienated resettled refugees, rather than integrated ones. Oral history is a tool *par excellence* here, for capturing narrators' misplaced and disappointed expectations. For instance in her book *US Media and Migration*, one researcher did oral histories in order to take a few steps back and find out how refugees' expectations of their destination in the US had been preshaped by media messages they had received back home, long before they ever even *knew* that they would have to flee there as refugees.[19] This project listened in depth to refugees' accounts of how international media had led them to *think* the US would be – and the serious contrasts with how they actually found it to be when they later had to try to build a new life there.

We know that this book is only about refugees, not economic migrants: our study stops at the fault line between refugees (who have to flee due to danger) and economic migrants (who travel to seek a better quality of life). But we can note here, in passing, that insightful applications of oral history have huge potential for *better informing* future waves of economic migrants who have not yet left home or reached their intended destinations. Yes, developed economies must do much more to share their wealth and build the economies of the poorest countries, and the best long-term solution to excessive economic migration is to help those societies build sustainable futures for their young people at home.[20] But, meanwhile, important oral history projects are currently busy capturing the often starkly unrealistic expectations of many young economic migrants, in particular those fleeing extreme poverty and climate change in sub-Saharan Africa. One example is with the predominantly African youth surviving outdoors at ports in northern France, hoping to smuggle themselves to Britain, who seem to have a distortedly optimistic perception of refugee and immigrant life there. This misplaced optimism is powerful enough to make them reject the option (in fact, a legal obligation) to request asylum in France, the European country where they are already safely arrived.[21]

Another example is *Mediterranean*, a BBC TV documentary by Simon Reeves that interviewed illegal migrants in Morocco. Though refused a filming permit, Reeves managed illicitly to interview the young illegal migrants hiding out in the forest, waiting for their chance to cross into Ceuta, the heavily fortified Spanish enclave within Morocco, where they would be on European Union soil. They had travelled a long and dangerous journey, crossing the Sahara to get this far, and felt they were now just a 20-foot, razor-wire fence away from their European dream. But Reeves himself then crossed over to the Spanish mainland and interviewed one of their peers who had 'succeeded' in crossing: he is now a slave worker trapped in subhuman conditions in the vast plastic polytunnel farms in Almeria, along the southern coast of Spain. In his interview, the young man fervently urges his peers not to come, as they have been seriously misled about what awaits them on the European side of the water.[22]

Because overoptimistic misinformation and misconceptions do seem to be driving some economic migrants from Africa, some projects are trying to open up a dialogue between oral testimonies gathered in Africa from youth considering making this dangerous migration from their homeland and these warning contrasts with testimonies from compatriots who have found themselves completely adrift and excluded from Western economies once they have got there. It can be a disincentive to hear firsthand the harsh reality of the Calais Jungle from a peer who heartily recommends that you instead stay at home and try to improve your circumstances and qualifications there. A beautiful example of this kind of work is *Lights in the Distance: Exile and Refuge at the Borders of Europe* by Daniel Trilling. The book is a set of sensitive, in-depth oral histories, done on the move with individuals – mostly refugees but some economic migrants too – across the various stages of their journeys. Jamal, one of the oral narrators in Daniel Trilling's *Lights in the Distance*, describes how shocked he was at the recession and poverty in parts of Europe, where he had expected a prosperous existence: 'You arrive in Athens and you see people sleeping in the street, eating from the garbage, shops closed down'.[23] This oral history that Jamal gave to Trilling is crucial. Jamal narrates his many points of disillusionment along the stages of his journey, and all that he would have done differently if he could have seen ahead. He concludes that he would have stayed at home and studied harder to get himself a place at his country's state university. As Fatima, another of Trilling's in-depth narrators, explains: 'This is why I am talking to girls on Facebook, telling them, "Don't come to Europe. Do you know what it's like? Do you really want to earn money this way?"… telling the girls in the (detention) center: "Tell your friends at home what it's like and not to come"'.[24]

Figure 5.1 shows some of the stages of the economic migrant journey where important further difficulties are often caused or compounded by a lack of accurate information and honest communication. Problems include: idealized media images of the future destination; peer pressure to go there and do well; shame and embarrassment at not succeeding at that; a social reality in the new life that can be grim and alienating, even if material needs are being met; the alienation and lack of integration for successive generations born in such a destination society. Applied oral histories can play a massively helpful role in disentangling these issues by:

- listening carefully to economic migrants' original beliefs and hopes at each stage of their journey;
- contrasting them, where necessary, with the actual experiences the migrants end up having;
- sharing these truths honestly with those considering migrating in the future;
- starting dialogue about more effective ways to move towards the desired prosperity and quality of life, whether back home or in the West.

**What you could do.** You could ask either refugees or economic migrants what their advice would be for compatriots thinking of making the long journey to the West. Obviously, this is especially relevant for economic migrants who are not entirely obliged to flee for their lives. What do they need to know, consider, prepare and take into account before leaving home? And what have refugees learnt

| → | | | | | |
|---|---|---|---|---|---|
| Economic migrants' unrealistic beliefs and lack of information about their destination | Their shock and disillusionment when they get there | Through pride and social pressure, not communicating this truth back to their peers at home | Accurate information about all they would realistically need in order to reach their aspirations in the West (e.g. qualifications, contacts, cultural attitudes, language skills, etc.) | Honest feedback about how unhappy and unfulfilled they may still feel even if they do get resettled in the West [25] | Listening closely to alienation among the second generation born into such unintegrated lifestyles in the West |

**FIGURE 5.1** Stages of economic migration where oral histories can communicate the truth back to those considering migrating in the future

along the way (knowledge, attitudes, skills, contacts) that could enable those back home to improve their chances if they have to make the same journey? You could extract their key recommendations and share them with a cultural organization that has links to their communities back home, and can get those recommendations disseminated there.

## 4. The Coping Strategies of Those Hosting the Most Refugees

One of the best places to look for and listen to tensions between host communities and refugees has got to be Lebanon. Years into the Syrian refugee crisis, and with war constantly on its doorstep, the tiny country of Lebanon hosts the most refugees per capita in the world: refugee numbers there now equal about one-third of what the Lebanese population was before the Syrian crisis. And a large proportion of those refugees in Lebanon are highly vulnerable, living in conditions of poverty and insecurity – not least because many native Lebanese were living that way already in this beleaguered, fragile nation.

So our next case study explores the challenges and coping strategies of the host community in Lebanon. The results contributed to an important international policy paper on the possible futures for Lebanon, entitled *Lebanon: Looking Ahead in Times of Crisis*.[26] The project did 97 interviews with host community members in Lebanon. But first, it segmented Lebanese society into a 'ladder' of four socioeconomic levels. The report explains why:

> The impact of the refugees from Syria is felt throughout Lebanon and Lebanese society. Yet the impact is experienced differently by different segments of society, and is disproportionately impacting upon the lower socio-economic segments since they are the part of the host communities who are co-living with the refugees ... As we move further down the socio-economic ladder, the directness of the impact tends to increase.[27]

So the project carefully selected its oral narrators from among the poorest (who, importantly, comprise over one-third of the country's population). Stark interviews captured the hosts' coping strategies, finding that

> like refugee households, poor Lebanese households control expenditure as a coping strategy to withstand stresses to their household economy. They reduce the number of meals they eat and the quantity they consume, and buy cheap and extremely low quality food (damaged and close to expiry). While adults in (host community) households prioritize the needs of children when it comes to reducing food expenditure, there are times when the entire household cuts its food consumption, surviving on bread and tea alone.[28]

The project used what it called 'open-ended, semi-structured interviews', taking care to let narrators define interview priorities for themselves, rather than responding to a checklist prepared by the interviewer. The researchers felt that this, along with the careful anonymization of interviews, allowed them 'to reach the parts which other methods cannot reach', accessing host narrators' 'thoughts, values, prejudices, perceptions, views, feelings and perspectives'.[29] The result is a 56-page report detailing the innermost thoughts, frustrations, concerns and coping strategies of Lebanon's most hard-pressed host communities. Many of the primary impacts on hosts were as one might predict – higher prices and rents, competition for work and housing, etc.[30] But the anonymized, high-trust nature of the interviews meant that narrators also confided and explored at length other specific things that pained them most about how their lives had been impacted by the refugees.

For some, it was the now incessant noise in their tiny, overcrowded streets. Or for many women in the Lebanese host community, it was an anxious belief that Syrian refugee women and war widows were 'stealing their men': Syrian refugee families were willing to accept little or no dowry, whereas, in the culture of Lebanese families getting married is an expensive business. Host women also confided about now having to flirt with soldiers to get past checkpoints when they didn't have proper identity papers. The report shows these host community narrators grappling with their own ambivalence: they are torn between the frustration of having such a reduced quality of life since the 2011 influx of Syrian refugees and trying to maintain a self-image as non-racist supporters of Syrians. As the report puts it,

> this is further exacerbated by the fact that most refugees receive some form of aid from international and local NGOs. The majority of members of the host communities in all the regions covered by this study expressed a sense of injustice in this regard, because they feel that their own situation is no better than that of the refugees, and yet they are left out of the distribution of aid. Even those narrators whose circumstances are better than those of the refugees expressed a sense of injustice at the fact that poorer host community members are not receiving aid.[31]

It is worth noting again that this project went on to help inform and shape an important policy document on future directions for Lebanon, one of the countries that is a key trigger point for stability in the Middle East.

**What you could do**. Basically, you could replicate a project like this anywhere that a host community is genuinely under pressure and experiencing a poorer quality of life due to an influx of refugees. Like this project, you could take the time to gain the trust of a host community that have not been much listened to, letting them know they can speak to you openly without being dismissed as ungenerous or simply 'anti-migrant'. (An example of this kind of work was an investigation by British TV's Channel 4 which revealed that Britain is housing asylumseekers primarily in its poorest areas, hence impacting most on the poorest of the British population, as we saw was also the case in Lebanon).[32]

## *5. When Refugees Host Other Refugees*

We can all understand the host community ambivalence revealed in the case study above: we would surely feel it too if, like the Lebanese poor, we saw our own children go hungry while incoming refugees got fed. But our next case study is about a very different hosting phenomenon that is also relatively common, though little publicized. This is when refugees themselves act as extraordinarily generous hosts towards other refugees.[33] In this uplifting example, Colombian refugees carry forward the refugee-friendly traditions of Latin America by choosing to offer up the very little they have to be shared with a new wave of refugees arriving from the now collapsing state of Venezuela.

After a 52-year civil war, Colombia has the most internally displaced persons in the world with 7.3 million individuals – more than 15% of the population – registered as such by 2016. In addition, hundreds of thousands of Colombians live abroad as refugees, mainly in neighboring countries. Most have found refuge in Ecuador, Venezuela, Panama and Costa Rica, but very few are officially registered as asylumseekers or refugees.[34] Meanwhile, neighboring Venezuela has been urgently diagnosed as having 'the largest growing refugee crisis in the world'.[35] As I write, 5,000 displaced Venezuelans are fleeing across the border into Colombia every day. By 2019, over 3 million had already fled the collapsing Venezuelan state, escaping into neighboring Brazil, Chile, Colombia and Peru. It is predicted that a further two million could join them by 2020.[36]

But one UN video report, called *Displaced Colombians Open Their Homes to Venezuelan Refugees and Migrants*, has focused on an uplifting microcosm within this great drama of human upheaval. In first-person video interviews, one couple explain how,

> having fled their own home in Colombia due to conflict, Alvis and Marnellis understood the struggles facing Venezuelan migrants and refugees. Now settled in Las Delicias near the Colombian/Venezuelan border, the couple have opened their home to Venezuelans seeking shelter.[37]

In the interviews, the narrators give their oral history of their own flight as refugees before explaining – as if it were to them the only, obvious logic – that having been refugees themselves, they feel it's only natural that they would now share everything they've got (down to the intimacy of their own home) with a new wave of refugees pouring in to the very place where they had found refuge themselves. Demonstrating the power of example, 23 other families in their town went on to do the same thing, taking into their homes a total of 130 refugee men, women and children displaced from Venezuela.[38]

In fact, as part of the world's new focus on the proactive resourcefulness of refugees, a whole field of oral history research is opening up to capture and document this sort of refugee-to-refugee hosting.[39] Otherwise, this phenomenon often passes under the radar, as refugees' individual lives and daily activities are so little documented.[40] In their crowded, impoverished environments, it is often not obvious to the passing eye that many of them are proactively going way out of their way to share their meager resources with other refugees. I saw this in action myself when interviewing a penniless Syrian war refugee who spent his days and nights in the camp methodically going about assisting others whom he considered to be even more vulnerable than himself, such as widows, the sick and unaccompanied children.

**What you could do.** You don't always have to have recorded an original oral history interview yourself. You can always take existing oral histories that have been captured by others and – with the relevant permissions – take steps to publicize and communicate their useful messages in ways that bring new perspectives to public perceptions of refugee situations. For instance, the story above about Colombian refugees Alvis and Marnellis sharing what they have with a new wave of refugees, sensitively recommunicated through a newspaper article, local radio slot or town hall exhibition in your local area, will inevitably set thoughts stirring about standards of universal generosity and dignity.

## *6. Listening to Anti-Migrant Communities in the West*

Our next case study could not be more different. This is applied oral history that listens to the right-wing, anti-migrant discontent of white populist voters in the West, most of whom have rarely, if ever, met a refugee face-to-face. Rather than just giving in to the scorn that left-wing intellectuals often feel for such groups, sociologist Arlie Russell Hochschild went and genuinely listened to these people for five years, in the Deep South state of Louisiana in the US. She went to investigate what she and other political scientists call 'the great paradox' – the fact that the lowest socioeconomic classes, whose material interests are most damaged by right-wing politics, persist in electing strong-arm, right-wing politicians, seeing them as some sort of cure-all. Her book, *Strangers in Their Own Land: Anger and Mourning on the American Right*, reveals what her narrators told her.[41] While acknowledging the 'large gap in life-worlds' between herself and them, she nonetheless listened respectfully and at length to their concerns. Those included deindustrialization; the wage squeeze of recent decades; robotization, with manufacturing and manual jobs getting left behind; and the rise of previously subordinate groups such as women, ethnic minorities and gays.

As her narrators see it, this has led to an unfair outcome in the competition for the 'American Dream'. They themselves hadn't received the rewards that they felt they were now due after a lifetime of hard work. And, above all, they perceived these newly prominent groups – women, immigrants, second-generation ethnic minorities, environmentalists – as getting to 'cut in line' unfairly and jump the queue. They explained to her that seeing these social groups exalted in the liberal media – while they themselves felt scorned as backward and uneducated, cast aside as ill-adapted for the future economy – left them feeling like '*strangers in their own land*'. Far-right movements are only too quick to step in towards such people, offering them a resurgence of collective dignity, supremacy and ethnonationalistic pride.

Commentators have praised Hochschild's method for 'the way it makes it possible to explore, see and even to empathize with the "anger and mourning" expressed behind these political attitudes and choices'.[42] Her interviews unearthed deep-seated emotions of loss, pain and fear of the future beneath this '*they're cutting in line*' narrative offered by her narrators. This notion of other groups jumping unfairly ahead of white, Western working-class males is what Hochschild feels her interviews located as 'the deep story' behind this rise in right-wing populism. (We saw in Chapter 2 that another such 'deep story' is the far-right's paranoid fantasy of the 'Great Replacement' of white workers by immigrants of color.)

A similar tranche of work has been done in the US by political scientist Katherine Cramer. Her book *The Politics of Resentment: Rural Consciousness in Wisconsin and the Rise of Scott Walker* is the fruit of a decade of listening closely to political attitudes in rural Wisconsin, US.[43] Like Hochschild, she too was motivated to investigate the 'great paradox' that perplexes many political scientists. Kramer defines the paradox as: 'Why do these people vote against their own interests, electing right wing politicians whose economic policies serve the interest of big business and employers, not of workers?'[44]

Kramer's long and careful listening process reveals these populist masses to be manipulated by 'political actors generating support by tapping into intergroup divides'. Like the perception of 'cutting in line' revealed by Hochschild's interviews, Kramer's narrators too are 'fueled by perceptions of distributive injustice'.[45] Cramer's research points out that these perceptions were often unfounded: her narrators' rural areas were often much better subsidized by public funding and services than her narrators either realized or were willing to admit. But in all the contemporary oral history being done with newly populist voters, it is clear that it is emotional belief and conviction that are directing their political choices, rather than rational facts.

**What you could do.** You could interview a host community to find out what things helped them most when they were expected to accept refugees resettled in their area. What social or cultural habits in either the host culture or refugee culture did they feel were helpful, to help them move forward and accept the incomers? Examples could be traditions of hospitality, neighborliness, faith practices, volunteering, sports, shared hobbies or interests. You could use their testimonies to create an exhibition in a local library, town hall or in the local press or media, communicating all this back to the host community, the refugee community and the agencies responsible for integrating them. Or you could interview members of each of those three groups, using the questions above. This would engage a triangular dialogue that could continue well beyond your own oral history project.

## *7. Tackling Anti-Migrant Prejudice in a Resistant Host Community in the West*

Inspired by projects like those above, I thought to myself: 'What could *I* do to help with the refugee crisis, while working here in a British city?' I decided to just follow where my interests led me, using my own time to do oral histories with the people in my immediate environment. Over 18 months I did in-depth oral histories with a dozen refugees from different countries who had political asylum in Cambridge, where my day job was. Their rich, diverse oral histories were published as the book *Asylum under Dreaming Spires: Refugees' Lives in Cambridge Today*.[46]

But I also analyzed their testimonies, extracting from them all the insights and recommendations that they had to offer about how their integration could be handled better. City government went on to implement a thorough program of policy actions based on these recommendations. The program included:

- publishing myth-busting facts in the municipal magazine, for instance debunking the myth that foreigners got preferential treatment in the city's social housing (in fact, 96% of the city's social housing tenants were British);
- a festival that the refugees held for the host community, with traditional dances, music and foods from their home cultures provided by the refugees;
- methodically supporting settled refugees to stand for local elections and gain political office in city government;
- providing training workshops that challenged prejudice among the most resistant parts of the host community, who in our setting were unemployed white English from working-class backgrounds.

My own past interviews with the latter community had shown me that their pride in the former British Empire fuelled in many of them a significant sense of entitlement that *they* should be able to travel and settle wherever they wanted abroad. When I questioned those double standards with one elderly lady, she answered, as if explaining something obvious to a slow child: 'But lovey, we're *British*: we can live wherever we *want*.' (She nostalgically believed this to be true, whereas it is, of course, factually incorrect: nowadays, international rules on visas and residency rights apply as much to Britons as to other Westerners.) I also knew that retiring to Spain was a cultural norm for many in this population group. There, they felt comfortable grouping together in completely British enclaves, not speaking the hosts' language yet receiving Spanish public services in ways carefully adapted to their needs (such as free medical services provided to them in English translation by the Spanish state).

So we designed a fun, role-play workshop for these English residents in Cambridge who were resistant to incoming refugees. First, the game – apparently about them retiring to Spain – cheerfully elicited from them the comprehensive list of services and supports that they felt should automatically be provided to them on their arrival in Spain, from free healthcare to interpreters, bin collections to public transport. But then we reversed the game's roles so that they played the role of migrants arriving in England: we asked what services and supports should be provided to those incomers. And they begrudgingly admitted that they held illogical, unsustainable double standards for themselves and for other nationalities.[47]

| Project's focus | Purpose of oral history project | With which host community? | Final product and outcomes | Type of oral history | Continent and country |
|---|---|---|---|---|---|
| **1. New ways of listening to host communities** | To get behind stereotypes and 'politically correct' language | Those hosting the most refugees | Reports, policy recommendations and publicity to raise awareness internationally | Interviews & life-story writing workshops | Middle East: Lebanon, Jordan and Turkey |
| **2. Hosts as poor as refugees are** | To uncover specific host grievances that could be addressed and to open a dialogue for conflict resolution | Locals near the refugee camps; women, elder males & male youth | Conflicts resolved; shared development projects going forward | Interviews listening to host community's concerns about refugees | Africa: Tanzania and South Sudan |
| **3. Reviewing a failed refugee program** | To find out what had gone wrong, for future reference | Aid-agency staff responsible for hosting refugees | Specific policies to do next refugee resettlements in a better way | Interviews listening to mistakes made by host aid agencies | South America: Brazil and Chile |
| **4. Those hosting the most refugees** | To reveal their coping strategies and needs | The poorest third of the host community population | Report of policy recommendations, to help address Lebanon's 'time bomb' pressures into the future | Anonymized interviews, targeted to reach the poorest; fluid enough to capture their ambivalent feelings | Middle East: Lebanon |
| **5. When refugees host other refugees** | To celebrate and publicize the generosity of refugees-turned-hosts | Former refugees, now hosting others | UN video interviews, broadcast on Youtube | Video interviews with hosts explaining why they're being so generous | South America: Colombia |
| **6. White anti-migrant voters in the West** | To better understand their motivation and their political mass movement | White working underclass who feel 'left behind' | Two mainstream books, plus much public debate on them | 'Deep immersion'; unhurried, high-trust interviews over five years | USA: rural Louisiana and Wisconsin |
| **7. A resistant host community in the West** | To engage with resistant host communities face-to-face, and shift prejudices | Poorest among host community, with an 'anti-migrant' culture | Trainings for this host community, delivered by city government | In-depth oral history interviews, published verbatim as a book | Europe: urban England |

**FIGURE 5.2** Case studies of oral history projects with host communities

**What you could do**. On this topic, anyone, anywhere, can get involved and help. Whether you are in a region that hosts a lot of refugees or one that hosts none, you could just start interviewing the home community around you to gather their thoughts, fears and concerns about refugees. No matter how unreasonable some of them might seem to you, it is crucial that this set of views be aired, so that those fears can be addressed. You could analyze these host community oral histories to extract a summary list, in priority order, of all their concerns, illustrated with heartfelt quotes in their own words. A package of reassuring facts and mythbusters could respond to those concerns, delivering public education and awareness through local newspapers, television and radio, schools, town halls, community centers, faith centers and libraries.

Before we move on to our how-to chapters, Figure 5.2 summarizes for you the sheer diversity of purpose, narrators and final products among these host community case studies that we've just explored.

## References

Berry, Leah, 'The Impact of Environmental Degradation on Refugee–Host Relations: A Case Study from Tanzania', *New Issues in Refugee Research*, Working Paper No.151. Geneva: UNHCR, 2008 [Available at www.unhcr.org/47a315c72.html; accessed on 21-6-2019].

Bishop, Sarah, *U.S. Media and Migration: Refugee Oral Histories*. Abingdon: Routledge, 2016.

Brenner, Mary and Kia-Keating, Maryam, 'Psychosocial and Academic Adjustment among Resettled Refugee Youth'. In *Annual Review of Comparative and International Education 2016 (International Perspectives on Education and Society, Vol. 30)* (pp 221–249). Bingley: Emerald Publishing, 2016.

Carvajal, Dayra, 'As Colombia Emerges from Decades of War, Migration Challenges Mount', *Migration Information Source* online, Migration Policy Institute, 13-4-2017 [Available at www.migrationpolicy.org/article/colombia-emerges-decades-war-migration-challenges-mount; accessed on 21-6-2019].

Collier, Paul, *Exodus: How Migration Is Changing our World*. Oxford: Oxford University Press, 2013.

CNN TV, 'Why You Should Care about Venezuela', online, 4-2-2019 [Available at https://edition.cnn.com/videos/world/2019/02/04/venezuela-refugee-crisis-walsh-orig.cnn; accessed on 21-6-2019].

Cramer, Katherine, *The Politics of Resentment: Rural Consciousness in Wisconsin and the Rise of Scott Walker*. Chicago: University of Chicago Press, 2016.

Cramer, Katherine, 'The Politics of Resentment: What I Learned by Listening', MIT online, 31-5-2017 [Available at https://civic.mit.edu/2017/05/31/kathy-cramer-on-the-politics-of-resentment-what-i-learned-from-listening/; accessed on 21-6-2019].

Espinoza, Marcia Vera, 'Extra-Regional Refugee Resettlement in South America: The Palestinian Experience', *Forced Migration Review*, 56: 47–49, Oct 2017.

Espinoza, Marcia Vera, 'The Politics of Resettlement: Expectations and Unfulfilled Promises in Chile and Brazil'. In *Refugee Resettlement: Power, Politics and Humanitarian Governance* (pp 222–243), edited by Jubilut Garnier and Sandvik Bergtora. New York: Berghahn Books, 2018.

Fiddian-Qasmiyeh, Elena, 'Refugees Helping Refugees: How a Palestinian Refugee Camp in Lebanon Is Welcoming Syrians', *The Conversation* online, 4-11-2015 [Available at http://

theconversation.com/refugees-helping-refugees-how-a-palestinian-camp-in-lebanon-is-welcoming-syrians-48056; accessed on 21-6-2019].

Fiddian-Qasmiyeh, Elena, 'Refugees Hosting Refugees', *Forced Migration Review*, 53: 25–27, Sept 2016.

Fiddian-Qasmiyeh, Elena, 'Refugee–Refugee Relations in Contexts of Overlapping Displacement', *International Journal of Urban and Regional Research*, 12-1-2016.

Fiddian-Qasmiyeh, Elena, 'Shadows and Echoes In/Of Displacement: Temporalities, Spatialities and Materialities of Displacement', *Refugee Hosts Project* online, 19-11-2018 [Available at https://refugeehosts.org/2018/11/19/shadows-and-echoes-in-of-displacement; accessed on 21-6-2019].

Gillespie, Marie, Ampofo, Lawrence, Cheesman, Margaret, Faith, Becky, Iliadou, Evgenia, Issa, Ali, Osseiran, Souad and Skleparis, Dimitris *Mapping Refugee Media Journeys: Smartphones and Social Media Networks*. Paris: Open University/ France Médias Monde, 2016 [Available at www.open.ac.uk/ccig/research/projects/mapping-refugee-media-journeys#; accessed on 21-6-2019].

Harsch, Leonie, 'Giving Refugees a Voice? Looking beyond "Refugee Stories"', *Refugee Hosts Project* online, 8-1-2018 [Available at https://refugeehosts.org/2018/01/08/giving-refugees-a-voice-looking-beyond-refugee-stories; accessed on 21-6-2019].

Hoffman, Marella, *Asylum under Dreaming Spires: Refugees' Lives in Cambridge Today*. Cambridge: Cambridge Editions in partnership with the Living Refugee Archive, University of East London, 2017.

Ikanda, Fred, 'Deteriorating Conditions of Hosting Refugees: A Case Study of the Dadaab Complex in Kenya', *African Study Monographs*, 29(1), 2008 [Available at http://jambo.africa.kyotou.ac.jp/kiroku/asm_normal/abstracts/pdf/29-1/07-14Ikanda.pdf; accessed on 21-6-2019].

Jacobsen, Karen, 'Livelihoods in Conflict: The Pursuit of Livelihoods by Refugees and the Impact on the Human Security of Host Communities', *International Migration*, 40(5), 2002 [Available at www.humanitarianinnovation.com/uploads/7/3/4/7/7347321/jacobsen_2002.pdf; accessed on 21-6-2019].

Lyons, Kate and Duncan, Pamela, 'It's a Shambles: Data Show Most Asylum Seekers Put in Poorest Parts of Britain', *The Guardian*, 9-4–2017.

Lyytinen, Eveliina, 'The Politics of Mistrust: Congolese Refugees and the Institutions Providing Refugee Protection in Kampala, Uganda'. In *Urban Refugees: Challenges in Protection, Services and Policy* (pp. 76–97), edited by Koichi Koizumi and Gerhard Hoffstaedter. Abingdon: Routledge, 2015.

Martinez, Marta, *Displaced Colombians Open Their Homes to Venezuelan Refugees and Migrants*, UN video report. Cúcuta, Colombia: UN, 2018 [Available at www.unhcr.org/uk/news/stories/2018/12/5c12bbae4/displaced-colombians-open-doors-venezuelan-refugees-migrants.html; accessed on 21-6-2019].

Maystadt, Jean Francois and Verwimp, Philip, 'Winners and Losers among a Refugee-Hosting Population', *Development and Cultural Change*, 62(4): 679–809, July 2014.

Oxfam GB, *Self-Protection and Coping Strategies of Refugees from Syria and Host Communities in Lebanon*. Nairobi: Oxfam GB, 2015.

Oxfam International, *Lebanon: Looking Ahead in Times of Crisis: Taking Stock of the Present to Urgently Build Sustainable Options for the Future*. Nairobi: Oxfam International, 2015.

*Refugee Hosts*, website [Available at https://refugeehosts.org/blog/contextualising-the-localisation-of-aid-agenda; accessed on 21-6-2019].

Revees, Simon, *Mediterranean*, Episode 4, BBC TV, 28-10–2018.

Russell Hochschild, Arlie, *Strangers in Their Own Land: Anger and Mourning on the American Right*. New York: The New Press, 2016.

Shenk, Timothy, 'Booked: Capitalizing on Rural Resentment with Katherine Cramer', *Dissent* magazine online, 7-2-2017 [Available at www.dissentmagazine.org/blog/booked-katherine-cramer-politics-resentment-rural-wisconsin-scott-walker-trump; accessed on 21-6-2019].

Staedicke, Sara, 'As Venezuelan Crisis Deepens, South America Braces for More Arrivals and Indefinite Stays', *Migration Information Source* online, Migration Policy Institute, 21-12-2018 [Available at: www.migrationpolicy.org/article/top-10-2018-issue-1-venezuelan-crisis-deepens-south-america-braces-more-arrivals-and; accessed on 21-6-2019].

Trilling, Daniel, *Lights in the Distance: Exile and Refuge at the Borders of Europe*. London: Picador, 2018.

UNHCR, *South Sudan Refugee Response: Mapping Tensions and Disputes between Refugees and Host Community in Gendrassa, Maban County*. Geneva: UNHCR, 2015.

Walton, Oliver, *Good Practice in Preventing Conflict between Refugees and Host Communities*. Birmingham: Governance and Social Development Resource Centre, University of Birmingham, 2012.

Winzler, Tim, 'Book Review: *Strangers in Their Own Land: Anger and Mourning on the American Right* by Arlie Russell Hochschild', *Review of Books*, London School of Economics and Political Science Blog [Available at https://blogs.lse.ac.uk/lsereviewofbooks/2019/01/14/book-review-strangers-in-their-own-land-anger-and-mourning-on-the-american-right-by-arlie-russell-hochschild; accessed on 21-6-2019].

World Humanitarian Summit 2016, *Agenda for Humanity: 5 Core Responsibilities, 24 Transformations*. New York: UN, 2016.

## Notes

1 Marella Hoffman, *Asylum under Dreaming Spires: Refugees' Lives in Cambridge Today*. Cambridge: Cambridge Editions in partnership with the Living Refugee Archive, University of East London, 2017; from this chapter's Case Study No. 7.

2 World Humanitarian Summit 2016, *Agenda for Humanity: 5 Core Responsibilities, 24 Transformations*. New York: UN, 2016.

3 *Refugee Hosts* website, 2018. Urls are given in this chapter's references.

4 Elena Fiddian-Qasmiyeh, 'Shadows and Echoes In/Of Displacement: Temporalities, Spatialities and Materialities of Displacement', *Refugee Hosts Project* online, 19-11-2018.

5 Leonie Harsch, 'Giving Refugees a Voice? Looking Beyond "Refugee Stories"', *Refugee Hosts* website, 2018.

6 Eveliina Lyytinen, 'The Politics of Mistrust: Congolese Refugees and the Institutions Providing Refugee Protection in Kampala, Uganda'. In *Urban Refugees: Challenges in Protection, Services and Policy*, edited by Koichi Koizumi and Gerhard Hoffstaedter. Abingdon: Routledge, 2015.

7 Elena Fiddian-Qasmiyeh, 'Shadows and Echoes', 2018.

8 Karen Jacobsen, 'Livelihoods in Conflict: The Pursuit of Livelihoods by Refugees and the Impact on the Human Security of Host Communities', *International Migration*, 40(5), 2002.

9 Fred Ikanda, 'Deteriorating Conditions of Hosting Refugees: A Case Study of the Dadaab Complex in Kenya', *African Study Monographs*, 29(1), 2008.

10 Oliver Walton, *Good Practice in Preventing Conflict between Refugees and Host Communities*. Birmingham: Governance and Social Development Resource Centre, University of Birmingham, 2012.

11 Leah Berry, 'The Impact of Environmental Degradation on Refugee–Host Relations: A Case Study from Tanzania', *New Issues in Refugee Research*, Working Paper No.151. Geneva: UNHCR, 2008.

12 UNHCR, *South Sudan Refugee Response: Mapping Tensions and Disputes between Refugees and Host Community in Gendrassa, Maban County*. Geneva: UNHCR 2015.
13 UNHCR, *South Sudan*, 2015.
14 UNHCR, *South Sudan*, 2015.
15 UNHCR, *South Sudan*, 2015.
16 Leah Berry, 'The Impact of Environmental Degradation', 2008.
17 Marcia Vera Espinoza, 'Extra-Regional Refugee Resettlement in South America: The Palestinian Experience', *Forced Migration Review*, Oct 2017.
18 Marcia Vera Espinoza, 'The Politics of Resettlement: Expectations and Unfulfilled Promises in Chile and Brazil'. In *Refugee Resettlement: Power, Politics and Humanitarian Governance*, edited by Jubilut Garnier and Sandvik Bergtora. New York: Berghahn Books, 2018.
19 Sarah Bishop, *U.S. Media and Migration: Refugee Oral Histories*. Abingdon: Routledge, 2016.
20 For insights on these dynamics, see the work of economist Paul Collier, in particular *Exodus: How Migration Is Changing our World*. Oxford: Oxford University Press, 2013.
21 Gillespie, Marie et al., 'From Paris to Cherbourg: Aspirations, Expectations and Realities'. In *Mapping Refugee Media Journeys: Smartphones and Social Media Networks*. Paris: Open University/ France Médias Monde, 2016.
22 Simon Reeves, *Mediterranean*, Episode 4, BBC TV, 28-10-2018.
23 Daniel Trilling, *Lights in the Distance: Exile and Refuge at the Borders of Europe*. London: Picador, 2018.
24 Trilling, *Lights*, 2018.
25 Mary Brenner and Maryam Kia-Keating, 'Psychosocial and Academic Adjustment among Resettled Refugee Youth'. In *Annual Review of International and Comparative Education 2016*. Bingley: Emerald Publishing, 2016.
26 Oxfam International, *Lebanon: Looking Ahead in Times of Crisis: Taking Stock of the Present to Urgently Build Sustainable Options for the Future*. Nairobi: Oxfam International, 2015.
27 Oxfam GB, *Self-Protection and Coping Strategies of Refugees from Syria and Host Communities in Lebanon*. Nairobi: Oxfam GB, 2015.
28 Oxfam GB, *Self-Protection*, 2015.
29 Oxfam GB, *Self-Protection*, 2015.
30 Jean Francois Maystadt and Philip Verwimp, 'Winners and Losers among a Refugee-Hosting Population', *Development and Cultural Change*, 62(4): 679–809, July 2014.
31 Oxfam GB, *Self-Protection*, 2015.
32 Kate Lyons and Pamela Duncan, 'It's a Shambles: Data Show Most Asylum Seekers Put in Poorest Parts of Britain', *The Guardian*, 9-4-2017.
33 Elena Fiddian-Qasmiyeh, 'Refugee–Refugee Relations in Contexts of Overlapping Displacement', *International Journal of Urban and Regional Research*, 12-1-2016.
34 Dayra Carvajal, 'As Colombia Emerges from Decades of War, Migration Challenges Mount', *Migration Information Source* online, Migration Policy Institute, 13-4-2017.
35 CNN TV, 'Why You Should Care about Venezuela', online, 4-2-2019.
36 Sara Staedicke, 'As Venezuelan Crisis Deepens, South America Braces for More Arrivals and Indefinite Stays', *Migration Information Source* online, Migration Policy Institute, 21-12-2018.
37 Marta Martinez, *Displaced Colombians Open Their Homes to Venezuelan Refugees and Migrants*, UN video report. Cúcuta, Colombia: UN, 2018.
38 Martinez, *Displaced Colombians*, 2018.
39 Elena Fiddian-Qasmiyeh, 'Refugees Helping Refugees: How a Palestinian Refugee Camp in Lebanon Is Welcoming Syrians', *The Conversation*, 4-11-2015.

40 Elena Fiddian-Qasmiyeh, 'Refugees Hosting Refugees', *Forced Migration Review*, 53: 25–27, Sept 2016.
41 Arlie Russell Hochschild, *Strangers in Their Own Land: Anger and Mourning on the American Right*. New York: The New Press, 2016.
42 Tim Winzler, 'Book Review: *Strangers in Their Own Land: Anger and Mourning on the American Right* by Arlie Russell Hochschild', *Review of Books*, London School of Economics and Political Science Blog.
43 Katherine Cramer, *The Politics of Resentment: Rural Consciousness in Wisconsin and the Rise of Scott Walker*. Chicago: University of Chicago Press, 2016.
44 Katherine Cramer, 'The Politics of Resentment: What I Learned by Listening', MIT online, 31-5-2017.
45 Timothy Shenk, 'Booked: Capitalizing on Rural Resentment with Katherine Cramer', *Dissent* magazine online, 7-2-2017.
46 Hoffman, *Asylum*, 2017.
47 Hoffman, *Asylum*, 2017.

# PART II

# Doing Your Own Oral Histories to Improve Outcomes for Refugees or Host Communities

## The Step-by-Step Guide

# 6

# THE ETHICS, RISKS AND LEGALITIES OF DOING ORAL HISTORY WITH REFUGEES OR HOST COMMUNITIES

This chapter overviews ethical, legal and behavioral protections needed around doing oral history with refugees and host communities. It will also walk you methodically through ethical technicalities that apply to doing any type of oral history. These include routine procedures around consent, permissions, data protection, anonymity, copyright, archiving, future access, freedom of information, defamation, criminality and safeguarding. Templates in the Appendices will guide you through applying them to your own project with full rigor and minimum fuss. But, importantly, neither this chapter nor this book constitute legal advice, which you must get from a legal professional where needed.

## Six Important '*PIECES*'

This section will highlight some *mental* preparations that you need to make before you can meet the specific ethical needs of refugees as narrators. (As we go through these preparations, you'll see that some logically apply to host community narrators too, especially when dealing with the small minority of them who could be involved with extremist views or organizations.) There's nothing technical about this exercise. These are just mental 'stretches' that activate the layers of emotional intelligence that – like layers of hidden muscles – you need for doing refugee oral histories.[1] We'll activate six faculties that, hopefully, you already have: **P**olitical awareness, **I**magination, **E**mpathy, **C**ommon sense, **E**quanimity and **S**elf-restraint. (The acronym '*PIECES*' will help you remember them.) Without them, I believe your oral history work cannot meet the ethical needs of refugee narrators. And keeping them activated throughout your contact with refugees will prevent you from stumbling naïvely into zones you shouldn't be in. Otherwise, like rushing out into a football game without warming up, you risk hurting yourself as well as those you're interacting with, and potentially getting you all into lots of trouble.

This whole section could be summarized under the old medical maxim '*First, do no harm*'. (There is actually a formal framework for measuring the impacts of aid in conflict zones that is called *The Do No Harm Handbook*.) [2] The simple mental exercises below will show you more than a dozen different ways that your interviews could unwittingly harm your narrators. But please don't be disturbed or daunted. These can all be avoided by consciously applying these six '*PIECES*' or aspects of intelligence that you already have. Your task here is just to run through the exercises below in a business-like way, knowing that the specific tool that you bring – applied oral history – can offer significant help and relief in these situations, and will be very welcome. But these exercises will show you how to '*stay in your own lane*', as North Americans put it. This means keeping to your own skill of doing quality oral history and maintaining respectful, pragmatic boundaries around refugee problems that are not in your domain but in the domain of *other* professionals (such as medical staff, psychotherapists, social workers, immigration officials, police and lawyers).

## *P: Political Awareness*

We've seen that the majority of refugees were ordinary people back home before crisis hit. But if it's war, persecution or a regime that they're fleeing from (rather than a natural disaster), you must maintain a background awareness of the politicized or even militarized activities that they could potentially have been involved in – whether willingly or not – before they fled. Stay aware that such people's background will lie somewhere along the very wide spectrum shown in Figure 6.1.

Crucially, it's not your role to aim to (a) 'find out' where they were on this spectrum or (b) do something about it. That's the role of specialized professionals such as asylum officers and surveillance police (although they too do their own specialized oral histories at times, as part of their intelligence-gathering techniques).[3] In the next chapter, you will clarify the precise goals of your own project: your role will then be to do ethically boundaried interviews that yield findings and insights that serve those public interest goals. But, in the background, you must stay quietly conscious of the political spectrum depicted in Figure 6.1. For instance, your

| ← | | | | → |
|---|---|---|---|---|
| Keenly liberal, actively campaigning for Western-style democracy and human rights | Ordinary people just trying to get on with their lives under regimes they don't particularly care for, but can do little about | Victims of radicalization, propaganda, threats or brainwashing; conscripted by force to support a regime or faction that is incompatible with Western society | Actively in combat as a soldier or paramilitary; forced to fight against their will; child soldiers | Keen fundamentalists, devoted to creating or spreading a regime or faction that is incompatible with Western values or laws |

**FIGURE 6.1** The spectrum of political activity among refugees before fleeing

narrator may be warm and friendly with you in their interview, but if they're fleeing a political or military conflict, they are likely to have lots of political pressures inside and around them. We know that all migrant nationalities tend to regroup abroad in informal networks that share language, information, advice, practical resources, temporary lodgings and other support. But I have seen in my own work that within such refugee communities abroad, political and ideological divisions can be at least as painful and divisive as they were back home, even if people have to try to paper over them to survive abroad.

And though they have fled a long way geographically, powerful states, militia or regimes may still seek to extradite, prosecute or punish them for a political stance that they held back home. For instance, a repressive regime may still be pursuing them – or may yet pursue them in the future – for having been a campaigner for reform back home or for continuing to campaign now, abroad. Or Western states might be pursuing them under suspicion of being extremist or radicalized. It would be naïve – both on your part and on the refugee's part – to ever think that any such dynamics are entirely 'behind them'. With the internet, social media, mobile phone links, surveillance methods, international data banks and the globally networked tentacles of many regimes now, these people are not totally 'safe' in any definitive sense: they're just a lot safer, for now, sitting in front of you, than they were before. And even if those tentacles never reach them personally, the anguish for many refugees is that families, friends and associates left behind may remain acutely vulnerable.

So every time you sit down to interview a refugee fleeing conflict, you're stepping into their own unique, post-war landscape, even if you've never been to a war zone yourself. You may both be in the physical safety of your office, in a law-abiding country, but for all the reasons above and further below, you have to discreetly assume that they're not safe, and that their future won't be totally safe either.[4] There are things that they will and won't – can and can't – tell you about the contours of their own individual war zone and its aftermaths, which travel on above their head like clouds. In our technologized global village, it's very hard to outrun a war zone entirely. Whoever they were *back there*, and the forces they're fleeing from, can pursue them and those they care about much more easily nowadays, wherever they all are.

## I: Imagination

In my experience, the most important thing to remember throughout your work with refugees is how little you can ever know about them. By definition your narrator is coming from a world of experiences that you can only ever imagine (unless you have lived such experiences too). The things you don't know about them yet *and the things you may never know* (all the evils that happened to them, and especially the worst of those evils) are the very reasons why they're a refugee and why you're trying to help. But as an oral history interviewer, it's not your job to push to get the whole story.[5] Your job is to enable them to tell you (a) whatever they want to tell you and (b) whatever will help improve policies, services, environments and outcomes for them and their host communities.

I really believe that in refugee interviews, it's not your role to dig into their personal story. I have found that every refugee narrator will do a very good job on the spot of regulating, editing and navigating for themselves how much they want to tell you or can tell you. Even after finishing your interviews together, you may not know all of what they were fleeing from. Yet, though they so often have to self-edit what they can confide, I have never met a refugee who didn't long to be interviewed and listened to, and who didn't have a lot of things to say that were important for refugee policies and services, as well as important to them.

This book doesn't have the space to explore the complexity of pain and frustration that refugees can experience around dilemmas of *telling*, *truth*, *identity* and *meaning*, but you need to have some awareness of those dilemmas before sitting down to listen to refugees.[6] Since the day they lost everything, leaving others behind in chaos and danger and laboring forward themselves into an alien world, '*regulating, editing and navigating*', to quote my own words from the paragraph above, are basically what they have to do now, all day, every day. Even an opening question like '*Who are you*?' can be deeply entangled for a refugee. Who they were back home before crisis, flight and losing everything was necessarily very different from the refugee they are in front of you today. Present appearances are almost always deceptive around these people. For instance, they may look well dressed, clean, smiling and engaging – but may also be deeply traumatized in their own psychological health. With Syrian refugees, in particular, their education and culture can often mean they come across as well educated, resourceful and positive – but they may also be walking towards you as a victim of some horror scene you can scarcely imagine. A young orphan reaching you from Honduras in Central America may reveal his wistful, gentle soul in your interview; but he may have been a drugged, conscripted gang member or child soldier. Or your narrator might be a kind and deeply courteous person; but they may hold cultural or religious views about women, gays or Sharia law that you would find unacceptable. And you may not end up knowing that, for instance if they tactfully choose to avoid those subjects. But, remember, your paths would never have crossed if they hadn't been obliged to flee from their home culture. And polite as they are, they may not think much of your home culture's values either!

Now that we've sharpened up our ***P***olitical awareness and our ***I***magination around refugees, you have a richer picture of who any given refugee narrator could be. So let's move on briefly to ***E***mpathy.

## *E: Empathy*

Basically, the refugee experience is a *four-stage trauma that* successively layers up:

1. the trauma that drove them from their home;
2. the traumas of the refugee journey;

3. the stresses of 'arriving', if they're lucky, at their hoped-for destination and applying to be allowed to stay, even temporarily;
4. the momentous challenge of rebuilding a new life there from scratch, if they are one of the small minority given asylum.

This next exercise is straightforward. Just take a moment to imagine for yourself all the possible points between the two extremes depicted in Figure 6.2 below, knowing that your narrator will be coming from one of those points. Imagine stepping in and walking along for a moment the whole spectrum that lies behind Figure 6.2, getting just a glimpse of what those experiences must be like.

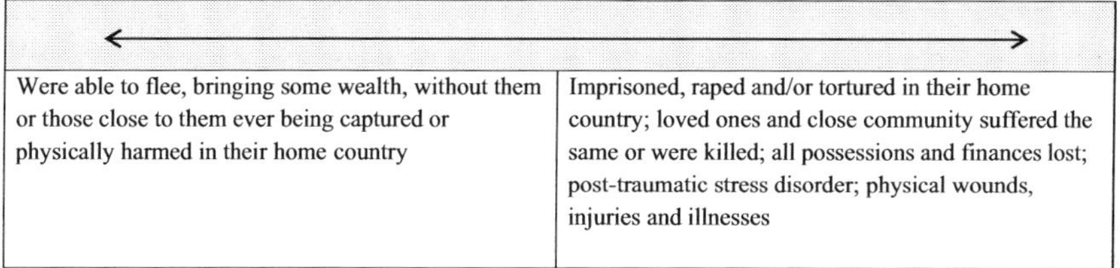

| ← | → |
|---|---|
| Were able to flee, bringing some wealth, without them or those close to them ever being captured or physically harmed in their home country | Imprisoned, raped and/or tortured in their home country; loved ones and close community suffered the same or were killed; all possessions and finances lost; post-traumatic stress disorder; physical wounds, injuries and illnesses |

**FIGURE 6.2** Extremes of variation in the amount of trauma refugees experienced before escaping

Then briefly do the same for this next table, Figure 6.3, aware that its hardships are layered *on top* of those in the previous spectrum, as the table focuses in on a range of traumas that refugees may suffer during their escape journey.

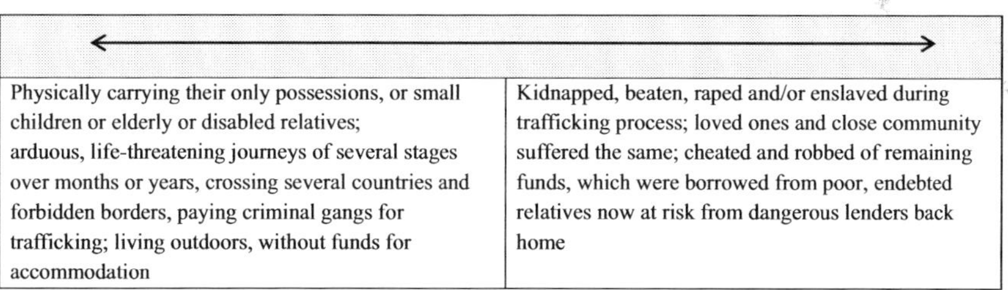

| ← | → |
|---|---|
| Physically carrying their only possessions, or small children or elderly or disabled relatives; arduous, life-threatening journeys of several stages over months or years, crossing several countries and forbidden borders, paying criminal gangs for trafficking; living outdoors, without funds for accommodation | Kidnapped, beaten, raped and/or enslaved during trafficking process; loved ones and close community suffered the same; cheated and robbed of remaining funds, which were borrowed from poor, endebted relatives now at risk from dangerous lenders back home |

**FIGURE 6.3** The range of traumas that refugees may experience during their escape journey

## *C: Common Sense*

In my experience, there are four levels of common sense that you must apply as you do this work. It can help to remember them as the *4 Cs*. The first is not to get too bogged down in or upset about these mental exercises that we're doing. Yes, you need *some* imaginative empathy but you also need healthy, down-to-earth boundaries. Remember that what's past is, fortunately, in the past. And it happened to them, not to you. You're just here to receive whatever useful oral history they want to give you.

The second level of common sense is to always respect refugees' hierarchy of needs. As with anyone else, a need for food, physical safety or medical attention, for instance, will always be more urgent than their need for oral history. Syrian refugee Hassan Akkad, a victim of the torture cells of the Syrian regime and one of the stars of the award-winning BBC documentary *Exodus: Our Journey to Europe*, describes finally getting smuggled into Britain after months of desperately trying. When the British police finally led him away for asylum interrogation, the first thing they said to him was: '*Are you hungry? Have you had enough to eat today?*' On hearing this he felt, for the first time in years: 'Things are going to get better from here on'.[7]

A third and crucial level of common sense is to manage refugee narrators' expectations of what you can achieve for them. This applies equally with host community narrators. When I gathered applied oral histories as a government employee, narrators from either community would sometimes assume I had the power to do much more for them than I actually could. If coming from certain developing countries, some refugees were used to corrupt government officials who had wide-ranging power to get things done – at a price. And even if they didn't think I would take bribes, they often still assumed that any government job in the West would be much more fluidly influential than it actually was. In the coming chapter, you will see how to communicate clearly to your narrators the precise level of influence that your oral history project aims to have. You can also explain that even its maximum influence is more likely to be about improving *collective* outcomes, services and opportunities for their community, rather than about individual outcomes.

The fourth level of common sense needed is to do your best to ensure that the resources that a refugee narrator, in particular, invests in your interview (which, at a minimum, will include their time, energy, trust, memory and emotion) will return proportional benefits to them in at least some way, and not just benefit your project or the institution you're working for. If you observe all the guidelines in this book, you will at least be giving them honesty, respect, quality listening, the sense that their story is of real value, that they are part of a larger positive project and that they are thanked.[8] If you do want to do something extra for them, what can be of real use to refugees is if, before meeting them, you spend some time researching in the public domain all the free and low-cost resources available and relevant to them in their current locality or online. These could include asylum support services, legal aid, resources for public housing, healthcare and schooling, free libraries, information centers and internet access, food banks, language classes, support groups, volunteering opportunities, work experience and specialist support for recovering from trauma or radicalization. You could type up this local resource list as an information sheet to give them as a gift when you meet.

So our *4 Cs* of common sense are:

1. don't get overly emotional around what's happened to your narrators in the past;
2. always respect their hierarchy of needs;
3. manage their expectations of you and your project;
4. ensure they get some return on their investment of effort.

Carefully observing these *4 Cs* of common sense puts boundaries around your oral history project that enable it to meet its goal of *returning tangible benefits to communities*, rather than trying to take on the whole world's problems or getting yourself depressed in the process.

## *E: Equanimity*

These last two '*PIECES*' are the easiest, as they just apply what you've already learned. You see now that you will *have* to practice equanimity because you simply cannot make it all okay for your narrators – neither in the past nor in the future. They may well be highly relieved and grateful to have survived this far to tell you their story. But, in your own mind, you must remain aware that being a refugee is, as we saw above, actually a *four-stage trauma*. So you know they are probably only partway through these long and arduous stages (even though they are probably very keen to get on with those stages). Most refugees that I've interviewed have what I privately in my own mind consider a kind of 'terrifying optimism'. I wince internally when I think of the statistics that are stacked against the chances of them (a) getting asylum, (b) in their chosen country and (c) ending up actually *liking* whatever life they might manage to rebuild there. But, as with a cancer patient battling tough odds, it is definitely not my business to discourage them with pessimistic statistics. In fact, I have never seen a refugee dwell negatively on the odds that are stacked up against them in the future. I suppose that would just be too discouraging. All the complaints I've ever heard from them have only ever been about the past or the present.

Nonetheless, please do take a moment to look across the spectrum of possible outcomes for any given refugee that is shown in Figure 6.4. Imagine too the many other points along it as well as the three that are described in the table.

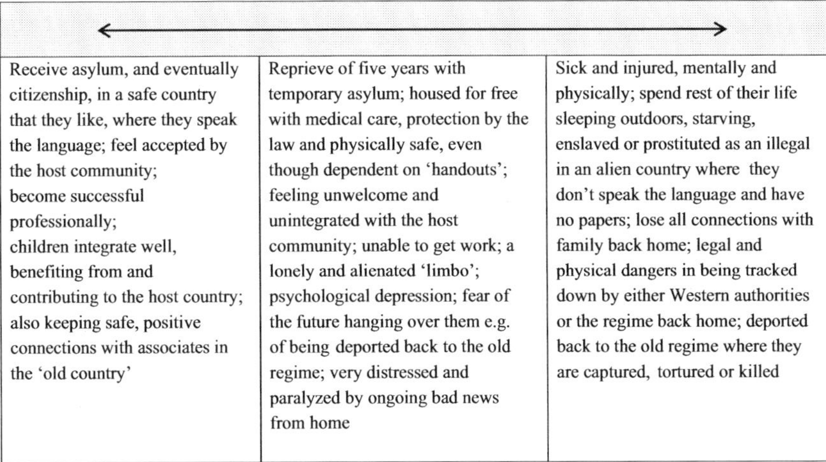

| ← | | → |
|---|---|---|
| Receive asylum, and eventually citizenship, in a safe country that they like, where they speak the language; feel accepted by the host community; become successful professionally; children integrate well, benefiting from and contributing to the host country; also keeping safe, positive connections with associates in the 'old country' | Reprieve of five years with temporary asylum; housed for free with medical care, protection by the law and physically safe, even though dependent on 'handouts'; feeling unwelcome and unintegrated with the host community; unable to get work; a lonely and alienated 'limbo'; psychological depression; fear of the future hanging over them e.g. of being deported back to the old regime; very distressed and paralyzed by ongoing bad news from home | Sick and injured, mentally and physically; spend rest of their life sleeping outdoors, starving, enslaved or prostituted as an illegal in an alien country where they don't speak the language and have no papers; lose all connections with family back home; legal and physical dangers in being tracked down by either Western authorities or the regime back home; deported back to the old regime where they are captured, tortured or killed |

**FIGURE 6.4** Extremes of variation in long-term outcomes for refugees

## *S: Self-restraint*

From its minor contours to its deepest chasms, you are now acquainted with the map of the 'refugee landscape': you see that it stretches out far behind a typical refugee, and far into the future ahead of them. You know that the person you'll be interviewing will have travelled their own unique route across this landscape, though you may never know all the details of that route.[9] As emphasized by Dr Richard Mollica, the world leader on using oral histories in clinical practice to help refugees heal from trauma: 'Survivors must be allowed to tell their stories their own way. We must not burden them with theories, interpretations, or opinions, especially if we have little knowledge of their cultural and political background.'[10]

So you know now why, as oral historians, we need self-restraint in our refugee interviews. One way to remember this, and to keep all six '*PIECES*' alert in your mind during your project (your **P**olitical awareness, **I**magination, **E**mpathy, **C**ommon sense, **E**quanimity and **S**elf-restraint), is to maintain a background awareness of *all the things that could go wrong* as a direct result of your oral history work with your narrators, from the mildest to the most deadly: see Figure 6.5 below.

Maintaining the six '*PIECES*' above, along with the standard guidelines below for doing any applied oral history, will help prevent you from contributing in any way to such unwanted outcomes for your narrators. But be aware that there can be dangers too for oral historians themselves as they do this sort of work, whether among refugees or host communities. Doing fieldwork with members of the public; being alone with distressed, traumatized or extremist people; recording testimonies about powerful regimes and radical movements, these are all situations where you must take all due safeguarding precautions, some of which we'll discuss later in this chapter.

One morning recently, over breakfast, I was leafing through the British *Oral History Review: Journal of the Oral History Association* which had just dropped through my letter box. Munching toast, I was musing sleepily over the usual genteel hand-wringing among oral historians about the finest nuances of narrator/interviewer relationships, or 'the risks that oral history poses as oral historians engage with

| ← | | | | | → |
|---|---|---|---|---|---|
| They feel you profited from them as a privileged Westerner and they got nothing in return; they had assumed you could help them more | Your work re-opens damaging rifts in the fragile connections they're trying to maintain with compatriots or the host community | You actively stir up mental traumas they can't cope with, and they get even more depressed, ill or incapable | Host authorities use your work to 'disprove' and reject their asylum claim | Host authorities locate them through your work and imprison them or deport them back to their home country | The regime they fled from finds them or their associates through your work and imprisons, tortures or kills them |

**FIGURE 6.5** Spectrum of ways that your oral history work could harm your narrators

human participants and often conduct their research outside of the academy'.[11] But I was shocked wide awake by the ensuing words about Giulio Regeni, an Italian doctoral student in oral history at Cambridge University, who was doing interviews in Egypt on trade unions and labor rights: 'Regeni believed that his Italian passport would protect him from state oppression (but) his corpse, showing signs of terrible torture, was found on January 25, 2016 on the outskirts of Egypt's capital'.[12]

The risks in doing challenging – or what's now even called 'dangerous' – oral history work have rightly attracted the interest of practitioners over the past few years. The British and Irish Oral History Society's annual conference in 2018 was on 'Dangerous Oral Histories: Risks, Responsibilities and Rewards'. And, as Alison Atkinson-Phillips' review of the year's oral history work in 2018 put it:

> With the growth of right wing populist movements in many areas of the globe, the critical thinking inherent in historical and academic investigation is under threat. This was brought starkly, and worryingly, into focus with the keynote lecture at the OHA conference (in America in 2018).[13]

That lecture, by oral historian Leyla Neyzi, told how authoritarianism was impacting on her oral history practice: she had recently been prosecuted in Turkey as 'promoting terrorism' by doing oral history work recognizing the Armenian Genocide.[14] Atkinson-Phillips adds: 'Given the growth of intolerance, including challenges to (and subversion of the meaning of) freedom of expression and academic investigation, the role of critical oral history is likely to increase in importance.'[15]

Atkinson also highlights that:

> Oral historians are increasingly working with people who have been involved in war, conflict or disaster situations. This leads to conversations about the safety of interviewers and narrators – both in practical and emotional terms – and potentially becomes even more pressing as climate change leads to increases in natural disaster and conflict.[16]

This dual sense both of the danger and the importance of their work may be relatively new to oral historians in Western democracies. But it has, of course, always been pressing for our oral history colleagues who were at work in countries ruled by totalitarian or corrupt regimes, where the rule of law was or is weak. The current sense of 'danger' is new only to those of us who, up until now, have had the luxury of being cocooned by the human rights, civil laws, tolerance and freedom of speech in free democracies.

But today, for the first time since World War II, far-right politics are becoming more mainstreamed, and future repression is foreseeable again in Western democracies. However, if our global village is making 'danger' a more universal experience, our responsibility and scope for action have also become more universal.

In the global village, we are all called upon and empowered to use the resources that we have to take positive actions that actually make a difference. And, as applied oral historians, we are well positioned to help by listening, defusing conflict and prejudice, and building understanding and collaborations across divides. These are the tools of our trade and we can put them to good use now.

## Legal and Ethical Protections

This section gives an introductory overview of issues like copyright, data protection, safeguarding of vulnerable people, and duties of confidentiality and of criminal disclosure. They apply equally to oral history with host communities or with refugees. But legislation varies across jurisdictions, and hence for oral history material disseminated across them, especially via the internet. So you must research and follow all the aspects of law in your country or jurisdiction that apply to your oral history activities. Neither this chapter nor this book constitutes legal advice, which you must get from a legal professional where needed.[17]

### *Informed Consent and Access to Interviews*

In any form of work with the public, there is a legal requirement to make clear to participants how any information that they give you and any personal data you hold on them will be used, processed, shared and disposed of.[18] The sample *Project Information Sheet* and *Consent Forms* in Appendices 1 and 2 (on pages 173 and 175) will help you to do that. If protecting narrators in this way is important in traditional oral history, it is even more so in applied oral history, where:

- you direct the interview more towards specific information that you hope to get from the narrator;
- you extract and use parts of their information for your project's aims;
- you are interviewing individuals, in the case of refugees, who are already vulnerable, traumatized and at risk.

At your first discussions with any potential narrator, you must explain in layperson's language who you are; what your project is doing and why; what you plan to do with its findings; the project's overall aims; and what role the person could potentially play in it. If you're employed by or affiliated to any organization in doing your oral histories, you must tell narrators honestly about that organization and your relationship to it. For better or for worse, this is likely to influence their perception of you, and affect how much they tell you. Explain to them the basic logistics of an oral history interview: where you'll do the interview, what it will be like, how long it will take, and what will happen to their interview afterwards.

After all this has been explained verbally – using an interpreter if there's any doubt about the person's ability to fully understand your language – you must then give these potential narrators a paper or electronic *Project Information Sheet* that confirms again in full:

- the purpose and scope of your project (its aims and intended outcomes, end products, duration and size of the project, how it's funded, etc.);
- who is involved (any organizations; project personnel and contact details; personnel's qualifications and affiliations, etc.);
- what you are looking for in narrators (their background, abilities, contribution, motivations and perspectives);
- what narrators can expect from you (*Code of Conduct*, confidentiality, practicalities of interviews, fact that they won't be paid, any expenses covered, etc.);
- all the legal parameters and protections around any information that they give you (the 'fine print' on issues like data protection, copyright, archiving, future access, freedom of information, publishing, defamation and safeguarding, explained below).

Obviously, if you don't speak your narrators' language, you won't have any choice but to use an interpreter as an intermediary throughout their interviews, as well as during these introductory processes. The ideal is to use a certified or chartered interpreter, as their state-approved qualification should mean that the interpreter will be completely objective, honest and accurate in translating between you and your narrators. But, of course, their services are likely to be fee-paying, adding costs to your project budget. On the other hand, it is quite common also to use a nonprofessional interpreter, such as a family member, community member or a charity staff member working in the community. This may add an ease, rapport and familiarity to the presence of the third-party interpreter. But you must stay aware that this interpreter is not an entirely objective presence: living or working within the community environment themselves, they will have their own responses to the issues discussed in your interviews, and may well color their translations with them. Or, if closely associated with the narrator, their translations may limit, censor or embellish upon what the narrator has actually said.

After the person has genuinely understood a layperson's version of the information above, they must then read and sign a *Consent Form* agreeing to release each of their interviews for you to use. Obviously, this must be translated into whatever language they do understand, or read to them by an interpreter if they are illiterate. *Consent Forms* can – and often need to be – further personalized with '*Restrictions*' that the narrator may need or request, whether on all or part of their interview. For instance, they might want to delay any public access to their recording – whether in an archive or by publication – for some years, or to refuse certain uses such as online access. (Freedom of information laws normally mean that most information held by publicly funded archives must be made available to anyone requesting it in writing, but not if the recording is 'closed' in this way due to a restriction in its *Consent Form*.) Another option on the *Consent Form* is to offer narrators complete anonymity or a pseudonym. This can be particularly necessary for refugees, as it often is:

- for narrators who have been victims of crime, trauma or oppressive regimes;
- if there is any 'whistle-blower' aspect to an interview and they could be pursued for their disclosures;
- for narrators on the edge of the law such as illegal immigrants, sex workers, school truants or users of illegal substances;
- around intimate topics like health, family, religion, relationships or sexuality.

Legally, it's your responsibility to anticipate whether a narrator might ever in the future need the protection of anonymity, even if they don't fully realize those implications at this present stage. Obviously a disadvantage of anonymity is that narrators cannot be publicly associated with their statement. Anonymized recordings can be publicly archived but they don't have the same status as signed ones, although they are very common in refugee oral histories.

A narrator's *Consent Form* summarizes again what they have seen on your *Project Information Sheet*, including the project's provisions for data protection, copyright, future use of the recording and so on as listed above. Basically, the *Consent Form* makes clear to a narrator:

- how widely what they say in their interview will be seen by others or the public;
- whether or not it will be anonymized;
- how their interview will be stored and who could access it in the future;
- how much they can change or control what they've told you, and the deadlines for any changes they may want to make to what they said in their interview;
- any practical applications that the project's interviews will have (such as being applied to influence a campaign or public service or policy);
- the potential extent and limits of the project's impact and influence.

You should, as far as possible, make clear to each narrator beforehand whether after their interview, they will:

- ever hear from you again;
- see your transcript of their interview, edited if, and as, you intend to edit it;
- get to keep a copy of their interview;
- receive ongoing updates on the project as it advances;
- hear about any final impacts and outcomes the project ends up having over time.

These issues will depend on the resources you have available to recontact and update them, and the interest and ability that they have to be contacted in this way.

If you do send them a copy of their interview shortly after they do it, you could – though you don't have to and must weigh up the pros and cons of this – offer them a limited right just to correct '*any factual errors or inaccuracies*', or the more extensive right to '*remove or change anything you feel uncomfortable with*'. Normally, narrators have copyright on recordings of their own words, but *Consent Forms* usually confer copyright over to the archiving institution or publisher. However, public funders increasingly expect oral history projects to use a 'Creative Commons' license, so that others can later go on to reuse the material for non-commercial purposes without permission.[19]

Everything about the speaker and their interview must remain confidential to you until they have signed or recorded their *Consent Form*. And the precise wording of the *Consent Form* must be approved in advance by any sponsoring organization and any archive that is to hold your interviews later. We have noted that all the project's main documents for narrators need to be translated if your narrators don't read English. Or if they can't read at all, you can use an interpreter to explain the documents' contents and do an audio recording of them giving their *informed* consent.

It is best practice to arrange beforehand for your interviews to be deposited in an archive, library, museum or university after you have also derived your own end products from them. Both funders and narrators tend to value this stage. But you must consult this archive at the early planning stage of your project, because they may want to specify very precise formats and documentation that they need in order to archive your interviews. They may well predefine for you much of the format of your *Consent Forms*, interview labels, interview summaries and so on. By far the most definitive, authoritative guide on what archives will need from you in order to take on your oral histories is the highly accessible *Curating Oral Histories: From Interview to Archive* by Nancy MacKay, backed up by further hands-on detail in her five-volume *Community Oral History Toolkit*.[20]

## *Data Protection and Safeguarding*

Data protection is an important and ever-growing field of law governing how we handle information about others. We know that information about individuals now has huge commercial value: it can be exploited to target advertising by tracking individuals' lifestyles and preferences. So data protection is an urgent legal duty for anyone holding even the simplest information about anyone else, even for a short period for a nonprofit oral history project.

This applies to both '*basic* personal data', such as a person's name, phone number or email address and to '*sensitive* personal data', such as information about a person's religion, health, sexuality, financial status, religious beliefs or political opinions. In oral history interviews, any 'sensitive' personal data that a narrator discloses in an interview needs to be covered, as appropriate, by special restrictions in the *Consent Form*. And to protect all the 'basic' personal data that your project handles – such as contact details of narrators and volunteers – you must observe the rules of data protection law. Fortunately, these mostly reflect fairness and common sense by insisting that you:

- gather or hold anyone's personal data only with the person's permission, only for the stated purpose and in as limited a way as possible;
- store it securely and confidentially, and for the shortest period possible;
- let them see at any time the data you hold about them;
- never share it with any party that the person hasn't approved for sharing;
- dispose of it securely as soon as possible;
- inform the person that you're protecting their data in this way.[21]

In recent years, the European Union's General Data Protection Regulation and Britain's Data Protection Act have greatly tightened their laws in this area. If dealing with personal data from or in those jurisdictions, the extra requirements are that:

- the onus is on *you* to really think about and justify how and why you use people's data, limiting its use as much as possible;
- people have to actively *opt in*, giving you informed consent to your handling of their data for the stated purpose and time period;
- people have the right to easily access all and any data you hold about them;
- there are fines of up to ten million euros for failing to comply;
- your project must have its own Data Protection Policy: at its simplest, this can be a short document clearly explaining how your project will meet all the requirements listed here.

In the US, there is a less stringent approach to data protection, with a lot of different legislation on it for different states, sectors and demographics. But whether you are in the US or elsewhere in the world, you must research and follow the data protection laws of your own jurisdiction. If you do choose to respect the spirit of the European and British laws just listed above, you would be unlikely to go wrong as they are currently the world's most stringent with regard to data protection.

Unlike data protection legislation, safeguarding laws are about how you handle people's safety and welfare, rather than their information. To stay safe while working with refugees or with host community members who may hold very strong views, you need extra layers of awareness around safeguarding, both towards narrators and towards everyone working for your project, including yourself. You must arrange venues that will be safe and appropriate for both narrators and interviewers. And whether there's just yourself interviewing or your project includes other interviewers – either professionals or volunteers – you should have in place some basic safeguarding arrangements for those doing the interviewing. I recommend you use a basic *Lone Working Protocol*.[22] This protocol ensures that you and anyone else going out to interview on behalf of your project know the basics of personal safety when working with the public, and especially with stressed populations like refugees or controversial or extreme groups such as organized anti-refugee movements within the host community. (You will have covered this in the *Training Workshop* for your personnel that we will discuss in Chapter 7). The basics of a *Lone Working Protocol* include common sense routines such as:

- giving to the project's *Safeguarding Contact* the exact details of where they're going, who they'll meet and when they'll be back;
- giving mobile phone contact details so they both can be in touch if needed, with '*Location visible*' software activated for the lone worker;
- sending a text message or quick call to confirm they got home safely and are 'logging off';
- sitting nearest the door at the interview venue so that they – rather than anyone else in the room – have first access to the exit;
- sending an agreed secret password or mobile phone message if they need to indicate that they're in trouble.

To safeguard narrators, do your best to discover and respect any needs or norms that they may have around language, dress, age, gender, body language, tone of voice or taboo topics or behaviors in the home or in public space. Implementing proper *Safeguarding Protocols* (Appendix 3, page 177) means you could defend yourself and your project if it was ever alleged that you had acted inappropriately towards a narrator or a volunteer (for instance by neglecting to cater for a disability or a cultural or gender-based taboo).

Interviews should, as far as possible, be in the physical environment, body language and tone that the narrator is most comfortable with, where they feel most culturally at home and have at least some positive associations. For instance in a refugee camp or encampment, that might be over tea on a rug on the ground in someone's tent, rather than in an official building. The venue must have the right degree of privacy and exposure for any cultural needs around age, gender, status, religious beliefs and chaperoning. And it needs to be easy to access in terms of distance and any mobility problems with steps or slopes. With young people, seniors and disabled or otherwise vulnerable people, it is good practice to let their family or guardian know that you'll be meeting them (if the person is happy for them to know). Explain your project to the family, giving them your *Project Information Sheet* too. Youngsters should ideally be accompanied. It is important to get written consent from parents or guardians for those under 16, as well as having the youngster themselves sign the *Consent Form* and doing the interview in an appropriately supervised place. While prioritizing all the needs above, you must balance them against the logistical limits of the interview, as well as the interviewer's own safety requirements. Ideally your interview requires minimum background noise, interruptions or distractions; whatever privacy they may need to speak openly; and sufficient space and light for recording equipment, video or photography.

Legally, oral history interviews should only be done with narrators who have the mental capacity to understand your project and give fully informed consent for their part in it. Every jurisdiction is different but, for instance, in Britain, the 2007 Mental Capacity Act provides this legal protection for those whose mental ability is limited, whether temporarily or permanently, by illness, accident, disability or another disorder or trauma. This is defined as their ability to understand and retain information, weigh it as part of decision-making and communicate those decisions. Oral history interviews should not be done with such people, as they cannot give fully informed consent.[23] Obviously, this is of particular relevance around refugees who are traumatized, may be minors or may have disorders or injuries that you don't know about. If in doubt, get formal approval from a medical professional before proceeding.

### *Defamation and Illegality*

Different jurisdictions have different definitions of libel and defamation. But, in general, a libelous or defamatory statement is understood to be (a) untrue and (b) damaging to the reputation of a living person or an organization. If a libelous statement in an oral history interview is made available to anyone, the libeled party could sue not only the narrator, but also the interviewer or the institution archiving or publishing the interview. In the course of an interview, if you think a narrator may be saying something that is libelous, these are the things you can do about it:

- politely ask the narrator to stop making any libelous statements, explaining the reasons above;
- later remove that section from any transcript or recording, and never publish or archive it;
- even if you consider the statement true and in the public interest, take legal advice before making that part of the interview available to anyone else;
- if someone ever threatens to sue over material already archived or published, you can apologize, explain that you had thought it was true and remove it from public access;
- if necessary, you can also publish a retraction.

In terms of any other sorts of illegalities, you need to know what to do in case you ever come across any in the course of your oral history work. Legal obligations on reporting illegalities vary across jurisdictions, so you must research and follow the laws of your country and state or region. First, let's consider general oral history work before we look at the more specialized issues around refugees. The training I have received is that you can usually choose to ignore minor law infringements you happen to come across that are outside your own area of expertise. Offences like littering, undeclared work, black market goods – we don't condone them but as oral historians it's not our job to scour for and report every petty law infringement that occurs around us.[24] (By contrast, it *is* the job of many types of officials who are trained, paid and required to do just that.)

However, in the course of oral history work, if you do become aware of any current mistreatment of vulnerable people or any serious criminal activity among those you are dealing with, you should:

- first protect yourself and those for whom your project has a safeguarding responsibility or a duty of care;
- arrange to part company with the offender(s), but in a way that doesn't alert them;
- report the issue *confidentially* to the relevant authorities.

In Western democratic societies, safeguarding legislation provides mechanisms against the mistreatment of vulnerable people. It enables anyone – simply and confidentially, via the police or local authorities, in person or online – to report any situation where they are concerned that a vulnerable person is at risk or being mistreated. It applies for instance to youth, elderly people, pregnant women, gay and transpeople and the disabled, who may be inherently vulnerable to harm or exploitation. But it also applies to anyone who is made vulnerable by a particular circumstance, such as through grooming, being trafficked, experiencing domestic violence or being stalked or harassed. The term safeguarding also applies in a contextual way to people whom one has employed or taken on as volunteers to do a particular task or project: taking them on also involves taking on a duty of care towards them under safeguarding requirements.

If you are doing oral history with either host communities or refugees in the setting of a Western democracy all these rules apply, and you should report confidentially to the authorities any instance you may come across where you suspect a vulnerable person is being exploited or harmed. But if working in a country where the rule of law is less well established, then unfortunately you need to use common sense to 'lower' your expected standards of safeguarding to the legal norms of that country. For instance, laws and norms around children attending school up to a certain age, children being employed, the minimum age for a girl to be married, whether she has to consent to the marriage – these sorts of safeguarding boundaries are obviously quite different in some of the poorest countries, compared to in the West. So it's crucial to be well informed about what to expect as to the legal thresholds on safeguarding within the jurisdiction that you are working in, especially if you're not deeply familiar with the culture there. Armed with that information, you can then at least try to report the issue if you come across mistreatment that falls below those local standards.

Meanwhile, when working around refugees even in Western settings, remember that you are entering a domain where so many aspects of their situation are already technically 'illegal'. For instance, people forcibly displaced from their home country are automatically turned into 'illegals' until and unless they eventually receive asylum or official permission to remain in a host country. And, until then, their innocent babe in arms – perhaps born on the road or in a camp – will be born 'illegal'! In some European countries, it's even illegal for a member of the host community to give refugees any kindly assistance before they have been registered by the state:

members of the host public have been prosecuted for giving such refugee families a lift in their car or inviting them into their home for a bite to eat.[25]

But it's also illegal under international law for a host country to leave refugees languishing in camps below certain substandard conditions. And it's illegal for governments to delay too long in processing their asylum applications. In the European Union, it's technically illegal for refugees not to apply for asylum in the first EU country they enter and to wait until they reach an EU country that they prefer. The list goes on. Clearly, most of these technical 'illegalities' are on a scale that you can do nothing about in the short-term. Instead, you've chosen to step up in a disciplined, professional way to offer your own assistance through your applied oral history skills, to slowly help clean up this world-scale mess.

Finally, ensure that you are a member of your country or region's oral history association, giving narrators and their entourage its *Code of Conduct* along with your *Project Information Sheet*. If you follow the *Code of Conduct* of a reputable oral history association, plus all the guidance in this chapter and the laws governing your own jurisdiction, I believe you can make a real contribution to the refugee situation, rather than adding to the problem. Appendix 4 on page 180 (*Checklist of Legal and Ethical Preparations*), gives you a basic reminder of all the issues we've looked at in this chapter, to help you apply them methodically to your own project.

## References


Akkad, Hassan, 'My Journey to Europe', video by digital storytelling agency sounddelivery [Available at http://beingthestory.org.uk/speakers/hassan-akkad; accessed on 21-6-2019].

Ashkanasy, Neal, Zerbe, Wilfred and Hartel, Charlene, editors, *Experiencing and Managing Emotions in the Workplace*. Bingley: Emerald Publishing, 2012.

Atkinson-Phillips, Alison, 'Oral History in 2018: What Did We Learn?', *News from the Oral History Unit and Collective* website, Newcastle University, 1-2-2019 [Available at https://blogs.ncl.ac.uk/oral-history/2019/02/01/2018conferenceroundup; accessed on 21-6-2019].

Bar-On, Reuven and Parker, James, *The Handbook of Emotional Intelligence: Theory, Development, Assessment, and Application at Home, School, and in the Workplace*. San Francisco: Jossey-Bass/ Wiley, 2012.

Blanch, Andrea, *Transcending Violence: Emerging Models for Trauma Healing in Refugee Communities*. Washington, DC: National Center for Trauma-Informed Care, 2008.

Bulman, May, 'Hundreds of Europeans Including Firefighters and Priests Arrested for "solidarity" with Refugees, Data Shows', *The Independent*, 18-5-2019.

Collaborative for Development Action, *The Do No Harm Handbook: Framework for Analyzing the Impact of Assistance on Conflict*. Cambridge, MA: Collaborative for Development Action Collaborative Learning Projects, 2004.

DLA Piper, *Global Data Protection Handbook*. Washington, DC: DLA Piper, 2019 [Available at www.dlapiperdataprotection.com; accessed on 21-6-2019].

BBC2 TV, *Exodus: Our Journey to Europe*. London: BBC, 2016.

Goleman, Daniel, *The Brain and Emotional Intelligence: New Insights*. Florence, MA: Key Step Media, 2011.

Hajek, Andrea and Serenelli, Sofia 'Inside the Interview: The Challenges of a Humanistic Oral History Approach in the Deep Exchange of Oral History: Guest Editors' Introduction',

*Oral History Review: Journal of the Oral History Association*, 45(2, Summer/Fall): 232–238, 2018. Oxford: Oxford University Press, 2018.

Krause, Ulrike, *Researching Forced Migration: Critical Reflections on Research Ethics during Fieldwork*. Oxford: Refugee Studies Centre, University of Oxford, 2017.

MacKay, Nancy, *Curating Oral Histories: From Interview to Archive, 2nd Edition*. Abingdon: Routledge, 2016.

MacKay, Nancy, Quinlan, Mary Kay and Sommer, Barbara, *Community Oral History Toolkit*. Abingdon: Routledge, 2013.

Mollica, Richard, *Healing Invisible Wounds: Paths to Hope and Recovery in a Violent World*. Nashville: Vanderbilt University Press, 2009.

Nayeri, Dina, *The Ungrateful Refugee*. London: Canongate, 2019.

Neuenschwander, John, *A Guide to Oral History and the Law, 2nd edition*. Oxford: Oxford University Press, 2014.

Neyzi, Leyla, 'Between "Democracy" and "Authoritarianism": Implications for Oral History Practice'. Keynote lecture at 2018 *American Oral History Association* Conference, Concordia University, Montreal.

Nguyen, Viet Thanh, editor, *The Displaced: Refugee Writers on Refugee Lives*. New York: Abrams Press, 2018.

Papadopoulos, Renos, 'Refugees, Trauma and Adversity-Activated Development', *European Journal of Psychotherapy and Counseling*, 9(3): 301–312, Sept 2007.

Suzy Lamplugh Trust, website [Available at www.suzylamplugh.org/Pages/Category/lone-worker-directory; accessed on 21-6-2019].

## Notes

1 Daniel Goleman, *The Brain and Emotional Intelligence: New Insights*. Florence, MA: Key Step Media, 2011. See also *Experiencing and Managing Emotions in the Workplace* edited by Neal Ashkanasy, Wilfred Zerbe and Charlene Hartel (Bingley, UK: Emerald Publishing, 2012) and *The Handbook of Emotional Intelligence: Theory, Development, Assessment, and Application at Home, School, and in the Workplace*, edited by Reuven Bar-On and James Parker (San Francisco: Jossey-Bass/Wiley, 2012).

2 Collaborative for Development Action, *The Do No Harm Handbook: Framework for Analyzing the Impact of Assistance on Conflict*. Cambridge, MA: Collaborative for Development Action Collaborative Learning Projects, 2004.

3 Later in this chapter, we will explore what you can do if you ever do need to report any illegality you come across during oral history work.

4 Ulrike Krause, *Researching Forced Migration: Critical Reflections on Research Ethics during Fieldwork*. Oxford: Refugee Studies Centre, University of Oxford, 2017.

5 That is the job of various other professionals such as medical experts, police, lawyers, asylum judges, etc., by whom refugees are thoroughly interviewed.

6 These issues are explored in books like *The Displaced: Refugee Writers on Refugee Lives* edited by Viet Thanh Nguyen (New York: Abrams Press, 2018) and Dina Nayeri's *The Ungrateful Refugee* (London: Canongate, 2019).

7 You can hear Hassan Akkad's story in the video 'My Journey to Europe' by digital storytelling agency sounddelivery. Urls are given in this chapter's references.

8 Andrea Blanch, *Transcending Violence: Emerging Models for Trauma Healing in Refugee Communities*. Washington, DC: National Center for Trauma-Informed Care, 2008.

9 Renos Papadopoulos, 'Refugees, Trauma and Adversity-Activated Development', *European Journal of Psychotherapy and Counseling*, 9(3): 301–312, Sept 2007.

10 Richard, Mollica, *Healing Invisible Wounds: Paths to Hope and Recovery in a Violent World*. Nashville:Vanderbilt University Press, 2009.
11 Andrea Hajek and Sofia Serenelli,'Inside the Interview:The Challenges of a Humanistic Oral History Approach in the Deep Exchange of Oral History: Guest Editors' Introduction', *Oral History Review: Journal of the Oral History Association*, 54(2, Summer/Fall), 2018. Oxford: Oxford University Press, 2018.
12 Hajek and Serenelli,'Inside the Interview', 2018.
13 Alison Atkinson-Phillips,'Oral History in 2018:What Did We learn?', *News from the Oral History Unit and Collective* website, Newcastle University, 1-2-2019.
14 Leyla Neyzi, 'Between "Democracy" and "Authoritarianism": Implications for Oral History Practice'. Keynote lecture at 2018 *American Oral History Association* Conference, Concordia University, Montreal.
15 Atkinson-Phillips,'Oral History in 2018', 2019.
16 Atkinson-Phillips,'Oral History in 2018', 2019.
17 Every effort has been made to ensure the accuracy of the information in this book but neither the author nor publisher accept liability for any consequences resulting from the use of this information for any purpose.
18 *A Guide to Oral History and the Law, 2nd edition* by John Neuenschwander in 2014 is an authoritative publications on the subject.
19 Available free at www.creativecommons.org, these licenses usually acknowledge the copyright holder with an '*Attribution*'.This is different from works in the public domain: those are completely free of copyright and do not have to be attributed.
20 Nancy MacKay, *Curating Oral Histories: From Interview to Archive, 2nd edition*. Abingdon: Routledge, 2016; and Nancy Mackay, Mary Kay Quinlan and Barbara Sommer, *Community Oral History Toolkit*. Abingdon: Routledge, 2013.
21 For an introductory overview, see the *2019 Global Data Protection Handbook*, by international law firm DLA Piper, 2014, a free A–Z summary, in over 800 pages, of data protection laws in a hundred jurisdictions and most countries.
22 Lone Working is a protocol or set of measures that plans for safeguarding employees and volunteers whose work duties take them away from official workplaces, especially when working alone; see the Suzy Lamplugh Trust website for resources.
23 Specialists could engage with such a person in a highly supervised environment, where relevant medical and legal authorities have authorized that some form of oral history interview would benefit the person.
24 My understanding is that under US, European and British law, for instance, there is usually no legal obligation to report such activity if it is not currently under police investigation, but if it is the subject of a current legal investigation, you must yield to the police on request any information that you may have about it.
25 May Bulman, 'Hundreds of Europeans Including Firefighters and Priests Arrested for "Solidarity" with Refugees, Data Shows', *The Independent*, 18-5-2019.

# 7

# STRATEGICALLY PLANNING AN ORAL HISTORY PROJECT THAT WILL IMPROVE OUTCOMES FOR REFUGEES AND HOST COMMUNITIES

In the words of Ai Weiwei, the world-famous Chinese refugee artist who made the refugee feature film *Human Flow*: 'We all have a short life. We have only a moment to speak out or to present what little skills we have'. Now that our case studies have shown you what can be achieved by even one person, you have real motivation to push on with your own oral history project to improve outcomes for refugees and host communities. The next three chapters will coach you through every detail of doing your project. This first chapter will show how you how to:

- choose and research a specific refugee or host community to interview;
- plan your project's intended outcomes and end products;
- select your narrators from a strategic, meaningful spread of ages, roles, genders and perspectives;
- plan all the logistics of your project, including budget, team, equipment, timeline and end products.

Appendices at the back of the book provide a toolbox of checklists, planners and forms with which you can plan all the logistics that you may need – from budgets, equipment, skills and training to background research, community outreach and using interpreters or translators. Subsequent chapters will talk you through all the details of actually doing interviews, analyzing your findings and disseminating them to achieve your project's goals.

## What Do You Want Your Project to Achieve?

To avoid wasting the time and resources of narrators who may already be vulnerable and under pressure, it's important that you get really clear beforehand about why you want to gather their oral histories. Remember that we are doing *applied* oral history here, not just gathering narrators' stories for the sake of it. So take some time to think clearly about the effects you would like your project to have – and on whom. This means answering the questions below for yourself, well before you ever meet your narrators:

1. What do you *aim to do* with these oral histories once you've gathered and edited them?
2. What target *audience(s)* do you want their *messages* to reach?
3. What *effect(s)* do you want those messages to have on that audience, and what would you like the audience to *do* as a result?

Your answers to these questions are very important, as they will define your project's *aims*, target *audience* and intended *effects* on that audience. Figure 7.1 will help you to think through your answers.

I recommend that you don't just answer 'I want to do *all* those things, and have all those effects.' Throughout this book you are seeing that different messages appeal to and impact upon different audiences; and different audiences have different means and leverage to affect specific different outcomes. It would seem to me irresponsible and wasteful to set out on any scale of refugee oral history project without first defining for it the three boundaries above: what you'll do with the oral histories; the intended audience for their messages; and the intended effect on that audience. All this strategic planning is the main difference between traditional oral history and the very applied oral history that we are doing here. So, to be effective, please take a streamlined, strategic approach by carefully plotting your own project's intended route across Figure 7.1.

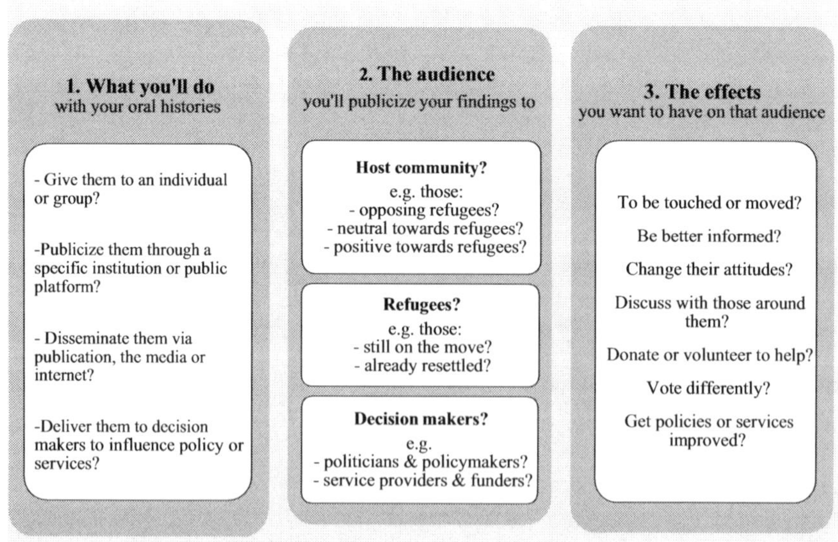


**FIGURE 7.1** Planning your project's aims, target audiences and intended effects

Also note that aims, audiences and effects can vary greatly across applied projects like these, depending on their size and scope. At one extreme, yours might be just a short project with just one narrator and a very specific intended outcome just for them. For instance, your modest goal might be just to capture the oral history of one refugee's experience in order to bring them some emotional relief, comfort and dignity as an individual, and to give their typed, bound testimony to their family as a keepsake. This can be well worth doing and of profound value and comfort to individuals (so long as full consent and ethical procedures are observed).

Or your project might have midsize goals. You might be planning to capture the views, concerns and grievances of both 'sides' in a specific refugee/host community location, and to air those views in a conflict-resolution setting that supports listening and dialogue, such as an exhibition in a library, a show on local radio or a series in a newspaper. Alternatively, your goal might be to capture the neglected concerns and grievances of the host community and deliver them to local politicians and public service providers in a meaningful, reasoned way. Your presentation of their views could: suggest ways that the authorities could respond directly to those grievances; respectfully dispel any myths that the grievances may be built upon; and improve relations between the home community and incoming refugees. Or, especially if you are a professional who is already delivering services to refugees, you may have the larger goal of applying refugee narrators' feedback strategically and methodically to improve the actual design and delivery of a specific refugee service in a specific setting. Or, like some of the case studies that we've examined, you may be designing a really big-budget, international project involving hundreds of narrators with large-scale, strategic outcomes that will influence the direction of refugee policy or the delivery of extensive refugee services. Importantly, the how-to chapters in this book are designed to be equally helpful for projects anywhere along this spectrum, from those with minimum to maximum goals and intended impacts.

Figure 7.2 depicts in graphic form the different scales of aim and outcome that any given refugee or host oral history project may have, from the smallest to the largest. If you think back over all the examples you saw in our case study chapters, you'll see that different projects had quite specific aims among those in this diagram. Hopefully, the seven aims or impacts depicted here will help you in turn to locate and define your own project's specific aims. And remember, it's fine to do a small local project that aims to just *contribute* in a small way towards a very big or even nationwide goal. But to ensure you achieve your goal, whatever it is, I'm just urging you to become very clear about it before you start. For instance, you might decide to interview just one refugee narrator, and to just display extracts from their story in a modest exhibition at your local library. But this project's overall *aim* or intention might still sit within any of the seven categories in Figure 7.2. Obviously, the smaller aims – like Aims 1 and 2 in the diagram – are ones you could achieve fully in this way. Or your small project could make a meaningful *contribution* towards Aims 3 or 4. Or, in the spirit of the 'think global, act local' movement, your modest project could make its drop of contribution to the bigger ocean of Aim 7.

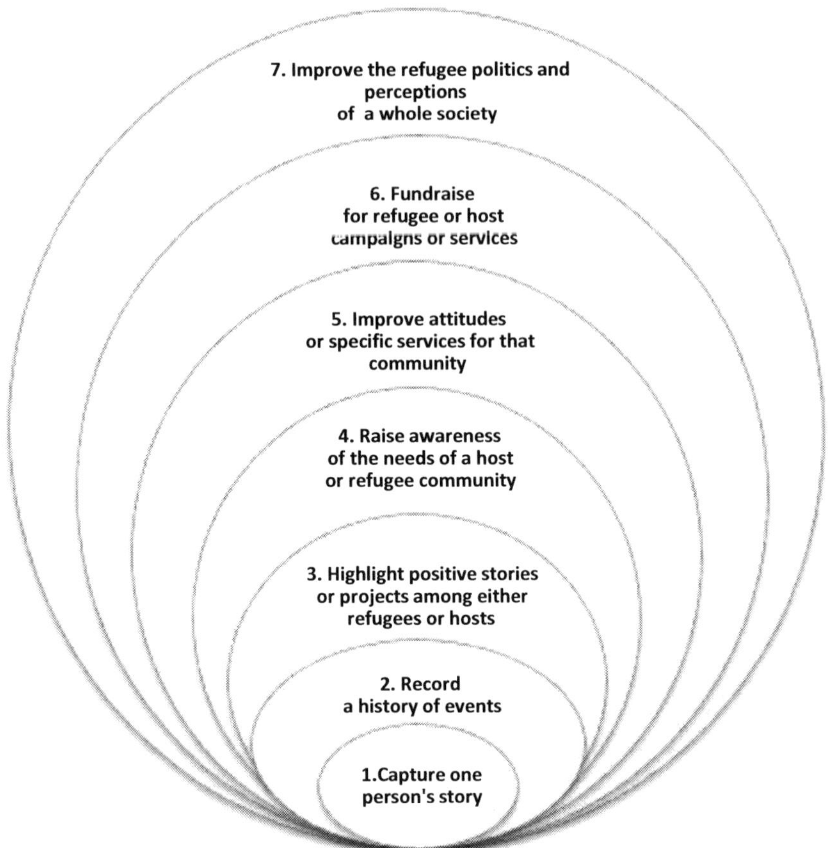


**FIGURE 7.2** Seven aims a refugee or host oral history project could have, from modest to ambitious

As I see it, any applied oral history project addressing the refugee crisis is essentially a 'message-carrying' exercise. Your project can carry and transmit important information, messages and new perspectives between categories of stakeholders who need these communication bridges built for them and who, without your project, might otherwise not receive these important truths and messages. In the planning that we are doing now, you are basically choosing the group that your project will listen to – and the group to whom your project will carry their messages. Figure 7.3 shows that within the great potential mass dialogue that is the refugee crisis, there are many possible combinations of speakers and listeners that you could bridge between: Figure 7.3 lists 20 of them.

Which group(s) do you feel drawn to interview? And which do you feel drawn to influence and have an effect upon, as the target audience for your findings? Logistics like geographical proximity, familiarity with a particular community and your own professional skills and interests will obviously help to narrow these fields.

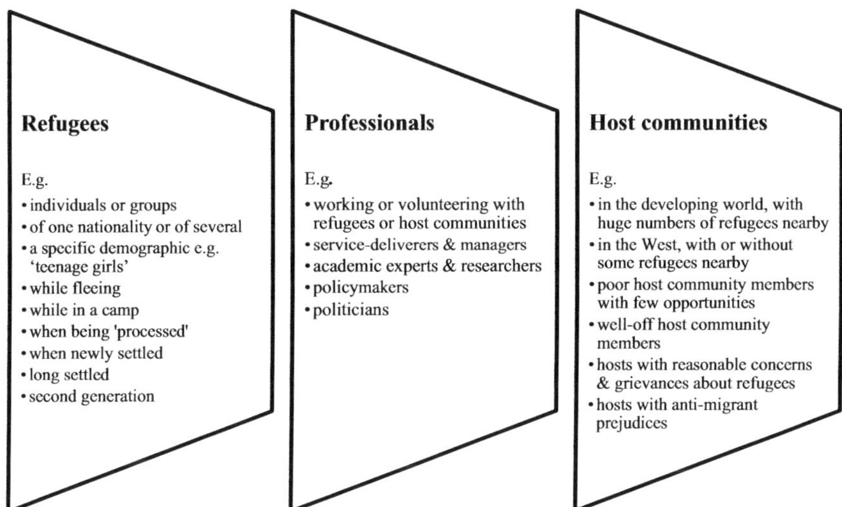


**FIGURE 7.3** Groups that your oral history project could (a) interview and (b) reach with its findings

Once you have decided on the specific refugee group or host community that you intend to interview, you will see further below how to select individual narrators among them. But first it's important that you establish some basic understanding of their community as a whole. Before interviewing individuals, you should first spend a bit of time finding out about:

- the group's geography (or geographical origins, if they're refugees), their language(s), economic status, educational levels, religion, culture and traditions;
- both the past and current nature of whatever political conflicts, wars or regimes caused them to flee if they're refugees – or the past and current nature of their local political landscape if they're a host community;
- for refugees: which stage of the refugee process they are at, on the long journey from fleeing to being long settled;
- for any given refugee group or host community: their particular needs, issues and concerns as a community at this time.

You should be able to find much of this information in the public domain, whether in current affairs bulletins, journalists' reports or on political or community websites. For the first three bullet points above, in particular, it's just common courtesy to inform yourself about this background context before narrators give you their time and trust going into more detail during interviews about the fourth bullet point.

Especially when interviewing host communities, it's a good idea to also first spend a little time looking around their local area anonymously, to get a sense of how life is there. How well cared for does this place seem? Do locals look happy, healthy and trusting, or downtrodden and anxious? Is there banter and ease in their public interactions, or noticeable tension between groups and in public life?

Similarly, before you approach any refugee community for interviews, you must first take some time to think through the major logistical and psychological impacts that they are likely to be experiencing, depending on where they are in the stages of the refugee process. There are massive differences, for instance, between the typical preoccupations of long-settled refugees, newly arrived ones and those still in transit or awaiting asylum. Figure 7.4 summarizes some of these typical worries that will tend to predominate the foreground for refugees at each phase of the refugee journey. You can expect these issues to be prominent in any interview you do with them in that phase.

| Journey stage | Refugee narrators' typical preoccupations at this stage |
|---|---|
| **While fleeing** | terror, escape, secrecy, transport, finances, safety, loss, grief, separation |
| **In a camp** | survival, physical & mental; cold, heat, hunger; lack of services<br>health problems, safety, privacy<br>future hopes & needs |
| **In transit** | transport, costs, physical dangers, evading police<br>mobile phone contacts; using traffickers or smugglers; illicitnetworks; dangerous people |
| **Being processed** | asylum rights, documentation, evidence, interviews, legal support<br>waiting, poverty, paralysis, hope<br>rejection, appeals, deportation or repatriation |
| **Newly settled** | housing, finding work, income, healthcare, public services<br>language learning, kids' schooling<br>isolation, new culture, alienation |
| **Long settled** | identity, memories, belonging, home<br>culture contrasts; pros & cons of each culture<br>links to the old country;regrets |
| **Second generation** | identity, not belonging, no clear 'homeland'<br>political resentments<br>links to the old country |

**FIGURE 7.4** Refugees' typical preoccupations at each stage of the refugee journey

Clearly, you need to take serious account of these phases and preoccupations when planning your interview questions.[1] For instance, in my view, it would be inappropriate to press refugee narrators with lots of questions about a phase they haven't reached yet. If they're still in a refugee camp (hence struggling for *survival, warmth* and a bit of *privacy*), I believe it's not appropriate to press them with questions about the further challenges that will come with a much later phase (such as weighing up the pros and cons between their home and host cultures once they are long settled). As an interviewer you must respect their natural human priorities of the moment, for instance by asking about them or letting the narrator pour them out at the beginning of their interview. But remember that your goal is not solely to make your narrators feel listened to (though that is indispensable). Your goal is to bridge between audiences, *carrying 'useful messages' that will help.*

Similarly, host communities have their own spectrum of preoccupations around the refugee crisis. Rather than varying across time as the stages of the refugee journey do, the variation here is more likely to be across the ideological spectrum. At one end are the benevolent host community members who initiate projects to assist refugees. And way over on the other end of the spectrum there are far-right white supremacists, who may even be involved in illegal 'hate crime' activities or memberships. Obviously, and thankfully, the vast majority of host populations occupy the more benign parts of this spectrum. In Chapters 3 and 4, we saw many dozens of examples of host communities' actions to help and benefit refugees. So, Figure 7.5 – with its spectrum gradually shading into the darker and illegal levels of opposition to refugees – gives more attention to the host preoccupations at that darker end of the spectrum. Fortunately, fewer people occupy those positions, but they are disproportionately dangerous and powerful. As with refugees, it's worth being aware of what these people's typical preoccupations are likely to be before you consider interviewing them.

| Spectrum of host community attitudes | Host community narrators' typical preoccupations about refugees |
|---|---|
| Proactively thinking up, designing and implementing projects to help refugees | Deeply stirred by a compulsion to 'improve the system'; sometimes putting their own life and job on hold to devote themselves to improving structures around how we integrate refugees |
| Lending a hand by joining in, e.g. by volunteering | Willing to give some of their time and energy to help a refugee project set up by someone else |
| Would like to help if they knew how | Feel refugees 'are human beings just like us'; particular sympathy for the same demographic as themselves among refugees e.g. host community mothers' sympathy for refugee mothers; host teens' sympathy for refugee teens, etc. |
| Neutral | Not particulary aware of or interested in refugees either way |
| Concerned over economic effects | Competition for jobs and housing; wages being undercut; rents and prices going up |
| Concerned over public resources | Competition for benefits and health services; crowding and degradation of public environments; policing stretched |
| Concerned for religious and cultural homogeneity | Fear of their country's religion or culture being diluted or challenged |
| Collective anxieties about sex and gender | Fears of refugees 'taking' host community women; of refugees reproducing rapidly to 'replace' host community; of refugees abusing host community women in the street; of refugees restricting liberties of women in the West |
| Ethno-nationalism for their own country | Wanting only their own 'race' in their own country; strong ethno-nationalist feelings for their own country |
| Illegal hate crime | Racist speech, behavior or publications that the law bans as 'hate-crime' |
| Part of international white supremacist or neo-Nazi movements, online, in person or through memberships, manifestos or marches, secretly or overtly | Wider affiliations and solidarities beyond just an ethno-nationalist vision for their own country; worldwide far-right ideas like the 'Great Replacement' or the 'Aryan Race', the self-imagined superiority of white people |

**FIGURE 7.5** Host communities' typical preoccupations along their spectrum of responses to refugees

## Gathering 'Useful Messages' that Will Make a Real Difference

This task requires a sort of layered or two-phase listening. First, you listen to narrators' urgent human concerns that are likely to 'pop out' at the beginning of your conversation. But you are also doing a kind of 'meta-listening' where, especially by the second half of the interview, you are scanning for the 'useful messages' that you could carry from this interview that could *make a measurable difference* to the situation, once received by your intended audience. I have found that these 'useful messages' fall broadly into these five categories:

1. the pain that narrators have been through, whether they are refugees or hosts;
2. the things they need now;
3. what they have to offer;
4. relations with the 'other' community, whether refugee or hosts;
5. how the services they receive could work better, either as refugees or as hosts.

Figure 7.6 overviews this spectrum of 'useful messages' and the effects each is likely to have on its intended audience. Whether coming from refugee narrators or from narrators in a host community, *Messages 1* and *2* often express the most urgent, immediate impacts and needs; *Messages 3* and *4* express more future-oriented attempts to improve the situation; and *Message 5* is always useful to policymakers and service-deliverers, at every stage of the situation.

While doing this 'meta-listening' for these 'useful messages', be aware that different messages may emerge from different demographic groups, even though they are in the same community and situation. For instance, let's say you interview, separately, four members of one family in a refugee camp. The grandmother might want to tell you all the pain they've all been through (*useful message 1*). The young mother might focus urgently on the material things her children need

| Types of **'useful messages'** | *1.The pain that narrators have been through* | *2. What narrators need now* | *3. What narrators' community have to has* | *4. Their relationship with the 'opposite' community (i.e. hosts or refugees)* | *5. How services for either community could be done better* |
|---|---|---|---|---|---|
| **Effects** you want to have on the audience receiving this message | Provoke some compassion & understanding | Show the audience the practical ways they could help | Show positive perspectives & examples | Improve relations, integrations & collaborations, for mutual benefit | Users' feedback can shape & improve policies & services |

**FIGURE 7.6** Five categories of 'useful messages' that an oral history project could carry to its chosen audience

right now (*useful message 2*). The young husband might want to show you all that their refugee community has to offer the host community in terms of professional skills, willingness to contribute and positive attitudes (*useful message 3*). And the grandfather might reflect more philosophically, with a bit more distance and overview, on how he feels they are viewed by the host community, and his memory of racist dynamics that stretch back into history between the two communities (*useful message 4*). With host communities, you'll see some techniques further below for steering narrators around to issues that you want them to address. But, with refugees, I believe it's best to mostly let *their* situation and emotions dictate which content they choose to give you. We already explored at length in Chapter 6 the ethical reasons why.

## Selecting Narrators Strategically

Hopefully, you are now clear about exactly which stakeholder group you want to interview, which type of useful information you want to get from them, which group you want to carry that information to, the effects you want it to have on them and what you'd like them to do as a result. The number of people that you go on to interview will partly depend on the scope of your project, as defined by logistics such as budget, intended outcomes, timescales and staffing. Certain types of oral history projects can function well with just a single narrator, if that person is an 'ideal' narrator. But in terms of maximum numbers, our case studies have included oral history projects that aimed to improve large-scale policies or public services by interviewing hundreds of individual oral history narrators.[2] Whether interviewing refugees or a host community, there are subgroups that you will need to zoom in on as narrators, depending on your aims and the information you seek to carry forward to your target audience. Perhaps you know already that you want to focus on a specific demographic, such as 'adolescent refugee girls' or 'unemployed working-class men in the host community'. Or, even if you decide to focus on the whole community, do still plan in advance to hear from a variety of ages, genders, disabilities and social classes among them – not just the most vocal and articulate. This is important because whether they're a refugee or a member of the host community, individuals are impacted by the refugee crisis in ways particular to their own role in life. So plan to hear from specific demographics such as:

- children, teens, young adults of both genders, parents, the elderly;
- the physically or mentally sick, injured or handicapped;
- women confiding on women's issues (e.g. women's health and hygiene; privacy and sexual safety; expected roles, etc.);
- men confiding on men's issues (e.g. violence; military activities; roles and responsibilities in family and community, etc.);
- those with vulnerable status through being gay or trans, the 'wrong' religion, apostates or politically or militarily active.

Your choice of narrators will also be led by your aims. If you are primarily aiming to provoke compassion in a host community audience, it's worth being aware of 'mirror neuron' psychology. Basically, this natural neurological function drives us to identify with and unconsciously imitate individuals that we perceive as similar to us.[3] This means that stories from our 'peer group' tend to be the ones we can most easily relate to and empathize with. Mothers tend to be most moved by the plight of other mothers. Fathers are particularly stirred by the struggle of another father to protect his brood. And teenagers may feel more empathy for fellow teens in any culture than they do for any other age-group in their own society! This is worth bearing in mind when selecting narrators for maximum impact, in terms of your project's 'message-carrying'.

Use the blank template Appendix 5 on page 182 to plan who your narrators will be. You can rank potential narrators as '*Must interview*' and '*Would be good to interview if I have time*'. Despite my warning above to avoid your project being dominated by the most vocal narrators, community leaders can nonetheless be a good place to start. Whether in a refugee population or in a host community, these people – whether formally or informally – are recognized as 'speaking for' their community. Appearing all across both refugee and host communities, they may be motivators, educators, propagandists, team leaders, campaigners, volunteers, community mentors or spiritual leaders. Whatever you may think of them, these figures tend to:

- hold a great deal of information about their community and its issues;
- have strong influence in the community, who may look to them for leadership on what to do and who to speak to;
- act as gatekeepers who can direct you to less accessible narrators, including 'protected' people they'll only let you access once they trust you.

But do retain a critical distance around community leaders, whether among refugees or host communities. Sometimes they will only tell you the official 'party line' of their community, rejecting or sidelining its nonconformists. Or sometimes they can be power-driven individuals, with vested interests of their own.

Whether you are interviewing refugees or a host community, it's also important to listen to their service providers. At once experts and insiders, these people know firsthand what their client group is experiencing, needs and lacks. In a host community, these people may be teachers, employers, community workers, social workers, unemployment advisors. They can often articulate with some objectivity the reasons why the host community feels so threatened by incoming refugees.

Around a refugee community, service providers may be volunteers, camp managers, healthcare workers, charity staff or state employees. These specialists have a painful awareness of gaps in provision as they struggle on with underfunded resources. I often consider their testimony to be as important as that of refugees themselves, because they hold a big-picture, expert overview of refugees' needs. Remember that until they are years into the sorry process, refugees themselves are new to the job of being refugees! They were never trained for the role. We saw in some of our case studies that refugees may have little knowledge of all the things that will be required for their arrival and integration into the culture, climate and politics of what is to them an alien place.

When planning who to interview, start deciding now whether you intend to do any group interviews. Think through the particular dynamics and the pros and cons for your specific project. For instance, why would you do group interviews as opposed to individual ones? One simple argument in favor of them might be that you feel you would save yourself time. You may feel that just an hour and a half interviewing a group of five refugee women will give you almost as much information as if you interviewed each alone. The group interview will take 7.5 hours of their time in all and 1.5 of yours; interviewing them individually would take the same amount of time from them, but 7.5 hours from you. But on this point of time saved, remember that in any 1.5 hour interview, only 1.5 hours of speech can actually be aired and recorded, regardless of which narrator is speaking it. You don't want narrators speaking simultaneously over each other, so you can only hear from each narrator one fifth of what you would have heard from her in a 1.5 hour interview dedicated to her alone.

That is assuming that in your group interview you will succeed in giving equal airtime to all five narrators. I can assure you that, given the natural flow of group conversations and group dynamics in any culture, this is much easier said than done, even for an experienced group interviewer. You may feel that the five refugee women will feel more encouraged and emboldened to speak by being together. But, in fact, group dynamics often mean that some speakers will be silenced by the presence of more dominant or inhibiting ones. You could try to combat this by 'imposing' equal airtime through scripted questions that you've prepared for each specific individual. But unless you know the individuals to some extent beforehand, it's not easy to know which questions it's best to target to which individual. Of course, an interviewer can always intervene like a compere or 'referee', distributing airtime fairly by interrupting the most vocal and actively calling on the quietest to speak up. This is done, for instance, in focus group interviews. And it is a role familiar to all in the 'anchorperson' of television interviews, whether those are challenging, political group interviews done for news broadcasts, or more leisurely chat show ones done for entertainment.

When interviewing communities for government, to gather their feedback to improve policies, I received a lot of training in running and moderating these 'focus group' style interviews. But playing that 'refereeing' role in a refugee or host community oral history interview is not so straightforward, and I would caution against it.[4] It would require you to be assertive and directive, controlling narrators' input as you move your attention methodically between narrators in the group interview. But that is far removed from the 'receptive following' technique taught in our previous chapter under the six '*PIECES*' heading. And it would significantly reduce the rapport and ease required for these much more delicate interview situations.

A relevant issue here is how differentiated your group narrators will be, demographically speaking. For instance, will the five of them be teenage refugee girls? Or will they be an average cross-section from the host community, such as an elderly man, a mother of three, a young boy, an unemployed drifter and the local policeman? Clearly, the latter group will each have very different perspectives to give, such that you would do best to hear from them all individually. And they will have hierarchically different levels of authority within their society, such that some will automatically tend to dominate others in the conversation. Compared with them, the five teenage refugee girls are likely to have more homogenous views about their experiences, which will be relatively similar to each other and might perhaps be more 'equal' and supportive about distributing airtime between themselves. Hence, they might be more suited to a group interview than the very mixed bunch of host narrators.

In any case, when doing any applied oral history project to improve a social or political situation, I often also recommend that you consider taking the trouble to interview those genuinely opposed to your own values. On a polarized subject like refugees, you can locate plenty of people opposed to their resettlement. It can be a noble task to go out there, find them and capture their views. We have seen that to achieve any kind of harmony in our future societies, these concerns will have to be aired and addressed, rather than suppressed in ways that will drive further wedges between populations and ideologies. Part of your important work in listening to host communities can be to sift and distinguish between their valid concerns – and the plain old racisms that do lurk behind some opposition to refugees. Applied oral historians can play an important part in locating and airing these two *different* voices within the opposition to refugees. Remember that all these voices are powerfully lobbying decision makers right now, and speaking loudly in the media. So knowing their arguments can only help us to refute them if necessary, and find better arguments.

## Planning How to Publicize Your Project's Findings

How you publicize your project's findings will depend on the aims that you set for the project at the beginning, in terms of the target audience you want to have an effect on, the effect you want to have on them and what you want them to do as a result. (Hopefully, you used Figures 7.1, 7.2, 7.3 and 7.6 to plan all these.) To prompt your thinking now about the final products that could disseminate your findings, Figure 7.7 shows five different spheres or domains in which you could communicate and apply them. These are the media, public education, the arts, public policy and academic research. There are others, but to stimulate your ideas, Figure 7.7 shows no fewer than 20 different formats and applications you could use to convey your findings in these five domains alone.

Hopefully you see by now how important it has been to first plan your project's aims right through to the end before you start the work. That way, you can select the right narrators and the right questions to ask them, to capture the types of 'useful messages' you are looking for, in ways suited to the publication medium

| | Through the media | As public education | Through the arts | For public policy | As academic research |
|---|---|---|---|---|---|
| Outlets | Newspaper articles | Exhibitions in public libraries | Theatre or street-performance | Use to improve design or delivery of a new or existing refugee service | Publish in an academic journal or book |
| | Radio interviews | Exhibitions in community centers | Novel, graphic novel, biography | Use to improve design or delivery of a new or existing public service for hosts resistant to refugees | Use to teach a course or qualification |
| | Website | Talks in schools | Film or video | Use as 'myth-busting' information to improve a host community's reception of refugees | Present as an engaging PowerPoint talk at academic conferences |
| | Online blog | Use to teach an evening course | Cartoons, quizzes, role-play games | Use to listen deeply to a resistant host community so that genuine grievances can be addressed | Deposit in an official archive |
| Audiences | General public<br><br>Could be localized or regional<br><br>Could be aimed at one demographic such as teenagers | More thoughtful publics<br><br>Specific age groups & levels of education<br><br>May be already a little 'open' to the subject | Anyone interested in those arts, even if they had no previous interest in refugees or host community issues | Service designers, service-deliverers, politicians, policymakers | Academics, policymakers, university students, future professionals |

**FIGURE 7.7** Some of the ways that you could publicize your findings

that you'll be using. For instance, let's say your final publication medium will be a cartoon story on *Save the Children*'s website, conveying true-life traumas told by child refugees in their oral histories. So you need to plan backward from that final medium, choosing locations, narrators and interview questions that will furnish the best material for that very specific publication medium.

Or let's say the final product of your applied oral history project will be a set of policy recommendations for local government in a Western city, to address a tide of anti-refugee sentiment that is becoming vocal in part of the local host community. You'll need to plan backward from the final policy document that you'll present to policymakers, which will have to contain highly relevant testimonies gathered from highly relevant narrators. For example, after 50 oral history interviews with the host community and some refugees, your main final product might be just a succinct four-page report of recommendations that you'll present to the policymakers using PowerPoint, backed up by hard-hitting quotes from your interviews. So use Figure 7.7 to get clear again about which audience you are aiming to influence, which medium is best for reaching them and which formats you're going to use within that medium.

## Planning Your Project's Logistics

The size of your budget will help define the scale and resources of your project. Budget obviously limits things like your project's amount of paid staffing, the amount of travel possible, the type of equipment you can have and the ways you can disseminate your project's findings. However, important as it is, remember that budget isn't everything. Many examples prove that even without a significant budget, other factors can prove more decisive and impactful. Your talent and imagination; the amount of free time you can dedicate to the project; contacts you might have who will do something for you for free; producing a story so compelling that the world media pick up on it and it goes viral... These factors have made world news of many refugee oral histories that were captured on a mobile phone by penniless people while fleeing. For instance, the near-drowning scenes filmed at sea on their mobile phones by refugees in the water as they sank, are the highlights of the BBC's film *Exodus: Our Journey to Europe*. And think of the wonderful work of Behrouz Boochani, the now world-famous refugee quoted in Chapters 1 and 4. His work was done in prison, on a remote island brutally cut off from the outside world, with absolutely no resources. Sheer talent, creativity, poetry, charisma and the help of a few willing outsiders smuggled his work out to become a famous, prizewinning book, a film and a movement.

Nonetheless, whatever your project's size, make a plan in writing now before you start for *every* aspect of its budget. On the budget template in Appendix 6 (p. 183) you can itemize every possible expense from equipment, software, printing and stationery to costs for travel, accommodation, communications, any staff or professional fees, and any publications or websites. List in your budget plan:

- all one-off costs, such as purchases of equipment;
- any costs ongoing for a time, such as wages, rentals, travel, accommodation or purchased services;
- any other costs that will require fundraising, grant applications or other external funding sources.

To help define your project team, list all the people who will do any sort of work for your project, other than narrators. Escalating from the most modest team to the most official, this could include any combination of:

- only yourself, working alone as an unpaid volunteer;
- you with the help of some volunteer(s), either trained or whom you'll train or get trained by someone else;
- a budget for some paid hours by yourself and/or other professionals;
- employing some professionals full-time for a fixed period.

Plan now how any volunteers will be trained: by whom, where, when, at what cost and on what precise topics. Even if they've already been trained to collect oral histories and abide by a *Code of Conduct*, they will still need induction sessions to be briefed on all the specifics of your project: its size and scope, goals, target audience, narrators, line of questioning, etc. If you intend to train or induct volunteers yourself, Appendix 7 (p. 184) gives a template for a simple *Training Workshop* to cover:

- the aims, ethos and intended outcomes of your project;
- the skills and awareness required for doing interviews;
- the practicalities of using equipment and keeping appropriate records;
- legal and ethical frameworks and codes of conduct;
- safeguarding for volunteers, staff and narrators.

When weighing up the benefits of using volunteers as opposed to professional interviewers, it may seem an obvious benefit that they bring free labor. But with fewer skills then professionals, they do take much more time to train and supervise. And all the various overhead costs for using them (such as office space, equipment, travel costs, catering, etc.) tend to be about the same as those for professionals. In fact, where volunteers often bring real advantages in oral history is when they are members of – and have the trust of – the community being interviewed. Their insider knowledge and the rapport they may have with narrators can be invaluable. But be aware that the opposite can also be true – that sometimes narrators won't want to disclose certain things to an interviewer coming from their own community and would prefer to speak to a complete outsider.

While volunteers will attend your *Training Workshop*, even professional staff will need a formal induction from you, clarifying everything about your project, its boundaries and its expectations of them. Type up a clear, succinct *Project Induction* sheet for all personnel on your team, defining your project's aims, values, intended outcomes, boundaries, *Lone Working Protocols* and *Code of Conduct*. As well as the basics, the *Code of Conduct* should also include guidelines or instructions defining the project's position on things like:

- sharing our views (social, political or cultural) and reacting to views we disagree with;
- being clear about the limits of what we can do for refugees (not promising the earth);
- personal boundaries for not getting over-involved emotionally with narrators (e.g. not giving our home contact details; not giving or lending money or gifts; not forming romantic relationships, etc.);
- not being intimidated by narrators with extreme or militant views, whether they are refugees or from the host community;
- managing our own emotions in a professional way;
- respecting confidentialities and other personal boundaries.

In terms of equipment, audio and video are the most common methods nowadays for recording oral history interviews, especially given the ubiquity of lightweight, affordable devices, from mobile phones to Dictaphones.

Compared to audio recordings, video has, in theory, certain advantages that should capture and convey more information for you, such as:

- narrators' facial expressions and body language, as well as the ways these change at different moments of their interview;
- a visible, atmospheric sense of their immediate surroundings;
- a more engaging intimacy and dramatic appeal for those watching the video in your project's final end product.

In today's highly visual media environment, clips of video are certainly more valued on the internet, for instance, or when displayed at a public talk or exhibition, compared to material that's solely in audio format. But getting the agreement of narrators to be filmed tends to be a much bigger step for them than just being audio-recorded. And even if they do agree, they may feel more inhibited and stilted with the camera focused on them. Filming also requires, on your part, a more intrusive setup that will be more visible and imposing in the eyes of those in the wider community. Audio, by contrast, can seem almost invisible, with just a small recorder sitting on the table between you during what can look to the outside eye like an ordinary conversation.

Whichever recording medium you choose, it can also be important to record your project photographically and through note-taking as you go along. Occasionally, a refugee or host narrator may simply be too nervous or intimidated to allow any mechanical recording, and you may decide that taking notes as they speak is the best that you can do.

Keep an orderly journal of your project as you go along, briefly noting *all* project activities, locations, names of those involved, dates and duration, and what was done. We will see later how important this *Project Logbook* can be. In Chapter 9, the records in this logbook will be crucial for totaling up the hours everybody put in so as to estimate the equivalent monetary value of your project and its impacts. You can also use the logbook immediately after interviews to capture any insights of your own, the next steps that occur to you, any points to follow up on after an interview or any connections with other aspects of the project.

Audio recording requires a reliable, portable voice recorder that you have already practiced using, ideally with an external microphone that you've tested for quality. Very small, good quality microphones can be pinned to the speaker's clothing or can lie on a table between you. Or some Dictaphone recorders now have quality internal microphones that can be set to different modes dependent on the number of people speaking, background ambient sounds and the speakers' distance from the recorder. Before doing interviews, ensure that you have also mastered the steps for uploading these audio recording files afterwards to a backup computer or to online storage.

For video recording, you will need a reliable video camera stabilized on a tripod. Practice the whole process beforehand to ensure you end up with appropriate lighting and good sound and picture quality, taken from appropriate angles. Nowadays, small digital cameras and mobile phones can also take shorter, more informal video clips of acceptable quality, to supplement your full audio recordings of an interview. For photos, you'll need a reliable camera that will work unobtrusively in spontaneous situations where there may be poor lighting, little time to set up or little space. With photos, as with other media, ensure beforehand that you have practiced using the software necessary to download and back up project photos, editing them for quality and content where necessary (e.g. cropping, lightening, removing irrelevant backgrounds, etc.).

The final, but in my view possibly the most important, stage of planning your project is to draw up your *Project Timeline*. This is basically a calendar where you plan in all the phases and stages of your project, the tasks within each phase and how long each of these tasks will take. The blank *Project Timeline* template in Appendix 8 (p. 186) allows you to write in all your own project's dates, timescales and deadlines. You can work progressively into finer detail as you plan the amount of time each task in your project will take. This kind of micro-planning is invaluable for getting your project finished in a timely, effective way.

For instance, to plan how much time you will spend with each narrator, you might decide that you will typically need:

- half an hour to introduce the project to them when you first meet;
- 1.5 hours to do the interview on another day;
- a follow-up one-hour interview on another day, if necessary;
- an hour for the journey to and from them on each of those three occasions;
- 15 minutes on another day to feed back to them by phone or in writing about the end outcomes of the project.

So your project's total time communicating with each narrator might be about six and a quarter hours. If you are planning to interview ten people, put a total of about 70 hours into your timeline for that (allowing some slack for hitches or overrunning). This level of planning also enables you to give polite clarity when requesting that narrators give you their time. For instance, you can explain that '*It will take up to three and a quarter hours of your time in all, but in slots that suit you, spread over ten days*'.

In the same way, go back to the *Project Timeline* template now and also estimate how long it will take to prepare all the thoughts, background information, questions and documents for each stage of those contacts with a given narrator. This includes the time needed for:

- preparing the written and verbal information that you'll need to give them at your first meeting;
- agreeing, booking and preparing the venue for the interview;
- planning specific interview questions to put to them;
- writing up your own notes after the interview;
- organizing a second interview if needed;
- editing, transcribing and analyzing their interview recordings.

Take the time to gradually layer into your timeline all the actions, timings and micro-deadlines of your project. This planner will be an invaluable asset for completing a successful project. If you have staff, volunteers or other helpers on the project, you can also write their names beside the tasks that they will do. This will build up a complete project plan showing exactly:

- who is going to do what;
- how long everything will take;
- a set of personal *To-Do* lists for everyone to tick off at every stage.

Without a planned timetable like this, an oral history project could spread out formlessly without any boundaries to prevent it from drifting on forever. Whether yours will be a big project or a small one, your *Project Timeline* will ensure that your project delivers its outcomes in the ways that you planned.

## References

BBC2 TV, *Exodus: Our Journey to Europe*. London: BBC, 2016.

Boochani, Behrouz, *No Friend but the Mountains*. Sydney: Pan Macmillan, 2018.

'Groundswell: Oral History for Social Change Network', *Reportback: Letting Go of the One-on-One Interview?*, 25-9-2014 [Available at www.oralhistoryforsocialchange.org/blog/2014/9/25/reportback; accessed on 21-6-2019].

International Rescue Commission (IRC), *Designing for a Change in Perspective: Embracing Client Perspectives in Humanitarian Project Design*. Nairobi & Geneva: IRC, 2017.

Kapiszewski, Diana, Maclean, Lauren and Read, Benjamin, 'Interviews, Oral Histories and Focus Groups'. In *Field Research in Political Science: Practices and Principle, edited by Diana Kapiszewski, LaurenLLauren Maclean and Benjamin Read*. Cambridge: Cambridge University Press, 2015.

Skoyles, John, 'Why Our Brains Cherish Humanity: Mirror Neurones and *Colamus Humanitatem*', *Avances in Psicologia Latinoamericana*, 26(1): 99–111, 2008.

## Notes

1 Diana Kapiszewski, Lauren Maclean and Benjamin Read 'Interviews, Oral Histories and Focus Groups'. In *Field Research in Political Science: Practices and Principle*, edited by Diana Kapiszewski, Lauren Maclean and Benjamin Read. Cambridge: Cambridge University Press, 2015.

2 International Rescue Commission (IRC), *Designing for a Change in Perspective: Embracing Client Perspectives in Humanitarian Project Design*. Nairobi & Geneva: IRC, 2017.

3 John Skoyles, 'Why Our Brains Cherish Humanity: Mirror Neurones and *Colamus Humanitatem*', *Avances in Psicologia Latinoamericana*, 26 (1), 2008.

4 For a discussion among oral historians of these dynamics, see *Reportback: Letting Go of the One-on-One Interview?* on the website of the network 'Groundswell: Oral History for Social Change', 25-9-2014. See also Diana Kapiszewski, Lauren Maclean and Benjamin Read, 'Interviews, Oral Histories and Focus Groups' in their *Field Research in Political Science: Practices and Principles* (Cambridge: Cambridge University Press, 2015).

# 8

# DOING INTERVIEWS THAT WILL MAKE A DIFFERENCE

In the last chapter you planned who you want to interview, what information you want to get from them, who you'll take that information to and the effects that you want it to have on them. This chapter will now talk you through all the details of:

- planning your interview questions;
- setting up and doing your oral history interviews;
- navigating dynamics inherent in interviews with specialist groups like refugees or anti-migrant campaigners in a host community.

This is where it starts to get really interesting, as you step out into the 'field', where you'll find strong emotions and controversial views blowing like powerful winds. This chapter will show you how to build rapport as best you can across either a refugee or host community interview, moving from closed to open questions while managing the interview's ethics and power balance. We explore the conversational techniques, body language, tones of voice and responses that can enhance interviews. We look at empathic receptivity, but also at how to challenge, if necessary, any views considered unacceptable. And you will learn how to handle the fact that a given narrator may be doing their own private editing process so as to share quite different narratives with peers and compatriots, police or immigration officials, and with you.[1]

Host communities are just as likely as refugees to tell you many different shades of 'truth', not least because different members of one host community may view and experience refugees in very different ways. One may be active in volunteer work to help settle refugees, while their next door neighbor may be leading a political movement against refugees being admitted at all. Some narrators who are opposed to refugees might withhold from you more extreme views that they know you might not like, or that might even be illegal to speak of openly. But as the current political environment is mainstreaming some views that used to be dismissed as fringe, you won't have to go far to find narrators who will give you their anti-migrant views full blast if you listen, as I have urged you to do.

Hopefully, you can see by now that applied, contemporary oral history is not a court of law where you seek to establish one truth: it's more like a kaleidoscope that's able to usefully capture multiple, different perspectives. This makes it an invaluable tool for listening methodically to complex public situations where competing viewpoints have to be reconciled, and for giving voice to more diverse stakeholders. This chapter will show you how to move safely and clearheadedly through the powerful winds of emotion, belief and experience that can blow through the interview process, whether with refugees or with hosts. The planning that you do here will help you keep to the ethical aims and intended outcomes that you set for your project.

## Preparing Interview Questions

In the previous chapter we looked at five different types of 'useful messages' that this sort of oral history project can carry, and you clarified which type yours will be. You are ready now to start planning which information you will seek from each narrator, and hence the questions you will need to put to them. The list below recaps the five types of messages and shows what type of questioning from you will best elicit that information during interviews:

1. *To provoke compassion in your target audience*: ask your narrators simple, empathic questions that allow them to share their pain, losses and injuries.
2. *To show the audience all the ways they can help*: ask narrators to say specifically what would help them most, from the smallest to the biggest examples.
3. *To present inspiring examples of positive behaviors in either refugees or hosts*: get your narrator to talk about their own and their peers' most positive behaviors and resourcefulness.
4. *To improve relations between refugees and their host communities*: ask narrators what specifically would help them most to get on better with the 'other side', from the smallest to the biggest examples.
5. *To gather end-user feedback that will improve services*: ask narrators to say specifically what changes would most improve the services and their effects for them.

These may seem simple or obvious lines of questioning, but it's worth thinking through beforehand which thread of questioning you intend to follow, as each comes from a specific approach to problem-solving. For instance, to inspire compassion in our target audience, our interview questions need to provoke *empathic listening*. To elicit accounts of positive projects and resourceful attitudes, we can ask questions that come from the *positive deviance* methodology explained below. To elicit really useful examples of 'the best ways to help', our questions come from techniques of *participant design* – an approach that involves service recipients in designing services from the outset. To elicit specific feedback to improve existing services, our questions can use even more specific techniques from participant design, aimed at capturing *end-user feedback* and reapplying it back into the service-design loop. In our concluding chapter, we will consider the wider importance of these technologies for tackling future problems.

Meanwhile, Figure 8.1 summarizes these lines of questioning and the methodologies they come from. Empathic listening actively addresses and engages those mirror neurons that cause audiences to identity with a narrator and feel their pain. (However, the line of questioning '*What hurt you the most?*' obviously needs to be used with enormous care and tact, and only in a 'safe space' of genuinely

| 'Useful message' | Type of interview questions | Problem-solving technique the questions come from |
|---|---|---|
| 1. **The pain that refugees have been through**<br><br>(Purpose: to provoke emotional compassion in the host community) | *What has hurt you the most?*<br>*What were the worst moments?*<br>*What do you miss most?*<br>(Questions to use only with great care) | Empathic listening; identifying and empathizing through mirror neurons |
| 2. **What refugees need now–and what the host community needs**<br><br>(Purpose: to show both audiences all the practical ways they can help the 'other side') | Ask each community:<br><br>*What would help you most, from the smallest help to the biggest help?* | Participant design |
| 3. **Positive examples & behaviors on both sides**<br><br>(Purpose: to show positive, resourceful behaviors & projects by both 'sides') | *How did you do it?*<br>*Why did you do it?*<br>*What kind of lateral thinking helped you to do it?* | Positive deviance methodology |
| **4. How to improve relations between refugees and host communities**<br><br>(Purpose: to show both sides what the other community needs from them) | Ask each community:<br>*What do you most want from that other community?*<br>*What could they do that would reassure you?*<br>*What could benefit both sides as a win/win?* | Mediation;<br>conflict resolution |
| **5. How services could be done better**<br><br>(Purpose: capture end-user knowledge and feedback to improve services for both communities) | *What changes would improve services and their effects for you?* | End-user feedback in participant design |

**FIGURE 8.1** Types of interview questions to capture specific 'useful messages'

empathic listening.) Meanwhile, the apparently simple question '*What would help you most?*' is from the field of participative design, which engages the narrator themselves to help define the solutions they need, rather than an expert doing it for them. The motto of this design approach is '*Don't decide about me without me*'.[2]

The technique of eliciting examples of positive, resourceful behaviors comes from the field of positive deviance.[3] This problem-solving method seeks out individuals who have bucked the trend of a problem and improvised their own ingenious solutions with limited resources. An example would be the music classes given by the Congolese refugee we saw in an earlier chapter: using borrowed and rented instruments, he created a music school that is now teaching 40 refugees as well as three native Kenyans from the host community![4] Eliciting from such individuals how and why they manifested more positive behaviors than others is done by asking them precise, cumulative '*How*' questions: *How did you do that? And how did you do this part? And how did you think of doing that aspect?* The positive deviance method uses their successes as a teaching model to motivate and inspire their peers.

The questions '*What do you most want from them?*' and '*What could they do that would reassure you?*' come from a mediation approach to conflict resolution. These questions can bring healing and resolution whether used between two individuals in conflict (as in divorce mediation, for example) or between two populations (as in the reconciliation processes that we saw done through oral history in our host community case studies).[5] Finally, the fifth type of questioning – *What changes would improve services and their effects for you?* – is from the participative design approach. Here, a product or service has been in use for some time and users can now, with hands-on experience of it, provide invaluable feedback to designers on how to improve its performance and smooth out glitches in its effectiveness. The technology industry relies on making constant use of feedback in this way to 'debug' services and increase customer satisfaction with them.[6]

The other reason why we plan our line of questioning like this is that real-life refugee situations can be so emotive and urgent for all 'sides' – affecting refugees, host community, aid agencies and yourself – that once an interview starts, it can be difficult to steer the direction it takes. Your refugee narrator might just want to just cry for the whole hour over the injustices and losses they've experienced – which isn't ideal though it might be some use for *useful message 1* – to provoke compassion. But if your goal is to publicize to the host community all the practical ways that they could help such refugees (*useful message 2*), that interview would be totally ineffective for that purpose.

Or perhaps your goal is to publicize the many inspiring examples where ingenious, resourceful, resilient refugees have proactively helped themselves and the host community by setting up new employment projects of their own (*useful message 3*). You have located and selected these 'positive deviant' refugees. You plan to interview them about their inspiring projects: how they thought up their ideas; what gave them the courage to do it; the motivation that keeps them going, and so on. But your chosen narrators may also be quite knowledgeable about the public services that are provided for refugees, and the gaps and failures in those services, and how they could be done much better (*useful message 5*). They may be burning with righteous desire to tell you about that. And that would indeed be invaluable material if that was what your project was for. But if your aim is to publicize their positive deviant projects and behaviors (*useful message 4*), you need to plan interview questions that will steer them towards answers about that.

So find your own project's position and goals within Figure 8.1. Given the 'useful messages' that you now know you want to convey through this project, take a sheet of paper with the names or roles of your intended narrators on it, and write under each name the types of questions from Figure 8.1 that you plan to put to them. Have these *scripted questions* to hand in the interview. You could even note beside these questions the approximate time that you plan to spend on each. For instance, an interview lasting an hour with five planned questions could mean ten minutes on each, leaving a few minutes to warm up and wind down. Or you might plan for just five minutes on some questions and 15 minutes on others.

## Doing Your Interviews

With all your paperwork prepared, you are now ready to get out there, see who's who in the community, make contacts and hopefully get recommended on to other narrators as well. Before setting off to do an interview, use the checklist in Appendix 10 (p. 186) to pack everything you'll need, such as forms, equipment, lists of questions, maps and contact details. Leave enough time to get the venue prepared (seating, equipment, any refreshments and so on). If possible, have the space fully ready before your narrator arrives, so you can focus on putting them at ease.

Before refugee interviews in particular, recall or review the six '*PIECES*' behavioral guidelines given in Chapter 6. Their core message is that refugees' past, present and future situations are probably all outside of your direct control and influence. Basically, you're just there for what your applied oral history skills can contribute to help with the wider refugee crisis. And that is why we have put so much planning and preparation into this interview *beforehand* (though hopefully, it will seem to the narrator to flow naturally and spontaneously). There are four valuable, meaningful things that you can do for them, if you follow the guidelines in this book. You can:

1. give top-quality listening that conveys to them dignity, respect, human attention and empathy;
2. skillfully extract their 'useful messages', as we have planned;
3. convey those messages to the world on their behalf, as planned in our next chapter;
4. remind them at the beginning and end of the interview that your main purpose is points 2 and 3.

On their own side, as we saw in Chapter 6, only the narrator can find their own point of balance between the benefits of talking about their woes to a caring listener and the downsides of restimulating trauma. Each person is different so let them lead on this. If you feel it's getting too traumatic for them, you can help them come away from the subject by gently talking about something else (good weather coming; children laughing outside; the hot soup that's for lunch; or something from your own daily life).

Begin your recording by stating aloud the names of all present, the time, date, place and intended topic. This constitutes an important reference record at the beginning of every interview recording. Remind your narrator how long their interview is likely to last. Work through your list of *scripted questions*. On your list, you had marked a provisional plan for how long to give to each question, though you must balance this against following the natural flow of the conversation and the importance of specific answers that they give. For instance, you might initially steer them onto a topic, give them full control on that for ten minutes, then you could shift to another topic by saying '*That's really valuable, to hear and record all these details of how dangerous your escape journey was. I'm wondering too what things were like while you went through the asylum application process later?*' And you might let them have the main control on that again for ten minutes. As each of your *scripted questions* is covered, consider whether it now needs a *checking question*, to verify the meaning of their answer. Try to avoid encouraging them by saying things like '*Uh-huh*', '*Yes*' or '*I see*', which are unhelpful when they appear in your recording later. Get used to encouraging narrators instead with silent nods, smiles and body language.

Figure 8.2 gives some guidance on how, in any oral history interview, you can gradually deepen the material being discussed. You can plan your *scripted questions* to move naturally from factual, ice-breaking information to a deeper exploration as trust grows in the course of the conversation. Appendix 9 (p. 188) is a blank template helping you to plan your *scripted questions* to move gradually through these five levels.

We saw above that even for practical reasons alone, level 1 questions identifying facts about the narrator should always be the launching pad of any oral history interview. You need those identifiers at the start of each recording because by the end of the project you may not remember exactly who this recording was with, nor when it was done, nor where, regardless of how interesting the content may seem now. But Figure 8.2 shows why this opening factual stage is also an 'icebreaker',

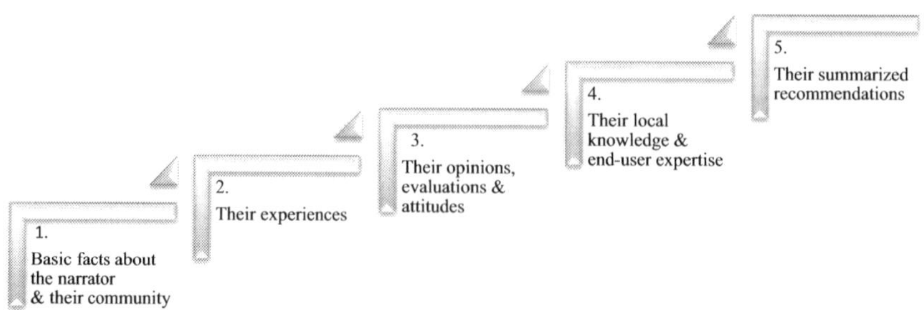


**FIGURE 8.2** Five chronological levels of an applied oral history interview[7]

giving narrators a bit of time to settle into the interview and get a feel for the conversation you're about to have.

As was mentioned earlier, both refugee and host narrators often need to pour out some of their experiences straight away (level 2), to release some of their frustrations and highlight the most urgent things they feel that they or those around them need. The conversation may then be able to 'mellow' a bit into standing back to give some reflections, assessments and thoughts on the situation (level 3). Again, it feels natural to do that before they finally come on to give their own recommendations about what the situation needs overall (level 4).

I feel it's important to take real care over level 4 in every interview. At this stage of the conversation you can afford to ask the narrator to list – specifically and concretely – all the ways they feel things could be done better, whether for example in terms of refugee services, refugees' relations with the host community or what the host community could do to help more. Our strategically chosen narrators will often have this sort of crucial, hands-on local knowledge about:

- what's really needed in their environment;
- where the obstacles and hitches are in the current provision;
- the most efficient, sustainable solutions for the long-term.

This is lived, *implicit* knowledge that your interview can uncover and make *explicit*. Remember that this knowledge is as yet 'hidden'. People with informal, end-user expertise tend to see themselves as 'just getting by', often not noticing that they have improvised low-tech solutions to problems that confound the experts.

The three insights listed above can turn mere policies or services into real solutions. Policymakers and service providers are always keen to hear them. So take care to always ask your narrators specifically: '*What do you feel is most needed? How could this be done better, in your opinion?*' Ask this methodically about each level of the situation. This draws out explicitly and records your narrator's local knowledge and expertise as an embedded end user. You will find these kind of points invaluable when you later analyze all your recordings to extract refugees' or host communities' recommendations that you can pass on to policymakers, service providers or the public. Finally, at level 5, you can start reviewing and summarizing the speaker's whole position back to them, to verify it, show them that you've captured their main points and prompt them to add anything else they feel is important.

Below is a list of interventions that can be used to help move any interview along. I teach these as classic interventions to use when doing oral history interviews for a specific purpose, to gather specific information and perspectives. You will find these particularly useful when interviewing either host communities or professionals who work with refugees. However, when interviewing refugees themselves, I feel you should use these 'steering' interventions much more gently, if at all. Traumatized by a long chain of challenges, refugees need to *self*-regulate their interviews. In my experience, a refugee's situation is so pressing and stressful that they're not just going to wander off topic and chatter on about something irrelevant. Refugees' minds tend to be very focused on the immediate challenges facing them. So, as we saw in Chapter 6, if they do avoid giving you certain information, it's likely to be because it's too traumatic for them, or there are logistical reasons why it would be dangerous or inappropriate for them to talk about it to you.

For instance, there is a profound tactfulness required around any discussion of beatings, incarcerations, torture or sexual violence while victims of all genders are trying to rebuild their dignity and self-image. For one refugee narrator I worked with, Adar, the humiliation, fear, embarrassment and helplessness he experienced during interrogations by the regime he fled from many years ago are *not part of his self-image now*, nor of the persona he inhabits in the rich relationships he has with those around him now, years later when settled elsewhere. He's a tall, cool, dignified, intellectual man who, over the years, has become a close friend of mine. But we have never referred directly to those interrogations, either in our oral history interviews about his life as a refugee, nor in the many hours that we later spent together socially. I can feel that that wouldn't be helpful to him; he would bring it up himself if he ever wanted to. But he survived to build a lifestyle of thriving new relationships beyond and without all that, and he doesn't want to mix those two different mental universes.

Refugee narrator Talya also did an excellent job of pre-editing those things she very much wanted and needed to tell me in our oral history interviews, and those things she couldn't talk about. A former human rights lawyer who had political asylum in the UK, she was receiving specialist treatment there for victims of torture, and she opened our meeting by handing me the medical specialists' long, typed report about her. During our interviews, she volunteered bits of her own choosing from her experiences at the hands of the regime of her home country, but not the worst of it. And it was of course crucial that I never probed that any further. She was receiving medicine, psychotherapy and social worker support, and it was imperative that I not wade into that delicate territory. Yet she was desperate to be part of my oral history project by telling her story. The solution, as with all my refugee narrators, was to let her do the pre-editing about what she told me, and what was best left out.

So your 'steering' of a refugee's interview should happen mostly within your own mind, using the six '*PIECES*' guidance taught in Chapter 6. If you'd love to know more about a specific event that they're steering away from or you're questioning the truth of what they're saying, you must *internally* regulate your own responses rather than just verbalizing the *Probe* or *Challenge* techniques that we'll see below. Over and over in the literature you see this gentle *unspoken* navigation being done by those who have published the best, most skillful oral histories with refugees, such as Daniel Trilling's *Lights In The Distance: Exile and Refuge at the Borders of Europe* or Charlotte McDonald-Gibson's *Cast Away: Stories of Survival from Europe's Refugee Crisis*. In the book that they publish later we, the audience, get to hear the author's internal mental commentary about how their refugee narrator was reacting on the spot: what they are avoiding, moments when they get upset or suddenly terminate the interview. But on the spot in the interview, the interviewer says nothing to the refugee narrator about that, and just respectfully follows the refugee narrator's lead. Later, when they write up and publish the project, they can tell you, their reader, what they noticed. But with the refugees they are interviewing, they intuit when it is important to just follow their lead on topics deliberately avoided.

By contrast, when you are interviewing host communities or professionals who work with refugees, I believe that the *Nine Steers* techniques below can help you *both* to get what you really need from the interview. They can improve the focus and thoroughness of whatever testimony the narrator *wants* to give you. Without some *steer, focus, probe, challenge* or *review* from you, they are unlikely to remember to make all the useful points they could potentially contribute.

## *Nine Steers:*[8]

1. Steer: politely steer the conversation onto a specific topic e.g. '*So how did your group come to organize marches against the resettling of refugees in your area?*' or '*Tell me a bit about your own upbringing*'.
2. Focus: focus discussion onto specific details of that topic, if the focus is inclined to wander.
3. Probe: gently dig a bit deeper on a point e.g. '*So tell me a bit more about what you think is going on behind the scenes in the anti-migrant movement*' or '*Why do you think the politicians are doing that?*' or '*What do* (name specific groups or people) *think of it all?*'.
4. Challenge: without losing rapport, a gentle, friendly skepticism can give the speaker the chance to refine or reconsider a point e.g. '*Was that really what was going on or do you think there was maybe something different happening behind the scenes?*'.
5. Reframe: mirror back a point they have made, but with a different meaning from the one they had intended e.g. to religious whites who are against having Muslim refugees in their area, you could say '*So I guess the refugees are religious, church-going people like yourselves, as they pray several times a day?*'.
6. Analyze: offer your own reading or interpretation of a situation they have described e.g. '*So you reckon what's really going on is that you skilled workers are being sidelined in favor of the cheap labor that refugees can provide?*'.
7. Summarize: briefly summarizing what they've just said can enable you to change topics politely (e.g. '*So you've really shown me there how you feel resettling refugees is a big threat to workers' livelihoods around here. Can you tell me a bit too about how your anti-refugee campaign got organized?*').
8. Review: briefly overview all the topics they've covered and the valuable main points that you've taken from them: this honors their contribution, gives them a sense of achievement and moves the conversation towards closure.
9. Give feedback: you can mention how informative it's been listening to them and when, and if, you'll get back to them with any outcomes or next steps.

You could keep a list of these *Nine Steers* on a small prompt card to glance at before or during interviews, especially when meeting an assertive narrator who holds views you may not agree with. That might also be a moment when you feel you ought to reveal your own views to challenge views you consider inappropriate, such as racist or homophobic ones. But narrators don't necessarily need to hear your own views on issues like this: there is always the option to just passively record theirs. If I am working on behalf of an organization that would wish me to, I will say: '*As an organization, we see that differently. Our view is that …*'. But if interviewing for oral history, I often just record narrators' opinions as significant data. Remember, your job is not to seek out and gather agreeable, politically correct views. Your project's purpose is to gather all relevant stakeholders' views so that they can be used to improve the overall situation. Your role is to carry those views (with permission) to audiences and decision makers who can respond to them in a healthy, critical way. For instance, if a wide range of narrators make racist remarks about a new facility put in place for refugees, this is useful information: it demonstrates to the authorities the extent of racist feeling, confirming why those facilities for refugees are badly needed. (Be aware that racism doesn't only happen in host communities: it can also be a problem between certain refugee groups and ethnicities who are accommodated together.)

There are various common sense ways to start drawing an interview to a close without seeming abrupt, rude or uncaring to your narrator. Starting to summarize in retrospect their main points already starts to give some sense of closure. You can also use body language, for instance by gently closing your notebook and putting it down. You could shift to a different posture – either a little more formal or more relaxed than before. Then draw their attention back to the present moment by gently shifting the conversation to something immediate or imminent, such as the weather outside or what they're doing for the rest of the day. Thank them, reminding them again how their information will be used and letting them know whether you'll be in contact again, and roughly when.

As soon as possible once you leave them, listen to the recording and look over any notes you made, to spot any areas important enough for a second interview if necessary. That should be done as soon as possible too, while the first interview is still fresh in their mind. Start any second interview by mentioning how useful the first one was, in case they think the first 'wasn't good enough'. Bring with you a new list of questions: you can steer even more tightly for relevance this second time, now that you know a bit about their thinking. Much more information may have surfaced in their mind since the first interview. But never underestimate either how much emotion that first conversation may have stirred up for them in the meantime, perhaps having spoken for the first time ever about certain intense experiences of loss or trauma.

## References

European Asylum Support Office, *Practical Guide: Personal Interview*. Brussels: European Union, 2015.

Grigoreanu, Valentina, Burnett, Margaret, Wiedenbeck, Susan, Cao, Jill, Rector, Kyle and Kwan, Irwin, 'End-User Debugging Strategies: A Sensemaking Perspective', *Transactions on Computer-Human Interaction*, 19(1), March, 2010.

Hoffman, Marella, *Practicing Oral History to Improve Public Policies and Programs*. Abingdon: Routledge, 2018.

Kelly, Anthony and Westoby, Peter, *Participatory Development Practice Using Traditional and Contemporary Frameworks*. Rugby, UK: Practical Action Publishing, 2018.

McDonald-Gibson, Charlotte, *Cast Away: Stories of Survival from Europe's Refugee Crisis*. London: Portobello Books, 2016.

Ndubi, Modesta, 'Congolese Asylum Seeker in Kenya Changing Lives through a Music School, despite Odds', UNHCR online, 25-10-2017 [Available at www.unhcr.org/ke/12535-congolese-asylum-seeker-kenya-changing-lives-music-school-despite-odds.html; accessed on 21-6-2019].

Pascale, Richard, Sternin, Jerry and Sternin, Monica, *The Power of Positive Deviance: How Unlikely Innovators Solve Some of the World's Toughest Problems*. Cambridge, MA: Harvard Business press, 2010.

Scharmer, Otto and Kaufer, Katrin, *Leading from the Emerging Future: From Ego-System to Eco-System Economies*. San Francisco: Berrett-Koehler, 2013.

Trilling, Daniel, *Lights in the Distance: Exile and Refuge at the Borders of Europe*. London: Picador, 2018.

## Notes

1 European Asylum Support Office, *Practical Guide: Personal Interview*. Brussels: European Union, 2015.

2 The approach is explained in works like Anthony Kelly and Peter Westoby, *Participatory Development Practice Using Traditional and Contemporary Frameworks*. Rugby, UK: Practical Action Publishing, 2018.

3 Richard Pascale, Jerry Sternin and Monica Sternin, *The Power of Positive Deviance: How Unlikely Innovators Solve Some of the World's Toughest Problems*. Cambridge, MA: Harvard Business press, 2010.

4 Modesta Ndubi, 'Congolese Asylum seeker in Kenya Changing Lives through a Music School, despite Odds', UNHCR online, 25-10-2017.

5 Otto Scharmer and Katrin Kaufer, *Leading from the Emerging Future: From Ego-System to Eco-System Economies*. San Francisco: Berrett-Koehler, 2013.

6 Valentina Grigoreanu et al., 'End-User Debugging Strategies: A Sensemaking Perspective', *Transactions on Computer-Human Interaction*, 19(1), March 2010.

7 Thanks to Routledge for permission to reproduce a version of this diagram adapted from my *Practicing Oral History to Improve Public Policies and Programs*. Abingdon: Routledge, 2018.

8 Thanks to Routledge for permission to reproduce a version of this list adapted from my *Practicing Oral History*, 2018.

# 9

# EDITING AND PUBLICIZING NARRATORS' INTERVIEWS IN WAYS THAT HELP IMPROVE OUTCOMES FOR COMMUNITIES

Ai Weiwei, the refugee artist who made the acclaimed refugee feature film *Human Flow*, has thought a lot about who actually needs to *see* projects about the world refugee crisis. He explains:

> All day long, the media ask me if I have shown (my) film to refugees. "When are the refugees going to see the film?", they ask. But that's the wrong question. The purpose is to show it to people *of influence* – people who are in a position to help and who have a responsibility to help. The refugees who need help – they don't need to see the film. They need dry shoes. They need soup.[1]

Now that you have done your interviews, this chapter will show you how to analyze, edit and communicate your best material to ensure that your end product, like that of Ai Weiwei, actually reaches and affects your target audience. This chapter, with templates appendiced, will coach you through the processes of:

- extracting from your interviews the testimonies that add the most value and solutions;
- choosing – or moving – between individual testimonies and the 'whole story' of a community over time;
- choosing the right medium to present your final product in, such as in audio or visual, digital or performance modes;
- navigating the ever-expanding options for sharing such testimonies, from blogs, social media, videos and websites to community exhibitions and public sector partnerships;
- concluding your project in ways that honor those involved and lay a basis for further successes in the future;

- calculating and demonstrating in hard financial terms the equivalent added value and savings that your oral history project has achieved for communities, organizations or funders.

## Designing Your End Products

In previous chapters you defined the effects that you wanted to have on a specific audience, and what you would like your target audience to do as a result. You planned which media you would use to communicate your final product, from traditional print outlets to street performances to policy reports. Here, in this chapter, your goal to have a specific desired effect on a specific audience using this particular medium will be the guiding force that shows you which extracts to select from your interview material, and how best to organize and present those extracts for your public.

In Chapters 2 to 5, we surveyed a great variety of different media that took refugee or host community oral histories and *re-presented* them in very diverse ways, without losing any of the impact or authenticity of the original accounts. (We noticed that refugee oral histories, as well as being much more numerous than host community ones, have also been communicated with much more artistry and technological innovation.) To awaken your own creative side, recall some of the innovative applications that we've seen. For instance, the *Refunite* project, cited in Chapter 3, reunited lost refugees by putting refugee testimonies on a giant hub online. Also in Chapter 3 the project *Longing* 'translated' the testimonies of Syrian child refugees into accompanying paintings by the host community. In Chapter 4, we saw *Wintegreat* used refugees' testimonies to get them jobs and university places.

But we've also seen that, in an important crosscurrent, some are now also listening more creatively to the testimonies of alienated, white host communities in the West who feel 'left behind' and are resistant to refugee resettlement (as well as to other results of globalization). We saw those testimonies aired through political oral histories like *Strangers in Their Own Land* by Arlie Russell Hochschild; in first-person life histories like *Hillbilly Elegy* by JD Vance or *The End of Eddie* by Édouard Louis from the French underclass; in televised road trips like the BBC's *Travels in Trumpland*. I hope you agree that the possibilities are endless for giving voice meaningfully to testimonies from either refugees or host communities.

Further below you will learn the mechanics of methodically extracting from your own interview material so that your project too can reach its audience. But to get to that point, you will have to stand back and be a bit inventive. Take some time to summon up in your mind all that you have heard while interviewing for your project, and all that you experienced while moving through your narrators' worlds. What comes back to you? What do you feel was most striking in that material? What scenes, sounds, faces, moments? What declarations, pleas or confessions? How best could you arrange your interview extracts so that your narrators' most important insights and messages reach your intended audience in the most impactful ways?

Yes, the final medium you've chosen will shape the answers to some extent but within any given medium you will also have to make editorial choices. Whether it's in print, in audio or in video, how long or short will your end product be? How many narrators will it quote directly from, and in what order and at what length? How will you divide up the narrative arc across the whole piece? For instance, whether your interviews were with host communities or refugees, you might choose to present them in any of the formats below – notice that all of them have appeared in the various books, videos and other projects that have been cited in this book:

- just one individual testimony, told to you in one session;
- one person's testimony across different phases of their refugee journey from flight to resettlement, or their changing experience as a member of a host community over the years;
- mixed testimonies from chains of people who know each other across a host community, or across a family of refugees who've been geographically separated;
- the 'whole story' of a community's exile as refugees, or their hosting of refugees, as told through a mosaic of different testimonies from different demographics – children, parents, the disabled, community leaders and so on;
- a range of testimonies from one demographic e.g. unemployed males of a host community or LGBTQ people among refugees;
- any of the formats above, but with narrators from a host community;
- any of the formats above, but with narrators who are 'positive deviants' in either refugee or host communities, i.e. showing exceptionally positive, resourceful behaviors and responses that can inspire others.

But how much 'wrapping' commentary or factual context should you add in around your narrators' extracts, by way of introduction, framing, explanation or argument? Should you paraphrase and summarize some narrators' points or should you quote from them all directly? As far as I'm concerned, in *applied* oral history it's fine to summarize, contextualize and paraphrase as much as necessary. The purpose of your project was to do interviews that gathered relevant information and perspectives that could help improve community outcomes: the content of these interviews is your research *data*. It can be appropriate to summarize some of it in your own words or in the language most suitable for your target audience.

If you have the time and resources, you might even decide to derive several different end products from your interview material. Really good interview material is like a gold mine that you can keep returning to, extracting different insights to present in different media to different audiences. For instance, when working with refugees and city government in Cambridge, my own primary goal was to tackle what I considered the hardest thing – to engage with resistant host communities and shift some of their prejudiced attitudes. But, extracted from the traditional oral history interviews that I did with refugees, we also produced:

- a full program of policy actions implemented by city government based on refugees' recommendations in the interviews;
- a public education program for the host community that included an exhibition, training workshops and 'myth-busting' articles in the municipal newspaper;
- an academic presentation at a sociology conference on refugee policy, presenting number-crunched data extracted from the interviews (the six strategies refugee narrators used to navigate infra-group tensions; the seven variables affecting whether they'll become politically active in the host country, etc.);
- a traditional oral history book of full-length interviews in all their eloquent, first-person glory;
- ethnographic observations before and after each interview in that book.

It's not that I had a lot of funding or staff for this work. But I knew that a single set of high-quality testimonies can yield many different types of useful information in many different media or voices, for many different audiences. So I decided to extract maximum value from that 'gold mine', rather than just going in once to get a single product out of it and leaving the rest of its potential applications 'in the ground'.

You, for instance, might decide to produce from your interview material a short book and an accompanying website. But you could also produce an 8-minute, multimedia video that you could show on different platforms to publicize your project. You could post it online, to front your project's website. You could show the video in person to a board of policymakers at local government level. And you could show it in schools, before you give a talk to pupils about your experiences in the field while recording your oral histories. Though brief, your video could include, for instance:

- atmospheric music, environmental sounds that you've recorded in refugee camps and visuals like photos or maps;
- slides bullet-pointing some hard data extracted from your interviews and research;
- audio extracts from your interviews, played over some video you took of scenes around the refugee camp and/or the host community neighbourhood;
- video footage of shorter and longer extracts from individual interviews;
- a brief voiceover from you, introducing your narrators at the beginning and at the end stating what became of them subsequently;
- introductory scene-setting, summaries and concluding recommendations from you, bookending the presentation.

With today's software options, it's easy to blend such elements into an engaging, informative video and to post it for free online. But remember that all these are just creative ways of editing and *re-presenting* narrators' interviews. All this extracting – and this cutting and splicing of different media – needn't take away from the beauty and emotion of direct quotes from your interviews: you should use the most relevant and convincing of those as highlights, convincers and examples.

## Editing and Extracting from Your Interviews

So, it's over to you now. The next step is to review all your own interview material and note down methodically as you go through it all the points, passages or moments that might make good material for your end product(s). At this stage, I suggest you note *all* passages that might be useful. And ensure you always jot down a few words or shorthand mentioning *how* you think this extract might be useful: for what effect or under what theme or heading? Otherwise, as I know from experience, you may return later to a sea of marked extracts and not be able to remember *why* you selected each one. And you may have to redo all that work of listening to the interviews again in order to note down what you intended to do with each extract. Later, when you start assembling your final product, you can do a final reedit that may exclude some of these marked passages. Figure 9.1 (and its blank template in Appendix 11 on page 190) will help you with that. So whether listening to your recordings or reading typed transcripts of them, make methodical notes now as you review them. You could, for instance, note:

- each narrator by their initials, with numbers if they did more than one interview e.g. marking the two interviews of a refugee narrator called Nadia Hussein as *NH1* and *NH2*;
- where the relevant passage in their interview starts, noted by time in audio recordings or by page number in typed transcripts e.g. *NH1 at 6 mins 18 secs* or *NH2, pg1 parag4;*

You should also watch out for what I call 'hotspots' in the interviews – zones that have emotional or even aesthetic impact, noting these for use as well. An example for me came from Kanwar Ali, a Syrian refugee whom I interviewed at some length. As a 'positive deviant', this young man had shown unfathomable resilience and selflessness across his many years in the refugee camps. But somehow the most poignant moment of his interviews with me came from the simple parting words that he said to one widow he came across in his refugee camp. Describing the moment when he discovered this woman's desperate situation one night, he said:

> As you know, I am a refugee myself, in the same situation, with my own wife and baby to feed. But I could not leave them there without giving them something. So I gave them the last 20 euros that I had left. That was all that I had – all I could give them.
>
> But you know, to live just for oneself must be a terrible existence. I always think: '*Give your life for something much larger than yourself. Live for a greater reality. Leave a legacy*'

I had nothing else to give her but I could also give her my name. I said to her: 'My name is Kanwar Ali. Please call me if you have such a night again.'[2]

The paradox is that what unearthed this poetic, culminating moment in his recordings was the very dry, analytic, methodical editing process explained above and summarized again in Figure 9.1. Figure 9.1 takes specific refugee examples or case studies that we have already seen across this book, and shows you how our editing process might have applied to those projects, selecting their narrators' most

| 'Useful message' and project's purpose | Name and role of narrator | Extract starts where in their interview recording? | How to present these extracts in your end product |
|---|---|---|---|
| 1. **The pain that refugees have been through**<br>**Purpose**: to provoke emotional compassion in the host community | *From Norwegian IKEA project in Chapter 3:*<br>Refugee mother Rana Hussein, surviving with her small children in a ruined, bombed-out building in Syria | RH1, 6 mins 18secs<br>RH1, 8 mins 54 secs | 1-minute video testimonies from Rana, plus a walk-in installation reconstructing their living quarters in detail, for visitors to explore in person |
| 2. **What refugees need now – and what the host community needs *from them***<br>**Purpose**: show both audiences all the practical ways they can help the 'other side' to cohabit better with them | *From Chapter Five case study on hosts/refugee conflict mediation in Tanzania:*<br>Host community farmer GF complaining about refugees using his field, which is outside their allotted camp border; his suggestions about what they could do instead of trespassing on his field | GF1, 1 min 4 secs<br>GF2, 0 min 40 secs | Bullet points listing:<br>–the ways that the refugees' behavior is impacting on him negatively and unfairly<br>–his practical suggestions for a win/win alternative behavior |
| 3. **Positive examples and behaviors on both sides**<br>**Purpose**: show positive, resourceful behaviours and projects by both 'sides' | *From Chapter Three:*<br>Refugee E. Museveni who set up a music school in his camp, now attended both by refugees and the Kenyan host community<br><br>*From Chapter Four:*<br>Host community students E. Guinet and T. Scubla who set up *Wintegreat* to give appropriate refugees university places and job placements | EM1, 6 mins 55 secs<br>EM2, 10 mins 42 secs<br><br>EG, 7 mins 20 secs<br>TS1, 8 mins 17 secs<br>TS2, 12 mins 32 secs | 30-second video testimonies from others about how EM's music school has changed their lives<br><br>Typed quotes from refugee recipients of *Wintegreat*, about how this assistance has improved their lives and future outcomes |
| **4. How to improve relations between refugees and host communities**<br>**Purpose**: show both sides what the other community wants from them so as to integrate and cohabit well | *From Cambridge project in Chapter Five:*<br>Resettled refugee Adar describing how he feels socially excluded by the host society around him<br><br>Insights from previously resistant host community member Tony, after a training workshop to overturn his racist views | Adar, 11 mins 35 secs<br><br>Tony, 4 mins 40 secs | Adar's testimony quoted verbatim in an oral history book aimed at the host community<br><br>Tony's reversed perspectives shown to hosts and re fugees as bullet-pointed quotes on PowerPoint slide at the next workshop |
| **5. How services could be done better**<br>**Purpose**: capture end-user knowledge and feedback to improve services for both communities | *From refugee contraception services project in Chapter Four:*<br>Refugee woman AGF explaining the cultural, religious and emotional reasons *why* she needs contraceptive services in the camp to be delivered differently, plus the specific changes that would help | AGF, 4 mins 36 secs<br>AGF, 8 mins, 7 secs | PowerPoint slide for service designers with bullet point list of obstacles in current policies and services, plus lists of solutions extracted from interviews |

**FIGURE 9.1** Analyzing interviews to extract the most useful material

'useful messages' and presenting them to the intended public in ways that help achieve the project's goals.

The important analytical work above can be done as you listen to your 'raw' audio recordings, entirely unedited. But will you also need to transcribe your recordings into type? In traditional oral history and the archiving of it, transcribing is best practice. But here it will depend on the goals that you planned for your project from the beginning. If your final end product will be one or more written documents, you will at a minimum need to type out all your chosen extracts, and you may decide it's worth transcribing the whole interviews as a further background product of your project. Or you may have arranged to deposit your material in an official archive that requires full transcription as well as audio formats. But if your final products will be primarily in audio or video format, you may not need to transcribe all your interviews into text.

To transcribe video recordings into type in the traditional way, by stop-start listening and typing, takes up to six hours per hour of recording. There is affordable software available now that potentially could seem to make this easier, with the audio and the typing appearing simultaneously on your computer screen. And there are apps that now transcribe speech into text reasonably accurately without any typing. However, for several reasons ranging from accuracy to data protection, many traditional oral historians prefer not to use these latest technologies for transcribing oral histories. Your most up-to-date and definitive guide on this whole subject is Teresa Bergen's *Transcribing Oral History*.[3]

Meanwhile, for those who do take an interest in testing the latest software, a large academic network called CLARIN (the Common Language Resources and Technology Infrastructure Network) can, at www.oralhistory.eu, introduce you to transcription innovations ranging from WebASR (Automatic Speech Recognition that's performed remotely online in The Cloud, and delivered back to you) to 'Speaker Diarization and Speaker Recognition' (automatic notation of who is speaking in an interview, and when).[4]

When transcribing, some oral historians do some editing to remove excessive '*ums*' and '*ahs*', pauses, repetitions or background noises, especially if recordings are going to be transcribed for publication. But for authenticity and transparency, you must highlight when extracts are from different speakers, and any editing must still ensure that narrators don't consider their intended meaning to have been distorted. It is best practice to ensure the unedited version remains available as a background reference.

When using oral history interviews to do applied work conveying specific messages, we often must extract from the longer interview. You needn't feel obliged to use all your material, just because your narrators gave you their time and the information means so much to them personally. Where appropriate, you can also produce one or more traditional oral history products that honor *all* the material you've gathered. This could be in a transcript, an exhibition or a public reading. You could get a slot on local radio celebrating your narrators' contributions or hold a celebratory get-together for the narrators.

As we've seen in Figure 9.1, everything in your more *strategic* end product should be edited for impact. Any 'filler' will detract from the influence that your project can achieve for communities. This kind of oral history for a social justice aim is in *addition* to traditional oral history – a further expression derived from the primary product, without taking anything away from the value of that primary source.

Any oral history that's been rigorously collected deserves to be formally preserved. Back when you were first planning your project, you arranged to consult an archive, library or museum to see what formats they would need in order to archive your material. But even if you don't deposit your interviews now with an official archive, they can still be confided to a relevant community center, school, charity or town hall that will keep them available to the public and future researchers. Explaining how to go about 'keeping oral histories close to home', archiving and curating expert Nancy MacKay points out that institutions like these often have a more informal archiving system that can accept your material with fewer restrictions and requirements than official archiving centers.[5] Nancy also advises:

> At the very least, I suggest the *LOCKSS* system ('*Lots of Copies Keep Stuff Safe*'), the cheapest, easiest and most effective of any preservation principles, used by diverse sources from Stanford University to Thomas Jefferson.[6] He more or less invented the idea, suggesting: 'Let us save what remains not by vaults and locks, which fence them from the public eye and use, … but by such a multiplication of copies, as shall place them beyond the reach of accident.'[7]

Meanwhile, do also store securely any other records that you have of your project, such as its *Information Sheets*, *Consent Forms*, *Codes of Conduct*, photos, emails and your *Project Logbook*. They provide evidence of your good practice, if the authenticity or purpose of your project were ever questioned in the future.

## Quantifying and Communicating the Financial Value of Your Applied Oral History Projects

In this section you'll find a simple but invaluable tool for demonstrating the financial value of your applied oral history projects. It enables you to measure and demonstrate in hard financial terms the added value and savings that your applied oral history project has achieved for communities or organizations. This tool analyzes and packages your oral history project in ways that will attract funding for your future projects. Taking the trouble to demonstrate in this way the financial-equivalent value of your work greatly increases its attractiveness to funders and employers.

Whenever you complete an applied oral history project, take half an hour at the end to fill your project's information into the simple table shown in Figure 9.2 (use the blank version in Appendix 12, p. 191). At this stage your *Project Logbook* – where you kept all the project's notes as you planned and did the work – will be an invaluable record of specific, practical details. In it you can find, add up and write into the blank Appendix 12:

- the total number of hours given to your oral history project by narrators;
- the total hours given by you and the rest of the team running the project;
- the financial scale of the refugee or host community situation, program, policy or service addressed by your oral histories (e.g. '*a one-off program/service costing £2,000*', or '*a 5-year program costing $1.5 million annually, totaling $7.5 million*');
- the numbers and types of stakeholders you reached in your interviews and community outreach (i.e. the number of potential users of the program, policy or service who became more engaged in it through your oral history project);
- how many pieces of key information narrators gave you about what would (a) improve the program, policy or service, and (b) make them use it to its full capacity and (c) recommend it to others in the target community;
- how many further service users your narrators each have around them to influence (e.g. '*an average of three additional individuals in each narrator's household*').

These are the concrete measures of the added value that your project contributes in terms of work put in and valuable outcomes extracted. Write them into the

| High-value services<br>provided by your oral history project | Financial savings for the organization<br>receiving your applied oral history findings<br>(your estimates) |
|---|---|
| Total hours of free expertise from narrators | Equivalent cost if they had to pay staff to do this |
| Total free hours from you and your team as providers of these 'consultation services' | Cost for consultation services:<br>• if your work had been done internally by the organization<br>• if hired in from a professional consultancy for market surveying |
| Total financial scale of the situation, program, policy or service addressed by your oral history project (e.g. cost of a refugee resettlement program; of a state service working to prevent illegal immigration; of rehabilitating refugee youths if they turn to crime) | Financial savings in waste avoided through useful suggestions made by your narrators e.g.:<br>• savings in wasted project time<br>• savings in wasted staff time<br>• savings in wasted materials and purchases |
| Your contribution to getting this situation, program, policy or service better accepted by its target communities:<br>• numbers and types of stakeholders your project reached<br>• numbers and types of potential service users each of your narrators can further influence | Financial savings compared to what it would cost the organization to achieve this 'buy-in' themselves through, for example:<br>• advertising, promotions and publicity<br>• PR<br>• outreach events |

**FIGURE 9.2** Quantifying the equivalent financial value that your work saves or gains for organizations

left-hand column of Appendix 12. Then 'translate' them into the approximate amount that it would have cost an organization or employer to pay someone else to do those hours of work if you hadn't provided them.

Naturally, your figures will be estimates. But this estimating of costs is normal practice in business, for instance when doing feasibility studies, starting to plan a project or assessing what a certain measure is likely to cost. You can add in notes showing how you arrived at your estimated figures, as is done in the sample estimates accompanying Appendix 12. The left-hand column is what your project has achieved; the right-hand column shows what it would have cost them to achieve it themselves without your project. So you 'translate':

- the hours put in by your narrators and your team – into *Savings on staffing*;
- the financial scale of the refugee or host community situation, program, policy or service addressed by your oral history project – into *Savings by helping to prevent that program, policy or service from failing*;
- the numbers of relevant stakeholders your project reached – into *Savings on PR, publicity and achieving 'buy-in'*;
- the information narrators gave about what would make them embrace and recommend the program, policy or service – into *Savings on PR and achieving 'buy-in'*.

For simplicity, Figure 9.2 assumes you weren't paid at all for doing your oral history project. If you were paid or funded by the organization that you're presenting these figures to, then just deduct that fee from the overall savings that your project ultimately achieved for them. If you were funded by someone else, don't deduct that from the savings you achieved for the organization that you're addressing now, as it didn't cost them anything – someone else paid for work to be done that benefits them.

When you are demonstrating the savings made like this, it doesn't matter if the organization you are addressing knew nothing about your project until you submitted your findings to them, or even if what your project is telling them is unwelcome news. If your oral histories highlight weaknesses and obstacles that need changing in a current policy, project or service, those responsible know that this can save them a lot of money and negative PR down the line in terms of wasted, unsuccessful services and outcomes. It is also important not to underestimate how much this kind of work costs organizations when they have to do it themselves or buy it in from expensive consultancies charging them by the hour for it. And remember that what matters most to organizations is *percentage* savings. For instance, using the schema of Figure 9.2, one very large, long-term project of applied oral history that I was involved in was able to demonstrate savings of over $500,000 through the strategic, focused input, suggestions and end-user advice gained from its oral history narrators. Yours might be a small applied oral history project that will save just $500 on an improved service or project. But if $500 is half of the whole budget put aside for that service, your input will be very much valued!

For your future funding applications, project proposals or job interviews, the ideal is to have some figures, like those in Figure 9.2, which are *retrospective* and drawn from your previous projects, showing the added value that they produced. But if you don't have any, even your *prospective* compiling of these figures as you estimate them for a forthcoming project is valuable. It demonstrates the potential savings that your future project could bring, and it shows that you have a mature, efficient, self-aware way of measuring up the resources that go into your projects as *inputs*, against the tangible benefits that come out of them as *outcomes*.

## References

Balls, Ed, *Travels in Trumpland*. London: BBC TV, 2018.

Bergen, Teresa, *Transcribing Oral History*. Abingdon: Routledge, 2019.

CLARIN, 'Common Language Resources and Technology Infrastructure Network', website [Available at www.oralhistory.eu; accessed on 21-6-2019].

Dekker, Stefanie, 'Haneen: Exhibition of Syrian Children's Longings in War', *Al-Jazeera* online, 23-2-2018 [Available at www.aljazeera.com/news/2018/02/haneen-exhibition-syrian-childrens-longings-war-180223151650843.html; accessed on 21-6-2019].

Hoffman, Marella, *Asylum under Dreaming Spires: Refugees' Lives in Cambridge Today*. Cambridge: Cambridge Editions in partnership with the Living Refugee Archive, University of East London, 2017.

Jefferson, Thomas in Letter to To Ebeneezer Hazard, 18-2-1791, In *The Letters of Thomas Jefferson, 1743–1826* on website of American History: From Revolution to Reconstruction and Beyond [Available at www.let.rug.nl/usa/presidents/thomas-jefferson/letters-of-thomas-jefferson; accessed on 21-6-2019].

Louis, Édouard, *The End of Eddy* translated by Michael Lucey. London: Harvill Secker, 2017.

Mackay, Nancy, *Curating Oral Histories: From Interview to Archive, 2nd edition*. Abingdon: Routledge, 2016.

*Refunite* website, 'Stories of Change', 2018 [Available at https://refunite.org/reconnection-stories/reunited-mother-community-leader-network-young-kenyan-wants-become-refunite-leader and https://refunite.org/testimonial/reconnected-after-22-years-of-separation; accessed on 21-6-2019].

Russell Hochschild, Arlie, *Strangers in Their Own Land: Anger and Mourning on the American Right*. New York: The New Press, 2016.

'Stanford University Libraries' Online *LOCKSS* System for Digital Preservation', [Available at https://library.stanford.edu/projects/lockss; accessed on 21-6-2019].

Vance, J.D., *Hillbilly Elegy: A Memoir of A Family and Culture in Crisis*. New York: HarperCollins, 2016.

Weiwei, Ai, 'Without The Prison Beatings, What Would I Be?', *The Guardian* online, 17-9-2017. [Available at www.theguardian.com/film/2017/sep/17/ai-weiwei-without-the-prison-the-beatings-what-would-i-be; accessed on 21-4-2019].

*Wintegreat* website [Available at www.wintegreat.org; accessed on 21-6-2019].

## Notes

1 Ai Weiwei interview, 'Without The Prison Beatings, What Would I Be?', *The Guardian* online, 17-9-2017; urls are given in this chapter's references.

2 Marella Hoffman, *Asylum under Dreaming Spires: Refugees' Lives in Cambridge Today*. Cambridge: Cambridge Editions in partnership with the Living Refugee Archive, University of East London, 2017.
3 Teresa Bergen, *Transcribing Oral History*. Abingdon: Routledge, 2019.
4 Website of CLARIN, the Common Language Resources and Technology Infrastructure Network.
5 Nancy Mackay, *Curating Oral Histories: From Interview to Archive, 2nd edition*. Abingdon: Routledge, 2016.
6 Stanford University Libraries' website offers their online *LOCKSS* system, 'open-source technologies for high-confidence, resilient, secure digital preservation'. In emailed communication from Nancy Mackay.
7 Letter from Thomas Jefferson to Ebeneezer Hazard, 18-2-1791. In *The Letters of Thomas Jefferson, 1743–1826* on website of American History: From Revolution to Reconstruction and Beyond.

# 10

# SOARING REFUGEE NUMBERS, A TWENTY-FIRST CENTURY *'MEGA-PROBLEM'*

## Applied Oral History Skills as Part of the Solution

### Why Now Is the Time

This book has set out ethical standards, a transdisciplinary methodology and a professional framework for those who want to learn or teach the ethical application of oral histories to improve outcomes for refugees or host communities. To conclude, we now take a wider lens to situate briefly all three aspects of our topic – refugees, host communities and applied oral history itself – within the sociopolitical movements and intellectual frameworks of the years ahead. As well as giving some wider context, this will also show how – whether as an oral historian or as a public service professional who has oral history skills – the methodology in this book will help future-proof your projects and your career.

We began with the United Nations High Commissioner for Refugees' (UNHCR) call for 'Humanitarian Innovation' – for every citizen in the world to engage their creativity and resources locally, where they are, to think up new ideas, perspectives and innovations that can help with the world's refugee crisis. And we have seen that anyone, anywhere, can help. You don't have to be a high-level expert. Even a single child, deciding to do something creative, can make an extraordinary difference. Think of the achievements of the Nobel Prize-winning young refugee girl Malala Yousafzai. Or of Greta Thunberg, the Swedish schoolgirl leading the world's youth against climate change. As Greta's book title puts it, *No One Is Too Small to Make a Difference*.[1] There is nothing whimsical or naïve about this approach. It's for logistical reasons that experts and top organizations are calling for local, improvised, synergistic innovations from the grassroots. This democratization and diversity of innovators is necessary now because all ages, backgrounds and levels of scale bring different perspectives and embedded knowledge. Every day, every one of us helps shape collective opinion by whatever perspective we express and demonstrate to those around us. Our thoughts and conversations weave up our collective values and expectations as a population, and we choose leaders to implement those values through policy. Norma Buckley is a community activist and oral historian in a quiet area of rural Ireland, where few refugees are settled. She was one of the manuscript reviewers of this book before publication, to ensure it felt relevant to the kinds of 'host communities' in the Western world who actually host very few refugees. Norma commented:

> Before reading the book, I had *no idea* that we in a place like this could do *anything* about refugee issues or have any influence on them. But of course I see now that there's no limit to what you can do even at neighborhood level, even in a place that's never actually seen a refugee. It was like a wake-up call, joining the dots together… I was already worried about the rise of the far right around the world. It's a threat everywhere, even here in Ireland where we're fairly compassionate and quite liberal now. But it's terrifying, the kind of far right politicians that some countries are electing now. But of course even that – we can actually be engaging with it every time we step outside our front door. In our local community projects, in the conversations we have at the shop about current affairs, the attitudes and values we teach our children at the local school… And of course, the politicians we vote for. I feel now more like there's actually an *unlimited* amount we can do, wherever we are.[2]

## Intervening at the Pressure Points

We will see further below how the necessary changes can happen, but first let's glance at the cascade of results that will unfold if we don't make those changes. In *The Future*, Al Gore pointed out that 'the fastest growing new category of refugees is climate refugees'.[3] In 2016 alone, over 24 million people were internally displaced due to natural disasters.[4]

> Almost 150 million people live in low-lying areas only one meter or less higher than the current sea level. For each additional meter of sea-level rise, roughly 100 million more people will be forced to abandon the places they call home.[5]

This is not counting the whole populations abandoning newly desertified drylands in the Global South, no longer cultivable due to global warming.

This is where the refugee problem intersects spectacularly with the environmental crisis. And yet there's one more vicious twist in this chain of cause and effect – namely, '*the role of climate change as a driver of conflict, which in turn drives displacement*'.[6] This means that if we don't act to halt climate change, climate wars will displace yet more waves of refugees as populations and nations conflict over the reduced resources of habitable land, water, food, security and quality of life.[7]

The reality is that if our nations and politicians don't start to make better decisions, then the current refugee crisis will pale in comparison with the bigger

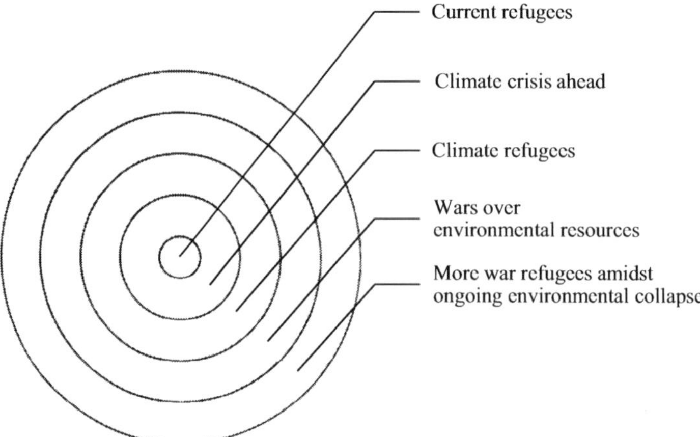


**FIGURE 10.1** The 'ripple' relationships between climate crisis and increasing waves of refugees

crises ahead, spreading out from each other like ripples in a pond.[8] As depicted in Figure 10.1, the current refugee problem, though serious, is nested on top of the much bigger problem that needs to be tackled even more urgently: if we don't halt climate change, it will generate many times more refugees than we currently have. And the resulting resource wars will in turn generate further refugees, amidst ongoing, exponential environmental collapse.[9]

## Bringing Oral History to the Populist Identity Crisis

So, in fact, halting climate change is actually the most important step for managing the refugee crisis in the future. But halting climate change requires us to look candidly at the chain of cause and effect that is currently preventing us from halting it. The green technology to halt climate change is already available, but we don't yet have sufficient political consensus to make that shift.

Meanwhile, far-right populist politics are on the rise across the developed economies. And the far right tends to oppose environmentalism, broadly rejecting the science of climate crisis as a leftist hoax exaggerated by liberal elites.[10] Populist governments will do little or nothing to slow or halt climate change. An era of rule by the far right would trigger further climate change, producing waves of climate refugees and resource wars. Figure 10.2 illustrates this cycle of how far-right governments would lead us to climate wars. It highlights the cycle's starting point – the collective identity crisis upon which far-right movements gain their populist foothold.

So where to intervene in order to slow or avert this chain of effects? The starting point – the crisis that's leaving Western populations prone to far-right populism – is described in continental Europe as an identity crisis or '*crise identitaire*'.[11] In Chapters 2 and 5, we saw that applied oral history is doing much-needed deep

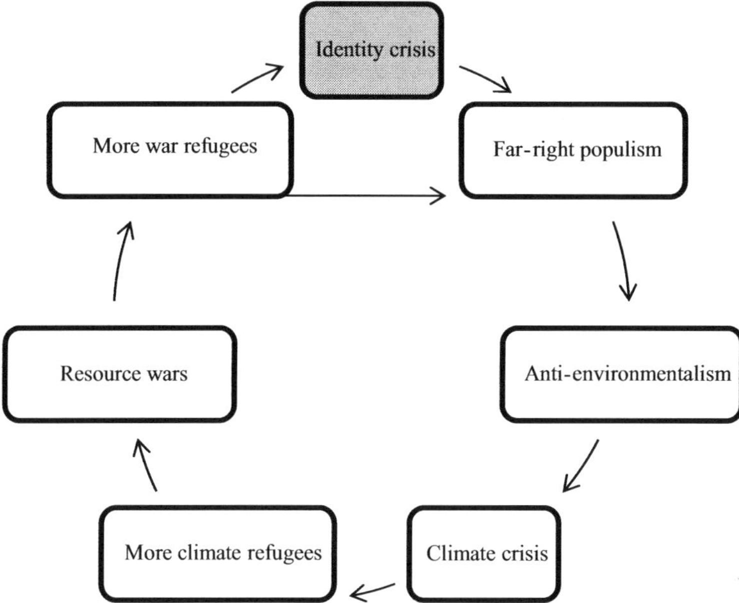


**FIGURE 10.2** Populism, environmental crisis and refugees: the chains of cause and effect

listening around the angst of these newly populist communities.[12] And this close listening shows that although demagogue leaders rouse these populations up against immigrants, they are in fact preying upon an identity crisis that runs much deeper, and has layers of deeper causes long before the question of migrants even arises. This current malaise among Western working classes and lower middle classes is comprised, like a multilayer sandwich, of:

1. the widening gap between rich and poor in developed economies; nations like Britain and the US are regressing towards Victorian-era levels of economic inequality, with the working and middle classes hard-pressed financially;[13]
2. globalized markets causing stiff competition for jobs, services and prices;
3. robotization set to wipe out most blue-collar and many white-collar employment roles within our lifetime;[14]
4. unprecedented amounts of time spent on-screen, with little 'downtime' and an epidemic of sleep loss;[15]
5. fewer human interactions, and less contact with nature and the outdoors;[16]
6. artificial intelligence increasingly valued over human workers and citizens; the widening gap ahead between elites who can afford to become 'enhanced humans' and those left behind by AI;
7. awareness of the environmental apocalypse ahead;
8. disenchantment with the political classes who have not helped significantly with any of these concerns;

9. the fact that before globalization, Western populations used to trusted their governments to protect their standard of living, quality of life and local culture from erosion;
10. this whole cocktail of grievances causing an acknowledged epidemic of depression and anxiety symptoms among both workers and children in Western populations.[17]

The trickle-down benefits of late-stage capitalism came to a faltering halt for this generation of working, unemployed or underemployed Westerners. They are the first generation in modern times to be less healthy than the previous one, and to have less buying power.[18] Those ten layers of anxieties are all burning away like acid for this population before 'the migrant question' even arises. Migrants are only the fine, visible tip of this iceberg – and the only part of it that populist demagogues choose to address. Meanwhile, leftist hand-wringing from the sidelines, criticizing this generation's swing to the right, doesn't help either. That knee-jerk reaction only widens the chasm of ideology in our increasingly polarized societies. The millions of neighbors alarming us now by voting for right-wing demagogues were until recently considered decent, hardworking communities. Political action is needed on all ten layers of this population's malaise. This is ideal terrain for applied oral history. It enables us to do the hard work – the deep listening that can unearth their core human concerns, find some common ground and see how their core needs could be met in positive, sustainable ways. Our Chapters 2 and 5 on host communities showed how applied oral history is already intervening, bringing:

- deep listening across what would otherwise remain 'divides';
- the ability to locate and air an underlying malaise that would otherwise not get heard;
- tolerance and suspension of judgment so that core issues can be aired and addressed even if the listener doesn't consider them fully justified or 'rational'.

## Oral History as Part of the Problem-Solving Frameworks of the Future

The encouraging reality is that the material means to solve all these world problems already exist. Experts agree that there is already sufficient technology, resources and knowledge to halt climate change, restore biodiversity and feed the world population sustainably.[19] For instance, *The Lancet*, one of the world's leading medical journals, recently clarified in detail how everyone on the planet could, *within our existing resources*, enjoy an environmentally friendly, affordable, tasty diet.[20]

Meanwhile, world-leading economists have designed new economic systems that can solve global economic problems while being environmentally sustainable, avoiding the boom and bust cycles, the desperate inequalities and the environmental destruction of previous economic models.[21] Green, sustainable and equitable economics is a well-established field now with projects already up and running, from the 'Prosperity without Growth' economy to Alternative Banking to the local currencies of Transition Towns.[22] Meanwhile, Bill Gates is pioneering a model of investment in the developing world that could restore equality to the 'poorest billion' while returning profits to investors.[23]

It is important not to be too daunted by the apparent size of the global changes needed. Consider the world-changing transformations already made in modern times to other social, political and economic aberrations that were once accepted norms. The African-American slave trade; women not being allowed to vote; gay relationships being criminalized, incurring long prison sentences; racial apartheid in the 1960s American South and in 1980s South Africa; not knowing that cigarettes were harmful to health. These vast historical mistakes had whole legal, scientific and economic worlds built upon them. Whether for slavery, tobacco, patriarchy or homophobia, the vested interests gaining from those systems thought: '*How could we possibly change all this? The costs to us would be too high – we have too much to lose*'. But all those things were changed (and applied oral history played its own part in each of these transformations).[24] Entire legal and economic systems ended up being dismantled and reassembled to give much better outcomes.

Like a ship navigating, society is able to correct its path when it drifts too dangerously off course. For instance, just as we eventually learned of the dangers of tobacco, we now know that the world's current cocktail of pesticides, herbicides, fertilizers, food additives and chemical pollutants are seriously harming both the environment and human health.[25] Does that system seem too big to tackle? There is no sound reason to think that way. So France recently went ahead and banned both home and professional gardeners from using chemical herbicides. Their ban on further herbicide products is set to follow.[26] The French governments' *Organic Ambition 2022* program has arranged for 15% of the country's huge agricultural surface to be fully organic by 2022. And, by then, 20% of the country's institutional catering – in places like public buildings, schools, hospitals, nursing homes – will be certified organic.[27]

These are the very cusps of transformation, the moments when profound, necessary change finally clicks into action, as it has done so many times before. But the only way to build this consensus needed for changing systems is by engaging with beliefs, values and choices. Carefully applied oral history, with its ability to deliver deep listening, collaboration, lateral thinking and an outcomes-focused approach, can help with that great work.

Fortunately, we have seen that the applied oral history skills in this book are working in tandem with a much bigger paradigm shift in government, industry, technology and the not-for-profit sectors. Whether newly designed or a tried and tested tradition, the following frameworks are being used as partners with oral history to tackle what sociologists are calling the 'wicked problems' of our global future.[28]

## Deep Listening

Characterized by the kind of work that we saw Arlie Russell Hochschild and Katherine Cramer[29] do in the populist US, deep listening allows us to touch and access what Hochschild calls the 'deep story' – whatever aching, fundamental belief is driving a particular set of resentments and political choices. This kind of oral history can capture a population's *deep stories* in an evidenced, empirical way that respects the facts as well as the different speakers and their emotions, however irrational they may seem. Deep listening enables dialogue, tolerance, compromises, and can build bridges across differences. In Chapter 4 we saw it used by the British security forces in their own subtle, effective *Prevent* program that attempts to prevent homegrown terrorism in the UK.[30] Deep listening asks: '*What are these narrators really looking for and needing? What natural human need is here? What forces are exploiting it harmfully? In what healthier ways could these needs be met?*'[31]

## Conflict Mediation and Nonviolent Communication

Experts agree that there will be an unprecedented need for conflict mediation amidst the resource conflicts of any climate-altered future.[32] It will also be indispensable before we get to that point, in order to achieve whatever political consensus we need in order to halt climate change before it goes too far. Conflict mediation and nonviolent communication are specialized methods of listening and negotiating that are practical and effective, and have long been used in fields from policing to family law. In Chapter 5 we saw them used to mediate resource conflicts between refugees and impoverished host communities in poor countries, where taking rigorous, well-organized oral histories has become the starting point for the negotiation process.[33]

## Participatory Design

This is part of what's known as the *participatory turn*, where we involve target audiences, end users and their local knowledge in design and decision-making processes previously reserved for specialists. Whether tackling social, political or technological problems, it's a practical, collaborative methodology for getting better outcomes. Academia has theorized it in fields such as participatory design theory, emergence theory and theories of generative learning.[34] And the method is taught in schools like the Institute for Development Studies, through their 'Participation, Inclusion and Social Change' group.[35]

## The Local

In Chapter 5, we saw the 2016 World Humanitarian Summit – described as 'a pivotal moment for the global humanitarian agenda' – announce that international aid and development must focus much more on *the local*.[36] Our chapters showed many examples of 'glocalization', the integrated approach that simultaneously uses local and global perspectives and resources.[37] In refugee settings, focusing on the local means also taking careful account of the place and the people who were there before refugees arrived: *What was this local community and landscape like before the refugee influx? What have been the impacts of the refugee crisis on host communities?*[38] *How is current aid addressing or neglecting those issues?*[39] Whether in white Western communities who rarely see refugees or in developing economies that are flooded by refugee numbers, oral history is a good tool for engaging with, tracking and giving voice to *the local* in this way.

Valuing the local is also a crucial step towards healing the national identity crises that lead to the populist right. Creative local listening can help us to develop in our neighborhoods, places and regions a sense of identity that is healthy, inclusive and evolving.[40] A love of one's own regional culture – its cuisine, language, music, sports or landscapes – need not become the preserve of isolationists and xenophobes. For instance, three countries that I have worked in – Ireland, France and Canada – each have unique, intense cultures that they are very proud of and for which they are much visited. Yet all three have in recent years been predominantly liberal and internationalist in their politics. They disprove the myth that strong national identity, pride and culture must go hand in hand with far-right politics.

## *Personal Testimony*

Both within academia and in the confessional, narcissistic focus on the self in popular culture, recent years have seen a boom in what experts call the *narrative turn*.[41] As a result, oral history in turn has boomed both inside and outside of academia. And it is true that 'selfies' and confessional blogs can indeed be narcissistic – a diversionary turning inward that distracts entertainingly from the nearly overwhelming, real-life problems facing the planet. However, in the years ahead the self will definitely need to speak and be heard in serious ways. With the further shrinking of the global village; the loss of diversity in local cultures under the homogenizing effect of globalization; the rise of artificial intelligence, robotization and enhanced human biology, our experience of self and identity will be constantly challenged, altered and displaced. To start facing, processing and managing such impacts on the self and on identity, just recounting one's experience is a good place to start. A rigorous, ethical practice of oral history will facilitate this process while humanity adapts or evolves across the twenty-first century. Quality oral history can act like a midwife, helping to develop new and healthier ways to experience the mid-twenty-first-century self.

## *Creativity*

As the UNHCR has put it with their call for 'Humanitarian Innovation', only new approaches from new perspectives can generate the solutions that we will need. This book's case studies and examples have shown waves of the new creativity in action. Chapter 3 highlighted dozens of innovative examples where arts and technologies are transporting and translating the core messages of refugee oral histories to much wider audiences.

### *Financially Valuable, Employable Skills*

Mindful that whole fields of previous employment will be lost to robotization, young people will increasingly need to choose fields of study and training that will not be automated. Robots could conceivably be trained to record basic or traditional oral histories. (And we saw that Stephen Spielberg's Shoah Foundation of oral histories uses artificial intelligence to enhance existing oral histories, enabling audiences to 'converse' one-to -one with narrators' holograms, even after those narrators are dead.[42]) But robots could not do the sort of applied oral history work that has been taught in this book: the planning, strategic design, analysis and interpretation of the findings, the reflexivity, the sensitive application of the findings to gaps in current services or understandings. Oral history that is applied for strategic problem-solving requires empathic, editorial and creative skills that robots will not in any foreseeable future provide.

Our methodology also helps to close the divide between academia and the needs of wider society. As such, it robustly meets the requirements of grant funders for projects that have measurable, positive impact. Funders see applied oral history as bringing added value to disciplines as diverse as clinical medicine and supermarket design.[43] It can provide a seam of well-funded employment, generating unlimited career opportunities for those with oral history skills, and an unlimited future for oral history as a methodology that serves the public interest across the coming century

*

Thank you for reading this book. Feel free to contact me any time for advice or dialogue about any aspect of this work. I leave the final word to David Miliband, head of the International Rescue Commission, whose short, simple book on refugees, *Rescue*, is one of the best:

> If you look at the statistics you get depressed, but if you look at the people you find hope.
>
> For every person who is afraid of refugees, there is someone who wants to offer a welcome. There is a discussion to be had, and now is the time to have it.
>
> Integration is up to all of us. It takes effort, street by street. That is how barriers are broken down and communities are built.[44]

## References

Alter, Adam, *Irresistible: Why You Are Addicted to Technology and How to Set Yourself Free*. London: Vintage, 2017.

Appel, Hannah, 'Finance, Figuration and the Alternative Banking Group of Occupy Wall Street', *Signs: Journal of Women and Culture in Society*, 40(1): 53–58, 2014.

Associated Press, 'Holocaust Survivors' Stories Are Being Preserved with Holograms', *New York Post* online, 14-1-2019 [Available at https://nypost.com/2019/01/14/holocaust-survivors-stories-are-being-preserved-with-holograms; accessed on 21-6-2019].

Balint, Peter, Stewart, Ronald, Desai, Anand and Walters, Lawrence, *Wicked Environmental Problems: Managing Uncertainty and Conflict*. New York: Springer, 2011.

Bancilhon, Charlotte and Prattico, Emilie, 'Four Obstacles Blocking Low-Carbon Technologies', *Green Biz* website [Available at www.greenbiz.com/article/4-obstacles-blocking-low-carbon-technologies; accessed on 21-6-2019].

Brahma, Rustam, *Globalization to Glocalisation: A Multidisciplinary Perspective*. Delhi: Akansha Publishing House, 2015.

Casassus, Barbara, 'French Court Bans Sale of Controversial Weedkiller', *Nature* science journal online 24-1-2019 [Available at www.nature.com/articles/d41586-019-00259-x; accessed on 21-6-2019].

Centre for Studies of Climate Change Denialism website, Chalmers University of Technology, 'Climate Change Denial Strongly Linked to Right-Wing Nationalism' [Available at www.chalmers.se/en/departments/tme/news/Pages/Climate-change-denial-strongly-linked-to-right-wing-nationalism.aspx; accessed on 21-6-2019].

Chalmers, Iain, 'Evidence-Based Medicine: An Oral History', *Journal of the American Medical Association*, 311(4): 365–367, 2014.

Cramer, Katherine, *The Politics of Resentment: Rural Consciousness in Wisconsin and the Rise of Scott Walker*. Chicago: University of Chicago Press, 2016.

Dorling, Danny, *Inequality and the 1%*. London: Verso, 2015.

Dupin, Éric, *La France Identitaire: Enquête sur la Réaction Qui Vient*. Paris: Editions La Découverte, 2017.

Federal Writers' Project, *Slave Narratives: A Folk History of Slavery in the United States: These are Our Lives*. Chapel Hill: University of North Carolina Press, 1939.

French Embassy website, 'France Unveils New Strategy for Organic Agriculture', Washington, DC online, 12-4-2018 [Available at https://frenchfoodintheus.org/3825; accessed on 21-6-2019].

French Government website, 'Le Programme Ambition Bio 2022: Transition Agro-Écologique', online 25-6-2018 [Available at https://agriculture.gouv.fr/le-programme-ambition-bio-2022-presente-lissue-du-grand-conseil-dorientation-de-lagence-bio; accessed on 21-6-2019].

Gates, Bill, 'How to Fix Capitalism', *Time*, 11-8-2008.

Gilding, Paul, *The Great Disruption: How the Climate Crisis Will Transform the Global Economy*. London: Bloomsbury, 2011.

Goodson, Ivor and Gill, Scherto, 'The Narrative Turn in Social Research'. In *Counterpoints: Narrative Pedagogy: Life History and Learning*, Vol. 86, (pp 17–34), edited by Ivor Goodson and Scherto Gill. New York: Peter Lang, 2011.

Gore, Al, *The Future*. New York: Random House, 2013.

Hamlett, Jane, Alexander, Andrew, Bailey, Adrian R. and Shaw, Gareth, *Regulating UK Supermarkets: An Oral History Perspective* on *History and Policy* website, 2008 [Available at www.history-and-policy.org/policy-papers/papers/regulating-uk-supermarkets-an-oral-history-perspective; accessed on 21-6-2019].

Harris, Jerry, 'Going Green to Stay in the Black: Transnational Capitalism and Renewable Energy', *Race & Class*, 52(2): 62–78, 2010.

Hartmann, Betsy, 'From Climate Refugees to Climate Conflict: Who Is Taking the Heat for Global Warming?'. In *Climate Change and Sustainable Development: New Challenges for Poverty Reduction* (pp 142–155), edited by Mohamed Salih. Cheltenham, UK: Edward Elgar Publishers, 2009.

Hultman, Martin, Björk, Olle and Viinikka, Katri, 'Far-Right and Climate Change Denial: Denouncing Environmental Challenges via Anti-Establishment Rhetoric, Marketing of Doubts, Industrial/Breadwinner Masculinities Enactments and Ethno-Nationalism'. In *The Far Right and the Environment: Politics, Discourse and Communication* (pp 121–135), edited by Bernhard Forchtner. Abingdon: Routledge, 2019.

Humanitarian Innovation Project, website [Available at www.oxhip.org/about/; accessed on 21-6-2019].

Jackson, Tim, *Prosperity without Growth: Economics for a Finite Planet*. Abingdon: Routledge Earthscan, 2011.

Kelly, Anthony and Westoby, Peter, *Participatory Development Practice Using Traditional and Contemporary Frameworks*. Rugby, UK: Practical Action Publishing, 2018 [Available at www.ids.ac.uk/clusters-and-teams/participation; accessed on 21-6-2019].

Klein, Naomi, *This Changes Everything: Capitalism versus the Climate*. New York: Simon & Schuster, 2014.

Korten, David, *Change the Story, Change the Future: A Living Economy for A Living Earth*. Auckland: Environmental Defence Publications, 2015.

Kurz, Christopher, Li, Geng and Vine, Daniel, *Are Millennials Different?*, Washington, DC: Board of Governors of the Federal Reserve System, 2018.

Logan, Fiorella and Mayer, Richard, 'Eight Ways to Promote Generative Learning', *Educational Psychology Review*, 28(4), 717–741, Dec 2016.

Manyika, Ames et al., *Jobs Lost, Jobs Gained: What the Future of Work Will Mean for Jobs, Skills and Wages*. New York: McKinsey Global Institute, 2017.

Martin, Adrian, 'Environmental Conflict between Refugee and Host Communities', *Journal of Peace Research*, 42(3): 329–346, 2005.

Miliband, David, *Rescue: Refugees and the Political Crisis of Our Time*. New York: Simon & Schuster, 2017.

Pickett, Kate and Wilkinson, Richard, *The Spirit Level: Why Equality Is Better for Everyone*. London: Penguin, 2010.

Pinker, Susan, *The Village Effect: Why Face-to-Face Contact Matters*. London: Atlantic Books, 2014.

Raine, Sarah, 'The Narrative Turn: Interdisciplinary Methods and Perspectives', *Student Anthropologist*, 3(3), 2013.

*Refugee Hosts*, website [Available at https://refugeehosts.org].

Reuell, Peter, 'Cities' Wealth Gap Is Growing Too: Separation between Rich and Poor Communities Has Increased in Past 40 Years', *The Harvard Gazette*, Harvard University, 2-5-2019.

Russell Hochschild, *Arlie, Strangers in Their Own Land: Anger and Mourning on the American Right*. New York: The New Press, 2016.

Scharmer, Otto and Kaufer, Katrin, *Leading from the Emerging Future: From Ego-System to Eco-System Economics*. San Francisco: Berrett-Koehler, 2013.

Schuler, Douglas and Namioka, Aki, editors, *Participatory Design: Principles and Practices*. Boca Raton: CRC Press, 1993.

Selhub Eva and Logan, Alan, *Your Brain on Nature: The Science of Nature's Influence on Your Health, Happiness and Vitality*. Toronto: HarperCollins, 2012.

Sivaram, Varun, *Taming the Sun: Innovations to Harness Solar Energy and Power the Planet*. Cambridge, MA: MIT Press, 2018.

Smith, Jessica and High, Mette, 'Exploring the Anthropology of Energy: Ethnography, Energy and Ethics', *Energy Research & Social Science*, 30:1–116, 2017.

Sophia Smith Collection, *Voices of Feminism Oral History Project*. Northampton, MA: Smith College, 2008.

Southern Oral History Program, *Tobacco, History and Memory: Storytelling and Cultural Grieving in Eastern North Carolina*. Chapel Hill: University of North Carolina, 1999.

Summerskill, Clare, *Gateway to Heaven: Fifty Years of Lesbian and Gay Oral History*. London: London School of Economics and Political Science, 2013.

*The Guardian* Letters, 'A Natural Solution to the Climate Disaster: Climate and Ecological Crises Can Be Tackled by Restoring Forests and Other Valuable Ecosystems, Say Scientists and Activists', collective letter by leading scientists to *The Guardian*, 3-4-2019.

Thunberg, Greta, *No One Is Too Small to Make a Difference*. London: Penguin, 2019.

UK Government, 'Let's Talk about It: Working Together to Prevent Terrorism', website [Available at www.ltai.info/what-is-prevent; accessed on 21-6-2019].

UN, *Agenda for Humanity: 5 Core Responsibilities, 24 Transformations*. New York: UN, 2016.

UN Environment Assembly website, 'National Academies Call for Immediate Action on Air Pollution', online 20-6-2019 [Available at www.unenvironment.org/news-and-stories/story/national-academies-call-immediate-action-air-pollution; accessed on 21-6-2019].

Walker, Matthew, *Why We Sleep: The New Science of Sleep and Dreams*. London: Penguin Random House, 2017.

Walloth, Christian, *Emergent Nested Systems: A Theory of Understanding and Influencing Complex Systems*. Switzerland: Springer, 2016.

Walton, Oliver, *Good Practice in Preventing Conflict between Refugees and Host Communities*. Birmingham: Governance and Social Development Resource Centre, University of Birmingham, 2012.

Wan, Deborah, *Depression: A Global Crisis*. Virginia, US: World Federation for Mental Health, 2012.

Whyte, William, editor, *Participatory Action Research*: Thousand Oaks Sage, 1991.

Willett, Walter et al., 'Food in the Anthropocene: The EAT-Lancet Commission on Healthy Diets from Sustainable Food Systems', *The Lancet Medical Journal*, 393(10170):386–387, 2-2- 2019.

Yousafzai, Malala, *We are Displaced: My Journey and Stories from Refugee Girls around the World*. New York: Little, Brown & Company, 2018.

## Notes

1 Malala Yousafzai, *We Are Displaced: My Journey and Stories from Refugee Girls around the World*. New York: Little, Brown & Company, 2018 and Greta Thunberg, *No One Is Too Small to Make a Difference*. London: Penguin, 2019.

2 Emailed communication from manuscript reviewer Norma Buckley of Glenville Community Council in Ireland.

3 Al Gore, *The Future*. New York: Random House, 2013.

4 David Miliband, *Rescue: Refugees and the Political Crisis of Our Time*. New York: Simon & Schuster, 2017.

5 David Miliband, *Rescue*, 2017.

6 David Miliband, *Rescue*, 2017. The italics are mine.

7 Naomi Klein, *This Changes Everything: Capitalism versus the Climate*. New York: Simon & Schuster, 2014.

8 Paul Gilding, *The Great Disruption: How the Climate Crisis Will Transform the Global Economy*. London: Bloomsbury, 2011.

9 Jerry Harris, 'Going Green to Stay in the Black: Transnational Capitalism and Renewable Energy', *Race & Class*, 52(2): 62–78, 2010.

10 Martin Hultman, Olle Björk and Katri Viinikka, 'Far-Right and Climate Change Denial: Denouncing Environmental Challenges via Anti-Establishment Rhetoric, Marketing of Doubts, Industrial/Breadwinner Masculinities Enactments and Ethno-Nationalism'. In *The Far Right and the Environment: Politics, Discourse and Communication,* edited by Bernhard Forchtner. Abingdon: Routledge, 2019. See also 'Climate Change Denial Strongly Linked to Right-Wing Nationalism' on website of Centre for Studies of Climate Change Denialism, Chalmers University of Technology. Urls are given in this chapter's references.

11 Éric Dupin, *La France Identitaire: Enquête sur la Réaction Qui Vient*. Paris: Editions La Découverte, 2017. This untranslated book title could be translated, for instance, as *French Identity: Examining the Backlash that's Coming* or *France's Identity Crisis: Looking Ahead to the Backlash..*

12 Katherine Cramer, *The Politics of Resentment: Rural Consciousness in Wisconsin and the Rise of Scott Walker*. Chicago: University of Chicago Press, 2016.

13 Peter Reuell, 'Cities' Wealth Gap Is Growing Too: Separation between Rich and Poor Communities Has Increased in Past 40 Years', *The Harvard Gazette*, Harvard University, 2-5-2019.

14 Ames Manyika et al., *Jobs Lost, Jobs Gained: What the Future of Work Will Mean for Jobs, Skills and Wages.* New York: McKinsey Global Institute, 2017.

15 Adam Alter, *Irresistible: Why You Are Addicted to Technology and How to Set Yourself Free.* London: Vintage, 2017; and Matthew Walker, *Why We Sleep: The New Science of Sleep and Dreams*. London: Penguin Random House, 2017.

16 Eva Selhub and Alan Logan, *Your Brain on Nature: The Science of Nature's Influence on Your Health, Happiness and Vitality*. Toronto: HarperCollins, 2012; also Susan Pinker, *The Village Effect: Why Face-to-Face Contact Matters*. London: Atlantic Books, 2014.

17 Deborah Wan, *Depression: A Global Crisis*. Virginia, US: World Federation for Mental Health, 2012.

18 Christopher Kurz, Geng Li and Daniel Vine, *Are Millennials Different?*, Washington, DC: Board of Governors of the Federal Reserve System, 2018.

19 *The Guardian* Letters, 'A Natural Solution to the Climate Disaster: Climate and Ecological Crises Can Be Tackled by Restoring Forests and Other Valuable Ecosystems, Say Scientists and Activists', collective letter by leading scientists to *The Guardian*, 3-4-2019; also Charlotte Bancilhon and Emilie Prattico, 'Four Obstacles Blocking Low-Carbon Technologies' on *Green Biz* website for green technologies; and David Korten, *Change the Story, Change the Future: A Living Economy for a Living Earth*. Auckland: Environmental Defence Publications, 2015.

20 Walter Willett et al., 'Food in the Anthropocene: The EAT-Lancet Commission on Healthy Diets from Sustainable Food Systems', *The Lancet Medical Journal*, 393(10170), 2-2-2019.

21 Dorling, Danny, *Inequality and the 1%*. London: Verso, 2015; Tim Jackson, *Prosperity without Growth: Economics for a Finite Planet*. Abingdon: Routledge Earthscan, 2011; and Kate Pickett and Richard Wilkinson, *The Spirit Level: Why Equality Is Better for Everyone*. London: Penguin, 2010; one of the field's journals is *The International Journal of Green Economics*, published by Inderscience in Geneva.

22 Hannah Appel, 'Finance, Figuration and the Alternative Banking Group of Occupy Wall Street', *Signs: Journal of Women and Culture in Society*, 40, 2014.

23 Bill Gates, 'How to Fix Capitalism', *Time*, 11-8-2008; see also Varun Sivaram, *Taming the Sun: Innovations to Harness Solar Energy and Power the Planet*. Cambridge, MA: MIT Press, 2018 and Jessica, Smith and Mette High, 'Exploring the Anthropology of Energy: Ethnography, Energy and Ethics', *Energy Research & Social Science*, 30, 2017.

24 Examples, respectively, are the Federal Writers' Project, *Slave Narratives: A Folk History of Slavery in the United States: These Are Our Lives*. Chapel Hill: University of North Carolina Press, 1939; Southern Oral History Program, *Tobacco, History and Memory: Storytelling and Cultural Grieving in Eastern North Carolina*. Chapel Hill: University of North Carolina, 1999; Sophia Smith Collection, *Voices of Feminism Oral History Project*. Northampton, MA: Smith College, 2008; and Clare Summerskill, *Gateway to Heaven: Fifty Years of Lesbian and Gay Oral History*. London: London School of Economics and Political Science, 2013.
25 UN Environment Assembly website, 'National Academies Call for Immediate Action on Air Pollution', online 20-6-2019.
26 Barbara Casassus, 'French Court Bans Sale of Controversial Weedkiller', *Nature* science journal online, 24-1-2019.
27 French Embassy website, 'France Unveils New Strategy for Organic Agriculture', Washington, DC online, 12-4-2018; also French Government website, 'Le Programme Ambition Bio 2022: Transition Agro-Écologique', online 25-06-2018.
28 Peter Balint, Ronald Stewart, Anand Desai and Lawrence Walters, *Wicked Environmental Problems: Managing Uncertainty and Conflict*. New York: Springer, 2011.
29 Arlie Russell Hochschild, *Strangers in Their Own Land: Anger and Mourning on the American Right*. New York: The New Press, 2016; Katherine Cramer, *The Politics of Resentment*, 2016.
30 UK Government, *Let's Talk about It: Working Together to Prevent Terrorism* website.
31 Otto Scharmer and Katrin Kaufer, *Leading from the Emerging Future: From Ego-System to Eco-System Economics*. San Francisco: Berrett-Koehler, 2013.
32 Betsy Hartmann, 'From Climate Refugees to Climate Conflict: Who is Taking the Heat for Global Warming?'. In *Climate Change and Sustainable Development: New Challenges for Poverty Reduction*, edited by Mohamed Salih. Cheltenham, UK: Edward Elgar Publishers, 2009.
33 Walton, Oliver, *Good Practice in Preventing Conflict between Refugees and Host Communities*. Birmingham: Governance and Social Development Resource Centre, University of Birmingham, 2012.
34 See, respectively, Schuler and Namioka, 1993; Walloth, 2016; and Logan and Mayer, 2015.
35 See Anthony Kelly and Peter Westoby, *Participatory Development Practice Using Traditional and Contemporary Frameworks*. Rugby, UK: Practical Action Publishing, 2018.
36 UN, *Agenda for Humanity: 5 Core Responsibilities, 24 Transformations*. New York: UN, 2016.
37 See Rustam Brahma, *Globalisation to Glocalisation: A Multidisciplinary Perspective*. Delhi: Akansha Publishing House, 2015.
38 Adrian Martin, 'Environmental Conflict between Refugee and Host Communities', *Journal of Peace Research*, 42(3): 329–346, 2005.
39 *Refugee Hosts* website, 2018.
40 William Whyte, editor, *Participatory Action Research*: Thousand Oaks Sage, 1991.
41 Ivor Goodson and Scherto Gill, 'The Narrative Turn in Social Research'. In *Counterpoints: Narrative Pedagogy: Life History and Learning*, Vol. 86, 2011: Sarah Raine, 'The Narrative Turn: Interdisciplinary Methods and Perspectives', *Student Anthropologist*, 3(3), University of Iowa 2013.
42 Associated Press, 'Holocaust Survivors' Stories Are Being Preserved with Holograms', *New York Post* online, 14-1-2019.
43 Iain Chalmers, 'Evidence-Based Medicine: An Oral History', *Journal of the American Medical* Association, 2014; and Jane Hamlett, Andrew Alexander, Adrian R. Bailey and Gareth Shaw, *Regulating UK Supermarkets: An Oral History Perspective* on *History and Policy* website, 2008.
44 David Miliband, *Rescue*, 2017.

# Appendix 1

## SAMPLE *PROJECT INFORMATION SHEET* (P.106)

**Project title**: *Asylum under Dreaming Spires: Refugees' Lives in Cambridge Today*

**Project organizers**: The project leader is researcher and oral historian Marella Hoffman, in partnership with the Living Refugee Archive of the University of East London, who hold the largest refugee archive in the UK.

**Purposes and outcomes of the project**:

1. To listen to, record and publish in book form the voices and experiences of 12 former refugees resettled in Cambridge.
2. To also gather their recommendations for policymakers and the society around them, implementing some of those recommendations into public policies and services in Cambridge.
3. To present academic summaries of the project's findings at conferences at the University of East London and Cambridge University.

**Your invitation**: You are invited to be one of the project's narrators, potentially becoming one of the 12 former-refugee speakers in the book. We believe that you could make a valuable contribution to the project.

But please read this *Project Information Sheet* carefully first and ask us any questions you like, so you know enough about it to decide whether or not you want to participate. You may also wish to discuss it with friends or family before deciding.

**Why this topic?** A lot of research is done on 'new' refugees, but not enough is known about the longer term experience of refugees after they are settled. This project will uncover the challenges they have faced around integrating into the host society. It will also explore how former refugees experience identity and belonging over the long-term. It is important to hear how refugees themselves view and experience these issues. Problems with identity and belonging in migrant communities have recently produced a tiny but dangerous radicalized minority, and a racist backlash against the peaceful majority of settled refugees. The project will also reveal the positive long-term legacies of peacefully settled refugees and their many contributions to the host society.

**Organizations involved in the project:** This project is independently funded, though in other contexts the researcher is employed by city government and has worked for Cambridge University. As a Fellow of the Royal Anthropological Institute and a member of the Oral History Society, she is bound by their *Codes of Conduct* (attached). The project book will carry a Foreword from the Living Refugee Archive at University of East London and an Afterword from a former Mayor of Cambridge and from the Cambridge Women's Resources Centre. If you wish, a chaperone could be present at all our meetings with you. And/or we could provide a certified translator, if you would prefer that to speaking in English.

**What would my involvement be?** After getting to know each other, we would arrange to record an interview or two with you, lasting about 1–1.5 hours each, at whatever times and places would suit you best. You could later add or remove anything you wanted for your interview, up until an agreed deadline before publication. Before your interview, you would sign a *Consent Form* (attached) agreeing to let us publish your interview in the project book, and for it to be held in the public archive if we so decide. We will discuss this in detail if you decide to be involved in the project.

**What are the possible benefits and disadvantages for me?** There is no payment, but people usually enjoy doing these interviews, which are very relaxed and full of respect for your experiences. They usually find it rewarding to have their voice, experiences and contributions recognized officially, published or perhaps deposited in an archive. But the interview may well remind you of some sad experiences too, or even some past events that you would not want the public or everyone around you today to know about. In those situations, we could partly or completely anonymize your interview. Or it could be excluded from the book and instead placed confidentially in the archive until a specific date of your choice in the future, when it would become available to the public in the archive.

**Keeping your personal information safe:** The project has a government approved Data Protection Policy in line with current European Union legislation. We would never share any aspect of your personal data with anyone. The researcher has received government training in data protection, and will hold your data securely and privately only for as long as it is needed for this project.

**Contact details for further information:** [ … ]

*Thank you for taking the time to consider participating –*
*and welcome to the project, if you decide to become involved*

# Appendix 2

## SAMPLE *CONSENT FORM* (P.106)

Name, address, logo of the organization or individual responsible for this project

Name of your oral history project

(e.g. '*Oral history project opposing/supporting/doing background research for policy proposal by* [name of public or nonprofit organization] *to build a new road/community centre in Jackson St, Sometown*')

### Oral History Recording & Release Agreement

I, the Oral Narrator, confirm that I have received and understood all the information in the *Project Information Sheet*. I have had the opportunity to consider the information, ask questions and have any questions answered satisfactorily.

My recorded interview, and typed transcripts of it, will become part of the collection cared for by [*name of archive or deposit location that will receive your interviews*], where it will be preserved as a permanent public reference resource for use in research, publication, education, lectures, broadcasting and on the internet. My participation in this project is entirely voluntary, and is not remunerated financially.

This Agreement is to ensure that my interview is added to the collection in strict accordance with my wishes. This Agreement is made between [*name and address of archive or deposit location*], referred to below as 'the archive' and me, referred to as 'the Narrator' or 'I':

Narrator's name:..........................................................................,

Narrator's address:.......................................................................,

in regard to my interview recorded by [*name of interviewer*] at [*place of interview*] on [*date*].

**Declaration:** I, the Narrator, confirm that I consented voluntarily to take part in the recording. I hereby assign to the archive all copyright on my contribution, for use and publication in all and any media. I understand that this will not affect my moral right to be identified as the 'performer' in accordance with the Copyright, Design and Patents Act 1988. I agree to refrain from making any libellous or defamatory remarks during the interview, and to those being removed if they occur inadvertently.

If you do not wish to hand over copyright to the archive, or you wish to limit public access to your interview for a period of years, please state those conditions here:

.............................................................................................................

.............................................................................................................

This Agreement will be governed by and construed in accordance with English law and the jurisdiction of the English courts. Both parties shall, by signing below, indicate acceptance of the Agreement.

By or on behalf of the Narrator:
Signed: ...........................................................
Name in block capitals: ....................................Date: ...................
On behalf of [*the archiving organization*]:
Signed: ...........................................................
Name in block capitals: ....................................Date: ...................

# Appendix 3

## SAMPLE *SAFEGUARDING PROTOCOLS* (P.111)

### Safeguarding Policy for (*NAME*) oral history project

**Definition of Safeguarding**

Safeguarding is a set of awarenesses and practices that help ensure the protection of children and vulnerable adults in the course of our work. It is a commitment to avoiding inflicting any harm, exploitation or abuse, and a set of procedures for preventing potential harm being done by anyone else, whenever we suspect or become aware of such harm.

Harm or abuse may be physical, sexual, emotional (e.g. involving bullying or neglect), financial or other. It can happen in any socioeconomic group, gender or culture. Those under 18 are particularly vulnerable, as well as those who are elderly or frail, or have a physical or mental illness or disability. But anyone can become vulnerable to abuse or exploitation, for instance through addiction, homelessness, trafficking, blackmail, domestic violence or harassment.

**Purpose of this Safeguarding Policy**

The (*NAME*) oral history project aims to make a positive contribution to a strong and safe community, and recognizes the right of every individual to stay safe. Our work could bring us into contact with children or vulnerable adults in the course of outreach, community meetings, interviews, follow-up meetings, publications or correspondence. This policy defines the commitments of the (*NAME*) oral history project for protecting children and vulnerable adults, and our expectations of our staff and volunteers in this area.

## Related legislation and policies

The principal pieces of legislation governing this policy are:
(*You may need to list here up to a dozen pieces of legislation that cover your geographical jurisdiction, stretching back over decades – an internet search for 'legislation related to safeguarding' in your region will name them for you*).

These cover related legal duties such as child protection and welfare, health and safety, duty of care, equal opportunities, data protection, obligations to disclose information in the public interest, mental healthcare duties and criminal records.

The internal policies of our organization that overlap with safeguarding are:

(*List your project's or organization's relevant related policies, e.g. on Codes of Conduct, Data Protection, Lone Working Procedures, etc.*, some of which will be described in your *Project Information Sheet* and *Consent Forms*)

**Safeguarding commitments from the (*NAME*) oral history project include:**

- 'Safer Recruitment' procedures and formal criminal record checks on staff and volunteers;
- *Code of Conduct* defining the professional boundaries and standards required from staff and volunteers;
- induction and training of staff and volunteers on these standards;
- an appropriately trained person as the named contact for safeguarding issues within our organization and project;
- regular discussion of safeguarding issues;
- disciplinary procedures and reporting mechanisms (listed below) to use if professional boundaries or conduct standards are breached by our own staff or volunteers, resulting in dismissal from the project or, if necessary, prosecution.

### Reporting procedures

The (*NAME*) oral history project recognizes its duty to report any safeguarding concerns or allegations made either about our own staff or volunteers, or about external parties.

Internal reporting lines & contact details for:

- person(s) responsible for safeguarding issues internally (*a flowchart defining these should be attached and used for training staff and volunteers*).

External reporting lines & contact details (*as above, a flowchart defining these should be attached and used for training*):

- local authority safeguarding contact for children and families;
- local authority safeguarding contact for vulnerable adults;
- Local Authority Safeguarding Incident Report Form;
- Form recording local authority's feedback.

### Individual commitment

I confirm that I have been made fully aware of the contents of this Safeguarding Policy, and how it applies to me.

Name:

Employee or Volunteer?:

Signature:

Date:

# Appendix 4

## CHECKLIST OF LEGAL AND ETHICAL PREPARATIONS (P.114); TICK WHEN TASK COMPLETED

| *Documents/tasks* | *Document ready or task completed?* | *Information given to all who need it, and/or stored securely?* |
|---|---|---|
| **Before your project's interviews:** | | |
| Membership of an oral history association, with its *Code of Conduct* printed out to share | √ | √ |
| All relevant legislation researched and legal advice sought where needed | | |
| Archiving agreed in advance with an institution | | |
| *Project Information Sheet* | | |
| *Consent Form* | | |
| Your project's *Data Protection Policy* typed up and all its measures in place | | |
| Your project's *Safeguarding Protocol* typed up and its measures put in place for staff and volunteers | | |
| Background police checks done on your staff and volunteers if/as needed | | |
| Every narrator's background researched where possible (e.g. for any physical, mental or political vulnerabilities; any traumatic topics to avoid; etc.) | | |

| *Documents/tasks* | *Document ready or task completed?* | *Information given to all who need it, and/or stored securely?* |
|---|---|---|
| Safeguarding planned for all your narrators (for their physical, emotional, cultural needs, etc.) | | |
| **After your project's interviews:** | | |
| Review interview recordings or transcripts for any potential libel or defamation | | |
| Your *Project Logbook* kept up to date throughout your whole project | | |

# Appendix 5

## PLANNING WHO TO INTERVIEW (P.126): YOUR BLANK TEMPLATE

| *Names of oral narrators* | *Their contact details* | *Meeting arranged? For when & where?* | *Info Sheet & Consent Form & your Code of Conduct ready to give them ?* |
|---|---|---|---|
| 1. '*Those most affected*' | | | |
| E.g. Tom Smith | Tom Smith's contact details | √ Date, time, address | √, √, √ |
| 2. '*Community leaders*' | | | |
| 3. '*Observant onlookers*' | | | |
| 4. '*Marginals*' | | | |
| 5. '*Policymakers*' | | | |

# Appendix 6

## *PROJECT BUDGET* (P.130): YOUR BLANK TEMPLATE

| *Project's needs* | *How to procure or fund (e.g. purchase, borrow, already available, etc.)* | *Estimated costs, and how to fund (e.g. funds secured, apply for grant, etc.)* | *Procuring and funding done?* |
|---|---|---|---|
| Staff hiring or salaries, if needed | | | |
| Any professional fees e.g. for interpreters or interview transcribers | | | |
| Workspace and overheads (e.g. utilities, furniture, filing, etc.) | | | |
| Equipment (e.g. computer, printer, recording equipment, camera, video camera, software, backup devices, etc.) | | | |
| Publications or websites | | | |
| Communication (e.g. phone bills, postage, computing costs, etc.) | | | |
| Stationery, printing, any design costs, etc. | | | |
| Travel (and related costs e.g. visas, vaccinations) | | | |
| Accommodation | | | |
| Other | | | |

# Appendix 7

## SAMPLE PLAN FOR WORKSHOP TO TRAIN VOLUNTEER INTERVIEWERS (P.131)

**Introduction to Oral History Interviewing** (workshop length, three hours to one day)

What is oral history and why do it?

Purpose and aims of oral history interviewing

Learning outcomes: what you will know, and be able to do, by the end of this workshop

**What oral history (OH) is**

- the tradition, and its wide applications nowadays (show photos of OH in action, from ethnic folklore to hip-hop refugee youth to cutting-edge medical laboratories);
- OH as a 'bottom-up' practice. *Group thought-shower*: Who doesn't often get listened to or have their voices heard? Why does OH listen to them?

### Skills and knowledge needed

**Ethical skills**

- Briefing oral narrators fully: your project's *Information Sheet* and *Consent and Release Form. Role-play*: take turns being the interviewer briefing a potential narrator using the forms.

- Avoiding libel or defamation. *Group thought-shower:* What could be examples of libel? What could I do if it happened?
- Safeguarding narrators: discovering and meeting their needs (physical, emotional, cultural, belief-based, etc.) *Roleplay:* take turns being the interviewer and narrator arranging to safeguard the narrator's needs.
- Safeguarding yourself and the team: protocols for staying safe. *Group thought-shower:* What are all the things that could possibly go wrong? List the preparations you can make to avoid them.

**Technical skills:** hands-on demo and practice session

- mastering the equipment (recording equipment, cameras, lights, etc.);
- setting up the space for an interview (health and safety, comfort, technical needs, etc.);
- recording, and returning recordings to the project in the safest, most usable way.

**Interpersonal skills**: the 5 Rs of interviewing: *Respect, Rapport, Relevance, Richness, Reward*

- preparing interview questions or using questions prewritten by the project organizer;
- expressing respect and building rapport;
- steering for relevance and getting to the richest material;
- ensuring interviews are rewarding for both the narrator and the project. *Roleplay:* plan questions for a ten-minute OH interview on a topic of your choice. Then take turns acting out being (a) the intervieweer and (b) the narrator.

**Opportunities and responsibilities**

- personal and career development through OH;
- resources and support available to you throughout the project;
- signing the project's *Code of Conduct for Volunteer Oral History Interviewers* (specially written for your project, e.g. adapted from the *Code of Conduct* of your region's professional oral history association);
- reviewing learning outcomes: what you've learned, and are now able to do, after this workshop.

# Appendix 8

## *PROJECT TIMELINE* WITH PHASED *'TO-DO'* LIST (P.133)

| *Project phases & tasks* | *Start & finish dates* | *Estimated time input (hours/ days/weeks)* | *Who will do it* | *Any equipment / info needed* | *Done?* |
|---|---|---|---|---|---|
| ***Planning the project*** | | | | | |
| Creating this *Project Timeline* | | | | | |
| Creating this *Project Budget* | | | | | |
| Recruiting/training any paid or volunteer helpers | | | | | |
| Researching the proposed public policy or programme | | | | | |
| Researching the local area and/or target community | | | | | |
| Arranging future depositing of interviews (with archive/library, etc.) | | | | | |
| ***Interviews*** | | | | | |
| Outreach to contact potential oral narrators | | | | | |
| Briefing potential narrators fully | | | | | |
| Arranging interviews | | | | | |

| *Project phases & tasks* | *Start & finish dates* | *Estimated time input (hours/ days/weeks)* | *Who will do it* | *Any equipment / info needed* | *Done?* |
|---|---|---|---|---|---|
| Preparing interview questions for each | | | | | |
| Doing interviews | | | | | |
| Any second-round interviews | | | | | |
| ***Extracting convincing data*** | | | | | |
| Transcribing recordings of interviews, if necessary | | | | | |
| Analysing interviews for data to extract | | | | | |
| Compiling presentation/ submission for decision makers | | | | | |
| Rehearsing giving the presentation, if it's in person | | | | | |
| ***Concluding the project*** | | | | | |
| Archiving, and publishing, if needed | | | | | |
| Feeding back policy outcomes to narrators and stakeholders | | | | | |
| Concluding and celebrating the project | | | | | |
| Quantifying the project's financial added value; adding it to your CV | | | | | |

# Appendix 9

## PLANNING INTERVIEW QUESTIONS (P.140): YOUR BLANK TEMPLATE

| | *Specific questions you could ask at this level* | *Approx. time for these questions or this 'level'* |
|---|---|---|
| 1. Basic facts about narrator & the community? | E.g. *'What's your address? How long have you lived round here?'* | |
| 2. Narrator's perceptions & attitudes? | E.g. *'So what do folks round here think about …?'* | |
| 3. Their specific points for or against the policy or programme? | E.g.*'What specifically do you dislike about the proposed policy?'* | |
| 4. Narrator's local knowledge & 'hidden expertise'? | E.g. *'If you were designing it, how would you get around the obstacles?'* | |
| 5. Their policy recommendations? | E.g.*'What are the best and worst things about the proposed policy, and what are the most important changes they should make to it?'* | |

# Appendix 10

## CHECKLIST FOR PREPARING TO GO TO INTERVIEWS (P.139)

| *Objects/Tasks* | *Packed or done?* |
|---|---|
| Date, address, tel. numbers, venue all confirmed; refreshments preorganized if needed | √ |
| *Safeguarding Protocol* for narrator arranged (their physical, social, cultural needs, etc.) | |
| Your *Safeguarding Protocol* done for yourself (informing your Key Person where you're going, etc.) | |
| Maps and timings of journey to get there early | |
| *Information Sheet*, *Consent/Release Form* & your own *Code of Conduct* | |
| Extra copies if needed for narrator's entourage | |
| List of pre-prepared interview questions | |
| *Project Logbook* & spare pens | |
| Recording equipment, microphone, spare batteries, extension leads | |
| Camera, spare batteries, lights if needed | |
| Video camera if needed, tripod, spare batteries | |

# Appendix 11

## ANALYSING INTERVIEWS TO EXTRACT DATA (P.150): YOUR BLANK TEMPLATE

| *Strategic information or perspective from narrator* | *Name and role of narrator* | *Starting where in their interview recording?* | *Importance for achieving project's goals, on scale of A–C* | *How to use in presentation to decision makers* |
|---|---|---|---|---|
| *User experience* | | | | |
| *Local knowledge* | | | | |
| *Hidden obstacles* (what will and won't work as solutions, and why) | | | | |
| *Long-term view* | | | | |
| *Affected directly* | | | | |
| *Influential* | | | | |

# Appendix 12

## QUANTIFYING THE EQUIVALENT FINANCIAL VALUE THAT ORGANIZATIONS GAIN FROM YOUR ORAL HISTORIES (P.153): YOUR BLANK TEMPLATE

| *High-value services provided by your oral history project* | *Financial savings for the organization receiving your applied oral history findings (your estimates)* |
|---|---|
| Total hours of free expertise from your narrators:<br>....... | Equivalent cost if they had to pay staff to do this:<br>....... |
| Total free hours from you and your team as providers of these 'consultation services':<br>....... | Cost for consultation services:<br>• if your work had been done internally by the organization .......<br>• if hired in from a professional consultancy for market surveying ....... |
| Total financial scale of the situation, program, policy or service addressed by your oral history project:....... | Financial savings in waste avoided through useful suggestions made by your narrators e.g.:<br>• savings in wasted project time .......<br>• savings in wasted staff time .......<br>• savings in wasted materials and purchases ....... |
| Your contribution to getting this situation, program, policy or service better accepted by its target communities:<br>• numbers and types of stakeholders your project reached .......<br>• numbers and types of potential service users ......... | Financial savings compared to what it would cost the organization to achieve this 'buy-in' themselves through, for example:<br>• advertising, promotions and publicity .......<br>• PR .......<br>• outreach events ...... |

A sample of the estimated savings to an organization delivering the refugee resettlement program studied by your oral history project (to help you fill in your own estimates into Appendix 12 above):

- if your volunteers did a total of 100 hours of unpaid work, that equates to *2.6 weeks of full-time staffing*;
- if paid @ $676 per week, that would have cost the organization *$1758*;
- plus staffing overheads of 25% for social insurance, employers' pension contributions, premises costs, etc. would have cost *$440*;
- totalling *$2198* of savings in staffing, due to your volunteers' input;
- your narrators exposing hidden obstacles in the program or policy helped avoid delays of 3–5 months in the delivery of the program – delays that would have cost *$12,500–$15,000* (calculated using the program's overall budget and duration);
- the materials wasted on that failed part of the program would have cost up to *$12,500* (again, calculated from the program's planned duration and budget for materials);
- your oral history work reached and involved about 120 stakeholders of the program (20 narrators and approximately five friends and family members that each of them discussed it with): this much outreach and publicity would usually cost the organization over *$3,750*;
- *Total savings to the organization due to your oral history project = approx. $32,000.*

# Appendix 13

## SOME RECOMMENDED RESOURCES:

### If You Want Just One from Each List, an Asterisk Marks Those I Found Most Engaging and Enlightening

**Powerful books by individual refugees**

Boochani, Bherouz and Tofighian, Omid, *No Friend but the Mountains*. Sydney: Pan Macmillan, 2018.

Mikhail, Dunya, *The Beekeeper of Sinjar*, translated by Max Weiss. London: Serpent's Tail, 2018.

Murad, Nadia and Krajeski, Jenna, *The Last Girl: My Story of Captivity, and My Fight against the Islamic State*. London: Penguin Random House, 2017. *

Yousafzai, Malala, *We Are Displaced: My Journey and Stories from Refugee Girls around the World*. New York: Little, Brown & Company, 2018.

**Books based on oral histories from a range of refugees**

Kingsley, Patrick, *The New Odyssey: The Story of Europe's Refugee Crisis*. London: Guardian Books, 2016.

McDonald-Gibson, Charlotte, *Cast Away: Stories of Survival from Europe's Refugee Crisis*. London: Portobello Books, 2016.

Trilling, Daniel, *Lights in the Distance: Exile and Refuge at the Borders of Europe*. London: Picador, 2018. *

**Explaining the issues around refugees**

Betts, Alexander and Collier, Paul, *Refuge: Transforming a Broken Refugee System*. London: Allen Lane, Penguin, 2017.

Betts, Alexander, Kaplan, Josiah, Bloom, Louise and Omata, Naohiko, *Refugee Economies: Forced Displacement and Development*. Oxford: Oxford University Press, 2016.

Collier, Paul, *The Bottom Billion: Why the Poorest Countries Are Failing and What Can Be Done about It*. Oxford: Oxford University Press, 2008.

Miliband, David, *Rescue: Refugees and the Political Crisis of our Time*. New York: Simon & Schuster, 2017.*

**Understanding the rise of anti-migrant populism in developed democracies**

Collier, Paul, *Exodus: How Migration Is Changing Our World*. Oxford: Oxford University Press, 2013.

Collier, Paul, *The Future of Capitalism: Facing the New Anxieties*. London: Penguin, 2018.

Goodhart, David, *The Road to Somewhere: The Populist Revolt and the Future of Politics*. London: Hurst, 2017.

Russell Hochschild, Arlie, *Strangers in Their Own Land: Anger and Mourning on the American Right*. New York: The New Press, 2016. *

Sparrow, Jeff, *Trigger Warnings: Political Correctness and the Rise of the Right*. Victoria: Scribe, 2018.

**On doing oral history**

Bryson, Anna and McConville, Sean, *The Routledge Guide to Interviewing: Oral History, Social Enquiry and Investigation*. Abingon: Routledge, 2014.

MacKay, Nancy, *Curating Oral Histories: From Interview to Archive, 2nd edition*. Abingdon: Routledge, 2016.

MacKay, Nancy, Quinlan, Mary Kay and Sommer, Barbara, *Community Oral History Toolkit*. Abingdon: Routledge, 2013.*

Perks, Robert and Thomson, Alistair, editors, *The Oral History Reader, 3rd edition*. Abingdon: Routledge, 2016.

Ritchie, Don, *Doing Oral History, 3rd edition*. New York: Oxford University Press, 2015.

Zusman, Angela, *Story Bridges: A Guide for Conducting Intergenerational Oral History*. Abingdon: Routledge, 2010.

**On doing applied oral history with refugees**

Cave, Mark and Sloan, Stephen, editors, *Listening on the Edge: Oral History in the Aftermath of Crisis*. Oxford and New York: Oxford University Press, 2014.

Krause, Ulrike, *Researching Forced Migration: Critical Reflections on Research Ethics during Fieldwork*. Oxford: Refugee Studies Centre, University of Oxford, 2017.

Mollica, Richard, *Healing Invisible Wounds: Paths to Hope and Recovery in a Violent World*. Nashville: Vanderbilt University Press, 2009.

Papadopoulos, Renos, 'Refugees, Trauma and Adversity-Activated Development', *European Journal of Psychotherapy and Counselling*, 9(3): 301–312, Sept 2007. Temple, Bogusia and Moran, Rhetta, *Doing Research with Refugees: Issues and Guidelines*. Bristol: Policy Press, 2011.

**On legalities, conduct and archiving**

DLA Piper, *2019 Global Data Protection Handbook*. Washington, DC: DLA Piper, 2019 [Available at www.dlapiperdataprotection.com; accessed on 21-6-2019].

MacKay, Nancy, *Curating Oral Histories: From Interview to Archive, 2nd edition.* Abingdon: Routledge, 2016.*

Neuenschwander, John, *A Guide to Oral History and the Law, 2nd edition.* Oxford: Oxford University Press, 2014.

Oral History Society (UK), *Is Your Oral History Ethical and Legal?* Introductory guide, 2012 [Available at www.ohs.org.uk/advice/ethical-and-legal; accessed on 21-6-2019].

**Future dynamics**

Bednar, Vasiliki, *Making Public Policy More Fun.* TED talk at TEDxToronto, 2017 [Available at www.youtube.com/watch?v=ZIroKbMniFM; accessed on 21-5-2019].

Dorling, Danny, *A Better Politics: How Government Can Make Us Happier.* London: London Publishing Partnership, 2016.

Ghosh, Amitav, *The Great Derangement: Climate Change and the Unthinkable.* London: Penguin, 2016.

Gilding, Paul, *The Great Disruption: How the Climate Crisis Will Transform the Global Economy.* London: Bloomsbury, 2011.

Kolbert, Elizabeth, *The Sixth Extinction: An Unnatural History.* New York: Henry Holt, 2014.

McKibben, Bill, *Eaarth: Making a Life on a Tough New Planet.* New York: Henry Holt, 2010.

**Films about the refugee crisis and experience**

Audiard, Jacques, *Dheepan*, 2015.

BBC2 TV, *Exodus: Our Journey to Europe.* London: BBC, 2016.*

Boochani, Behrouz and Sarvestani, Arash Kamali, *Chauka, Please Tell Us the Time*, 2017.

Carpignano, Jonas, *Mediterranean*, 2015.

Fedele, David, *The Land Between*, 2013.

Makhmalbaf, Monsen, *Kandahar*, 2001.

Rosi, Gianfranco, *Fire at Sea*, 2016.

Weiwei, Ai, *Human Flow,* 2017.

**Online immersion and experiences**

*Clouds over Sidra* is a groundbreaking, immersive online experience created by the United Nations Virtual Reality department. Seeing through the eyes of a young refugee girl from Syria, this 8-minute virtual reality film takes you on a 3-D journey. Clicking your way along the routes you choose through this refugee camp, you go on a quirky, inspiring walkabout. The place is alive with the sounds, images and engaging testimonies of interesting refugee characters going about their daily lives there [Available at www.unvr.sdgactioncampaign.org; accessed on 21-6-2019].

*The Refugee Project* uses attractive interactive maps and stories to communicate UNHCR data [Available at www.refugeeproject.org; accessed on 21-6-2019].

*TED* hosts videos of short, entertaining talks by the world's top thinkers. On and from refugees, it has a range of uplifting, inspiring talks. Some are by resettled refugees active in the arts, politics, business or charities. An example is refugee Saba Abraham's own oral history – performed live as a talk on the TED stage – about going from being a refugee to a resettled, integrated businesswoman [Available at https://ideas.ted.com/8-practical-ways-to-help-refugees and www.unhcr.org/innovation/15-ted-talks-on-refugee-resilience; accessed on 21-6-2019].*

# GLOSSARY

## Some Key Concepts Used in this Book

**applied oral history** – when interviews are not just preserved or published for the historical record, but findings, insights and recommendations from the interviews are also extracted and applied to inform or improve projects, services or situations

**asset-based** – a problem-solving approach that starts by doing an inventory of what's positive and resourceful about a problem situation or community, rather than by focusing on the challenges and difficulties; drawn from the positive psychology movement, it can be used with either an individual or a sector of the community

**asylum** – when a government approves an asylum seeker to stay in their country, after vetting them within that country (see versus *resettlement*)

**asylum seeker** – someone who had to flee to a foreign country to escape harm or persecution in their own, and is now applying for political asylum in the foreign country on the grounds that they would face persecution if sent back to their own

***bricolage*** – the grassroots art of resourcefully combining objects or parts of objects – often discarded or without apparent value – to improvise items with new functions or applications

**conflict societies** – societies where the population, environment and infrastructure remain affected by the impacts of present or past armed conflict

**crowdfunded** – internet practice of raising funding for a project through an online appeal; can amass significant amounts of funding through very small donations from large numbers of online followers or enthusiasts

**deportation** – forcible removal of a migrant by a host country, whether sending them to their country of origin or another country

**detention centre** – facility where asylum seekers are housed and constrained while their asylum applications are being processed; usually involves some restrictions on movement, ranging from being refused the right to work to complete incarceration away from the host community

**economic migrant** – someone who migrates to a location that they expect will improve their economic situation, usually through improved employment opportunities

**emotional intelligence** – ability to consciously regulate one's own emotional responses for the benefit of a given situation or interlocutor

**end user** – the person at whom a service, product or policy is targeted, and for whom it is designed; as distinct from the designers and providers of the service, product or policy

**expatriate** – polite, high-status term for a person living in a foreign country; traditionally used by the British to refer to themselves abroad

**forcibly displaced person** – someone displaced from their home by conflict or natural disaster, and obliged to seek refuge either elsewhere within their own country or abroad

**'glocalization'** – a dual approach that blends insights from globalization with local needs and culture; can be used in research, service provision or work with communities

**human smuggling** – an illegal, paid service provided to consenting migrants to transport them across territories or borders that, for physical, financial or legal reasons, they couldn't cross unaided

**human trafficker** – the illegal smuggling of kidnapped or captured people against their will, for financial exploitation as slaves or ransom

**humanitarian innovation** – term launched by the UNHCR to promote innovative thinking and new perspectives for humanitarian interventions, especially produced by new synergies and new partners, from grassroots to multinationals

**internally displaced person** – person forcibly displaced to another part of their own country by conflict or natural disaster

**intersectionality** – when several vulnerable characteristics coincide in one person's identity, such as being at once gay, disabled and a refugee

**IRC** – International Rescue Commission, an independent charity or nongovernmental organization; and the second-largest body responsible for assisting refugees after the United Nations High Commissioner for Refugees

**ISIS** – the so-called '*Islamic State*' terrorist group who impose the extremely brutal fundamentalist laws of the Salafi branch of Sunni Islam

**lateral thinking** – creative approach to problem-solving that looks at the issues from new perspectives, combining elements in new ways

**localization** – a problem-solving approach that starts from the uniqueness, resources and needs of the local context (population, economy, landscape, ecology and culture), rather than starting with the viewpoints of international elites such as donor governments, global agencies and international charities

**migrant** – a person who has moved from their own country or region; strictly speaking, includes refugees who are forcibly displaced but most used for non-refugees, moving by choice to improve their economic situation

**narrator** – the speaker in an oral history interview; less passive than 'interviewee', the term recognizes that the speaker's responses weave their own narrative or story, regardless of the questions asked by the interviewer

**NGO** – literally a 'nongovernmental organisation', meaning a not-for-profit or charitable organization independent of both the state sector and private industry

**'No-Borders'** – an ideological movement that believes all national borders should be abolished, as doing more harm than good for human society overall

**participatory design** – a collaborative methodology for improving the effectiveness of a product or service by involving target audiences, end users and their local knowledge in the design process

**positive deviance** – a problem-solving methodology that seeks out individuals who are 'exceptions to the rule', improvising their own, homegrown but reproducible solutions and ways of thriving in a difficult situation where everyone else is struggling or failing

**preparedness** – foreseeing future threats to civil society, with precautionary measures ready to be implemented when a threat is imminent

**public good** – of benefit for society, communities and public services rather than for private interests or profit

**refugee** – a person forced by conflict or natural disaster to flee from their home and seek refuge in another country, or another part of their own country

**refugee economy** – the sphere of economic activity, local or global, generated specifically by the presence of refugees

**'Refugee Nation'** – the concept of viewing all the world's refugees as members of a single, notional 'Refugee Nation'

**repatriation** – enforced removal of a migrant or refugee back to their country of origin

**resettlement** – international agreements whereby a country offers a refugee asylum, after they have been vetted in another country (see versus *asylum*)

**robotization** – the process of artificial intelligence taking over functions and employment roles previously done by human beings

**scaling up** – taking a solution from a very grassroots level, and reproducing it elsewhere to solve similar problems

**stakeholder** – every party who will be affected by a situation and its outcomes; 'stakeholder mapping' takes a 360-degree approach to try to ensure that every stakeholder is recognized, not just those that are high status, vocal or most visible

**'thinking through oceans'** – a shift in perspective that ignores land and national borders to instead view the seas and oceans as virtual countries, with whole populations occupying and travelling their sea-routes; phrase coined by Refugee Studies academic Peter Gatrell (citation given in references list of Chapter 1)

**translocal** – a subset of the 'transnational' approach below, the 'translocal' zooms in on the links connecting localities far apart geographically; an example would be rural Sicily, off southern Italy, and the Bronx ghetto of downtown New York where Sicilians settled across the twentieth century; the two localities are densely bound by migration, family relationships, visits and exchanges of money, as well as links of language, culture and collective memory

**transnational** – a perspective that ignores national boundaries to trace instead other connections that transcend them, such as travel-routes, export-routes and international communications and relationships; particularly important when describing the networks, movements and relationships of migrant diasporas, which can often stretch around the globe, well beyond a small country of origin

**UNHCR** – United Nations High Commissioner for Refugees

**UNRWA** – United Nations Relief and Works Agency for Palestine Refugees, a distinct branch of the United Nations created in 1949 to assist Palestinian refugees who had just been expelled from their homeland; originally created as a temporary agency, as the UN never expected the Palestinians' statelessness to last so long

**upcycling** – repurposing old, cheap or discarded materials, using creativity and manual skills to upgrade them for a new and more valuable purpose

# INDEX

Page numbers in italic refer to figures.


academic investigation 105
academic research: publicizing findings as *129*
access: to the internet 51; to interviews, informed consent and 106–9
accessibility: of interview venues 111; of oral histories 109
adaptation 8
Adar (refugee) 142
added material value: through integration 23; *see also* financial value
*Addicted to Hate: Identity Residual among Former White Supremacists* 27
adolescents *see* teenage refugees
Afghanistan 21
Africa 6; host community oral histories 77–9; refugee camps, and 'time bomb' of likely radicalization 15; wars and displacement 38; *see also individual countries*
African Artists for Development 49
African youth: unrealistic expectations 81–3
age: and experience of violent conflict 12
agency 67
aggrieved host communities: oral histories 73–90, *see also* grievances (host community)
agreement (narrator): to filming 132
aid *see* refugee aid
aims/goals (project) 117–18, 119–20, 126, 128, 138, 139
Akkad, Hassan 101
Al-Qaeda 69
al-Qunun, Rahaf Mohammad 44
al-Rashid, Ahmad 45
Ali, Kanwar 150–1
*Ali and the Long Journey to Australia* 47
amateur reportage 52
American Council on Foreign Relations 28
American Dream 87
American Horse 35
*American Journal of International Law* 38
*American Women of the Far Right* 29
Amsterdam 48
analysis of testimonies 88, 90, 143, 151–2, 190
Angola 39
animation 44, 47
anonymity 108
anonymization 84
anthropologists' interviews 41
anti-migrant communities: leftist interviews with 28; listening to concerns of 26, 86–8; tackling prejudice 88–90, *see also* resistance to refugees
anti-terrorism: applied oral history as a strategy for 27
applied oral history(ies): for assisting refugees and communities *10*; communicating level of influence of 102; and constructive public conversations 24; defined 197; and engagement with host communities 30–1; as fundamental in 'processing' refugees and providing services 10; and improved public policy and services 9; and maintenance of civil democracy 22; as part of the problem-solving framework 162–6; participatory approach 8–9; and populist identity crisis 160–2; and resolution of refugee crisis 30; suitability to refugee environments 10–11, *see also*

case studies; oral history interviews; oral history projects
archives/archiving 40, 41, 109, 153
Arian, Moutaz 6
artificial intelligence 165, 166
the arts: publicizing testimonies/findings through 43–9, *129*
'asset-based' approach 7, 197
asylum: defined 197; numbers of forcibly displaced people with 4; refusal of, Japan 9–10; teaching refugees the price of 23
asylum application 114
asylum applications 4
asylum seekers 4, 197
*Asylum under Dreaming Spires: Refugees' Lives in Cambridge Today* 88
Atkinson-Phillips, Alison 105
attribution 41
audio recordings 131, 132, 152
Australia 3, 28, 46, 47, 65, 66, 67
authenticity 152
authoritarianism 105

'backwards and forwards' approach 67
Balls, Ed 28
Bangladesh 4
barter 8
'basic' personal data 109
*The Beekeeper of Sinjar* 63
benefit(s): of oral histories 102, 103; of using volunteers 131
Bergen, Teresa 152
Berlin 5, 46, 67–8
Betts, Alexander 5, 8
body language 111, 132, 140, 144
Boochani, Behrouz 3–4, 65–6, 130
'bottom-up' innovation 8
boundaries: community-refugee 79; emotional 101; of project aims, audiences and effects 118; transnational perspective 6, 200
brainwashing 13
Brazil 79–83, 85
bricolage 8, 197
Britain *see* United Kingdom
British and Irish Oral History Society: annual conference (2018) 105
Buckley, Norma 159
budgets (project) 130, 183
Burundi refugees 77

Cambodian Khmer Rouge *36*
Cambridge: oral histories 73–4, 88–90
Camus, Renaud 29, 30
Canada 5, 44, 50, 165, *see also* Montreal
case studies: host community oral histories 73–90; refugee oral histories 60–9
*Cast Away: Stories of Survival from Europe's Refugee Crisis* 142
Central America 4, 39, 49, *see also individual countries*
centre right-wing interviewers 28
centrist think tanks 28
certified/chartered interpreters 107
challenge: in interviews 143
Charlottesville (Virginia) 29
*Chauka, Please Tell Us the Time* 3
checking questions 140
Checklist of Legal and Ethical Preparations 114, 180–1
Checklist for Preparing to go to Interviews 189
chemical herbicides: banning of 163
child refugees: numbers 4; oral histories publicized through the arts 44, 47, 48; risks to unaccompanied 12
Chile 79–83, 85
civil wars: as obstacles to peace 38
CLARIN 152
claymation 47
climate change: far right rejection of science of 160; and refugee crisis 4, 159–60
climate refugees *36*
Clooney, Amal 62–3
closing interviews 144
Code of Conduct 114, 130, 131
collaboration 7, 43, 63, 163
collective outcomes: oral histories and improved 102
Collier, Paul 25
Colombia 4, 39, 85–6
comic strips 46
common sense 101–3
communication: nonviolent 164; of project value 153–6, 191–2, *see also* body language; language; media; publicization; voice
community leaders: retaining a critical distance around 126
*Community Oral History Toolkit* 109
community outreach 68
community theatre program 44
compassion: provoking *124*, 126, 136, *137*
competition *see* job competition; unfair competition
compromise 164
confidentiality 109, 113
conflict: refugee experience of violent 12
conflict resolution 77–9, *see also* mediation

conflict societies 197
conflict zones: amateur reportage in 52
Congolese refugee's music classes 49, 138
conscription 13
Consent Forms 106, 107–8, 109, 111, 175–6
consultation 8, 9
contextualizing interview data 148
contraceptive and reproductive health services: using testimonies to improve 64–5
contribution: project aims and meaningful 119
control: and choice, over resettlement process 80; of expenditure, as a coping strategy 84; of interview material 41
conversations: steering 143
copies (interview): keeping multiple 153; offering a limited right to correct 109
coping strategies: of those hosting the most refugees 75, 83–5
copyright 109
corruption 39, 102, 105
cost estimation 155
Costa Rica 85
costs: of failing to manage refugee crisis 14–16
Cramer, Katherine 28, 87, 164
creative approaches: to editing and re-presenting interviews 149; to listening 165; to refugee issue 5–7; writing workshops for host communities 76, *see also* the arts
Creative Commons license 109
criminal intelligence 68–9
criminal justice: testimonies used in 61–3
Crisis Info Hub 64
critical distance: around community leaders 126
critical thinking: populism as threat to 105
crowdfunded 197
cultural diversity: loss of 165
cultural habits: helpful 87–8
cultural integration 67
cultural sensitivity 65, 69
cultural taboos 63, 65
cultural values: addressing differences in 23
culture: of creativity and collaboration 7
*Curating Oral Histories: From Interview to Archive* 109

Dadaab refugee camp (Eastern Kenya) 15
dance 49
Dangerous Oral Histories: Risks, Responsibilities and Rewards 105
data protection 109–10, 152
Data Protection Act (British) 110
deep listening 78, 162, 163, 164
deep story 87, 164
defamation 112
deindustrialization 86
*The Deindustrialized World: Confronting Ruination in Postindustrial Places* 28
Democratic Republic of Congo 39, 49, 77
demographic groups: awareness of different messages that emerge from 124–5; narrator selection 125, 128; refugee theatre groups 44; risks of refugee journeys 12
Department for International Development (UK) 27
deportation 4, 197
design: of refugee services 8, 9
designer objects: made by Amsterdam refugees 48
detective work: oral history as 75
detention centre: defined 197–8
developed economies: and the Great Replacement theory 29; left-wing movements and loss of white working class allegiance 28; need for wealth sharing 81; percentage of refugees hosted by 21; rise of far right politics 160
dialogue 6, 7, 24, 44, 49, 76, 82, 88, 120, 164
Dictaphones 132
Diffa region 78
difference: doing interviews that will make a 135–44; gathering 'useful messages' that will make a 124–5
differences: deep listening and building bridges across 164
digital cameras 132–3
digital mapping/maps 35, 64
Digital Migration Studies 50
*Dimensions in Testimony* 49
disillusionment 82
*Displaced Colombians Open Their Homes to Venezuelan Refugees and Migrants* 85
displacement *36*; average length of 15; climate crisis and 159; wars and 4
disposable income: spent on staying connected 51
distance: through writing 76
distributive injustice 87
diversity: of needs 11, 12; of personal finances 12, *13*
Do, Anh 46
*Do You See What I See?* 48
doctors' interviews 41
'*Don't decide about me without me*' 138

double standards 88, 89
Doucet, Lyse 52

ecological metaphors 63
economic actors: refugees as 7
economic migrants: defined 198; difficulties compounded by lack of accurate information 82; distinguished from refugees 11; helpful role of applied oral history 82–3; long-term future of 25; potential of oral history for informing 81
economic power 23
economics: green, sustainable and equitable 162–3
economies: refugee intake and boost in 7, 23
*The Economist* 62–3
Ecuador 85
editing: interview data 150–3, *see also* pre-editing; self-editing
education: extremes of variation in 12, *13*; school set up by refugees, Zimbabwe 7
emotion (interviewer) 101
emotional intelligence 97, 198
empathic double vision 68
empathic listening 136, 137–8
empathy: among peer groups 126; in doing oral history 100–1; for political ideological positions 26
employable skills 50, 166
end user: defined 198
end user feedback: useful messages *124*, 136, 137, 138
*The End of Eddy* 30, 147
enslavement: girls, women and likelihood of 12, *see also* Yezidi women
entitlement 4, 88
environmental migration 4
equanimity 103
Eritrea 13
ethical protections 40, 106–14; checklist 114, 180–1
Ethiopia 21
ethnic minorities 30
Europe: community theatre group 44; oral histories 30; perpetrators of terror attacks 15; risk of radicalization among 'second generation' born to refugee parents 15; shock at poverty and recession in 82; technical illegalities 113–14
European Union 26; asylum applications 114; disagreement of refugee policies 38; General Data Protection Regulation (EU) 110
Examining Local Community Experiences of and Responses to Displacement from Syria 75
exchange 8
Exil Ensemble 46
*Exodus: How Migration is Changing the World* 25, 64
*Exodus: Our Journey to Europe* 45, 101, 130
expatriate 5, 198
expectations (refugees): of future destinations 80–1; managing, in doing oral history 101–2, *see also* false hopes
explicit knowledge 141
extreme ideologies: unhelpfulness of 25, *see also* far left; far right
extreme violence 39
extremist networks 29

Facebook 82
failed projects/programs: interviewing host agencies about 79–83; lessons learned from 9–10
fake news 52
false hopes 64
far left: migration and spectrum of political ideology 25
far right: awareness of seed ideas 28–9; ideology 22; interviews by centrist/moderate right-wingers concerning drift towards 28; migration and spectrum of political ideology 25; myth of national identity, pride and culture as hand in hand with 165; opposition to refugees driven by 27, 29; politics, mainstreaming of 105; and populist communities 87; rejection of science of climate crisis 160; rise of 14, 26; and terrorist attacks, United States 15
Fatima (refugee) 82
feedback: giving, in interviews 143; useful messages *124*, 136, 137, 138
feminists 30
films 45, 46, 47, 49, *see also* animation; video recordings
financial ability: inverse relationship between actual help and 21
financial advantages *13*
financial disadvantages 12, *13*
financial value (project): quantifying and communicating 153–6, 191–2
financially valuable, employable skills 166
Finland 49
'*First, do no harm*' 98
first-person life histories 29–30

fleeing: using the theme of 77
focus of discussions: steering 143
focus group interviews 127
forcibly displaced persons: defined 198; numbers 4; online movement and potent reuse of language 6
*Four Golden Pillars* 40–1, 52
four-stage trauma: refugee experience as a 100–1
France 30, 67, 81, 163, 165
freedom of expression 105
freedom of information 107–8
From Paris to Cherbourg: Aspirations, Expectations and Realities 64
funding applications: figures for future 156
*The Future* 159

gang gun violence 49
Gates, Bill 50, 163
Gatrell, Peter 37
gender: and experience of violent conflict 12
Gendrassa camp 78
General Assembly (UN) 38
General Data Protection Regulation (EU) 110
Geneva Convention (fourth) 38
Gest, Justin 28
Gillespie, Marie 64
girls: likelihood of rape and enslavement 12
*Global Compact on Refugees* 8
global humanitarian agenda 164
global transformations 163
globalization 165
glocalization 6, 164, 198
Goodhart, David 28
Gordon, Glenna 29
Gore, Al 159
government: interviewing communities for 127
Gramsci, Antonio 66
graphic novels 47
the great paradox 86, 87
*The Great Replacement* 29, 87
grievances (host community): aid organizations and awareness of 27; listening to 22, 26, 27, 75–7, 79, 86–8, 128; rise of far right fueled by dismissal of 14, *see also* aggrieved host communities
group dynamics 127
group interviews 127
group narrators 128
Guinet, Eymeric 67

*The Happiest Refugee: Live* 46
harm to narrators: history work and spectrum of possible *104*
Harvard Program in Refugee Trauma 68
help: inverse relationship between financial ability and actual 21; useful messages 124–5, 136, *137*, 138
High, Stephen 28
*Hillbilly Elegy: A Memoir of a Family and Culture in Crisis* 29, 147
historical records: oral histories as 60
*History of Violence* 30
Holocaust survivors *36*, 37, 49
holograms 49
honesty: about one's political ideology 25
hospitality 77, 88
host communities: attending to 'the local' 74; complaints of lack of voice 27; different types of 21–2; differing shades of truth 135; engagement with 30–1; finding out about, before interviews 121–2; grievances/concerns *see* grievances; percentage of refugees in 21; refugee innovators in 7–8; refugee theatre and building bridges with 44; refugee's account of, Cambridge 73–4; refugees' socioeconomic contributions to 7; rise of the far right fueled by dismissal of grievances 14; spectrum of political reactions among 24–6; statistics 21; as target audiences *121*; typical preoccupations along their spectrum of responses *123*
host community oral histories: case studies 73–90; recent 26–30, *see also* oral history projects
hosting: using the theme of 77
hotspots (interview) 150
human 'caravan' 39
*Human Flow* 45, 64, 117, 146
human smuggling *36*, 198
human trafficking *36*, 198
humanitarian aid 22–3, 76
humanitarian crisis: and political instability 15
humanitarian innovation 8, 198
Humanitarian Innovation Project (Oxford University) 7
Humanitarian Innovation (UN): global call 5, 75, 158, 165
humanitarian narrative 76
humanitarian system 5

'icebreaker' stage (interviews) 140–1
identity: experience of 165; reconstruction of sense of 46

identity crisis (populist) 160–2, 165
ideology *see* political ideology
IKEA 48
ILLEGAL 46
ILLEGAL: One boy's Epic Journey of Hope and Survival 47
illegal incarceration: smuggled testimony exposing 3, 65–6
illegal migrants: Morocco 81
illegalities 112–14
imagination: in oral history 99–100
impact: of oral histories 35, 42
implicit knowledge 141
improvised theatre 46
independent listeners 80
India *36*, 49
induction: of volunteers 130–1
informal networks: migrant nationalities 99
information: informing narrators of the future use of 106, *see also* personal data
information provision 80
information technology: and migration 50–2
informed consent 106–9, 111–12
injustice: host communities' sense of 84, 87
innocents: first-person life histories by ambivalent 29–30
innovation: concerning refugee issue 4–11; in tech industry with refugees' oral histories 50–2, *see also* humanitarian innovation
Innovation Service (UNHCR) 7
innovators: democratization and diversity of 158–9, *see also* refugee innovators
insider knowledge (volunteers) 131
Institute for Development Studies 164
integration: added value through 23; history of, Latin America 39; multimedia histories as tools for 66–8; and negligible terrorism 14; using the theme of seeking 77
intended effects: history projects 118, 119, *124*
interior décor design 48
internal regulation (interviewer) 142
internally displaced persons 4, 198; due to natural disasters 159; Latin America 39, 85; Syria 48
international aid 84, 164
international aid organizations 27, 76
international legislation 37
International Refugee Organization 39
International Rescue Commission (IRC) 8, 15, 198
internationalism 12, *13*
internet 99, 132
internet access 51
interpreters 106–7
intersectionality 198
interviews *see* oral history interviews
intolerance 22, 105
investment: new model of 163
Iran 21
Ireland 165
ISIS: defined 198; oral testimonies and prosecution of war crimes 61–3
Israeli occupation of Palestine 37, 38
Italy 6

Jamal (refugee) 82
Japan 9–10
Jewish refugees *36*, 37, 49
job competition 23
Jordan 21, 75
journalists' interviews 41
journals (project) 132
*Journey: Helen's Story* 46
The Jungle (Calais) 64, 82
justice *see* criminal justice; injustice; social justice
Justice Department (US) 27

Kauffman, Eric 28
Kenya 15, 21, 49
Key Informant Interviews, Africa 78
Kongo Drama 49
Kyangwali (Uganda) 7

Lampadusa 6
*The Lancet* 162
language: creative shifts in use of 5–7, *see also* interpreters; translation
language teaching 80
late-stage capitalism 161
lateral thinking 4, 7, 8, 60, 163, 198
Latin America: history of openness and integration 39; numbers displaced *36*; refugee crisis 4, 39, *see also individual countries*
learning approach 80
Lebanon 21, 47, 75, 83–5
*Lebanon: Looking Ahead in Times of Crisis* 83
leftist interviews: with anti-migrant communities 28
legal documentation 78
legal processes: smoother 80
legal protections 106–14; checklist 114, 180–1

legal testimony: oral histories as 60
*Let's Tech the Borders Down* 50
libel 112
liberal political leaders: rejection of 29
libraries: depositing interviews in 109
*Lights in the Distance: Exile and Refuge at the Borders of Europe* 82, 142
liquid cemetery 6
listening: creative local 165; failure in, Japan 10; gathering 'useful messages' 124–5; to concerns/grievances of host communities 22, 26, 27, 75–7, 79, 86–8, 128; to hopes and beliefs of economic migrants 82; to the masses who elect Western politicians 23; to service providers 126, *see also* deep listening; empathic listening; meta-listening
lived knowledge 141
livestreaming 49
local: the need for more focus on 74, 164–5, *see also* 'translocal' perspective
local economy: refugee intake and boost in 23
local knowledge 75, 141
localization 6, 198–9
localization of aid 74
'location visible' software 111
*LOCKSS* system 153
logbooks (project) 132, 153–4
logistics (project) 130–4
London School of Economics and Political Science 28
Lone Working Protocol 110–11, 131
long-term settled refugees *36*, 68–9
*Longing* (art exhibition) 47, 147
*Los Comandos* 49
Louis, Édouard 30, 147
Louisiana 86–7
loved ones: website for separated 50–1
Lucify 49

McDonald-Gibson, Charlotte 142
MacKay, Nancy 109, 153
Makers Unite 48
Manus Island 3, 65, 66
Mapping Memories: Participatory Media, Place-Based Stories and Refugee Youth 66
media: and the distortion of reality 21; and false expectations 81; idealized images of future destinations 82; publicizing findings through *129*; radicalization battle 69; refugee marches as rich fodder for 39; reversal of preconceptions presented by 7; whipping up resistance into right-wing politics 22, *see also* social media
mediation 75, 77–9, *137*, 138, 164
Mediterranean 6
*Mediterranean* (documentary) 81
Mental Capacity Act (2007) 112
mental capacity (narrator) 111–12
mental health issues 68
mental preparations: for oral histories 97–8
message-carrying exercise: oral history projects as a 120, 122, 126, *see also* useful messages
meta-listening 124
Mexico 39
micro-planning 133
microphones 132
Middle East: humanitarian crisis and political instability 15; refugee camps, and 'time bomb' of likely radicalization 15; refugee crisis 38; wars and displacement 4, 38, *see also individual countries*
Middle Eastern refugees: improvised theatre with 46, *see also* Palestinian refugees; Syrian refugees
migrant nationalities: informal networks 99
migrants 11, 199
Migrants (rap video) 49
migration 50; environmental 4; spectrum of political positions on 24, *25*; studies, and innovative shift in looking at people and places 5–6, *see also* Digital Migration Studies; refugee journeys
Mikhail, Dunya 63
Mikkelsenng, David and Christopher 50
Miliband, David 166
military/paramilitary activity 13
'mirror neuron' psychology 126, 137
misconceptions 64, 81
misinformation 81
misplaced optimism 81
missing persons website 51
mobile phones: use of 42, 51, 52, 65–6, 132–3
Mollica, Dr Richard 68, 104
Montreal 50, 66
Morocco 81
The Movement 29
multimedia oral histories 44, 66–8
Murad, Nadia 60, 61–3
museums: depositing interviews in 109
Museveni, Eric 49

music classes 49, 138
myths: debunking 88

Namibia 48
narrative turn 165
narrators: agreement to filming 132; defined 199; oral history work and spectrum of possible harm to *104*; pre-editing 142; ranking potential 126; researching/finding out about 121; safety/safeguarding 105, 111; selecting 125–8; self-editing 100; truths and views from 135–6, *see also* host community oral histories; refugee oral histories
'National Anthem' for the 'Refugee Nation' 6
national consultations 8
national economy: refugee intake and boost in 7
national identity 165
Native American refugees 35, *36*, 37, 56n1
needs: refugees and diversity of 11, 12; respect for hierarchy of 101; useful messages *124*, 136, *137*, *see also* help
neighbouring countries: refugees settled in 21, 85
neo-Nazis (American) 29
networks/networking: *Prevent* program 68; for refugee entrepreneurs 50; for safer refugee journeys 64; of Syrian expatriates 5, *see also* extremist networks; informal networks; Makers Unite; social media
New Berliners 5
New Canadians 5
*The New Minority White: White Working-Class Politics in an Age of Immigration and Inequality* 28
New York City 4
newcomers 5
newly settled refugees: multimedia histories 66–8
Neyzi, Leyla 105
NGO 199
Nigeria 4
*No Friend but the Mountains* 3, 66
*No One is Too Small to Make a Difference* 158
'No-Borders' 6, 25, 199
Nobel Peace Prize (2018) 63
non-settled refugees 15
nonprofessional interpreters 107
nonviolent communication 164
*Not just a refugee* 6
*Not Just Victims* approach 67
note-taking 132

'one-size-fits-all' solutions 10
online connection 51, 66
open-ended interviews 84
optimism (refugee) 81, 103
Ora, Rita 48
oral histories *see* applied oral history(ies); host community oral histories; refugee oral histories
oral history interviews 135–44; checklist for preparing to go to 189; chronological levels 140–1; editing and reviewing material 150–3; extracting testimonies that add the most value and solutions 147–50; genuine power-sharing in 40; hotspots 150; informed consent and access to 106–9; interviewers and methods 40–3; offering a limited right to correct copies 109; open-ended, semi-structured 84; question preparation 136–9, 188; setting up and doing 139–44; storing project records 153, *see also* Key Informant Interviews
oral history projects: aims, target audiences and intended effects 117–23; common sense 101–3; designing end products 147–50; empathy 100–1; equanimity 103; gathering 'useful messages' that will make a real difference 124–5; imagination 99–100; importance 105; legal and ethical protections 106–14; light-bulb moments 61; logistics 130–4; main groups involved in 60; mental preparation 97–8; political awareness 98–9; professionals involved in 9, 40, 60; publicizing findings 128–9; quantifying and communicating financial value of 153–6, 191–2; selecting narrators strategically 125–8; self-restraint 104–6; ten variables in the methodology of 41–2
*Organic Ambition 2022* program 163
organised crime 39
Oslo 48
outcomes (refugee): extremes in variation in long-term *103*; oral histories and improved collective 102
outcomes-focused approach 163
ownership 40, 41
Oxfam 27
Oxford University 7, 8

pain (refugee): useful messages *124*, 136, *137*
paintings 47
Pakistan 21, *36*

Palestinian refugees 37–8; craftswomen and creative expression through textiles 48; failed resettlement, South America 79–83; oral history project *36*, 37, *see also* United Nations Relief and Works Agency for Palestine Refugees (UNRWA)
Panama 85
paraphrasing 148
Participation, Inclusion and Social Change group 164
participatory approaches 5, 8, 64–5
participatory design 136–7, 138, 164, 199
participatory maps 78
participatory turn 164
partnerships 5, 44, 69, 74
peer groups: stories from 126
permission: in writing testimonies 76
personal (body) technologies 52
personal data: informing narrators of the future use of 106, *see also* data protection
personal finances 12, *13*
personal safety 110–11
personal testimony 165
perspective: creative shifts in 6–7
Peru 85
photo exhibitions 48
photographic recording 132, 133
pictogram 49
PIECES behavioural guidelines 97–114, 139
Pilot Refugee Resettlement Program (Japan) 9–10
planning: how to publicize findings 128–9; project aims, audiences and effects *118*; project logistics 130–4
Planning Interview Questions 188
Planning Who to Interview 182
Playback Theatre 46
plays 43–4, 46
political activity (refugee): spectrum of, before fleeing 98
political asylum *see* asylum
political awareness (interviewer) 28–9, 98–9
political consensus 160, 163, 164
political ideology: among host communities 24–6; divisions among refugees 99; honesty about one's own personal 25; host communities and spectrum of responses to refugees *123*; interviewer's awareness of 28–9; and resistance to refugees 22, *see also* far left; far right
political instability 15
political power 23
political responses: to refugee populations 37–9
political rhetoric: and the distortion of reality 21
political vulnerabilities 12–14
political will 22–3
politicians: listening to the masses who elect 23; whipping up resistance into right-wing politics 22
*The Politics of Resentment: Rural Consciousness in Wisconsin and the Rise of Scott Walker* 28, 87
poorest communities: oral histories 77–9, 85
poorest countries: percentage of refugees in 21
pop star's oral history 48
populists/populism: danger of ignoring concerns of 26; environmental crisis and refugees 160, *161*; identity crisis 160–2, 165; interviews with 28, 86–8; politics 27, 38, 39, 87, 160; strategy for avoiding terrorism 14–15; as threat to critical thinking in academic investigation 105
portable voice recorders 132
positive behaviours/examples: useful messages *124*, 136, *137*, 138
positive deviance 136, *137*, 138, 139, 150–1, 199
poverty: Europe 82
power-sharing 40, 41
pre-editing (narrator) 142
preconceptions: reversal of 7, 74
prejudice: tackling 88–90
preoccupations: at each stage of the refugee journey *122*; host communities' typical *123*
preparedness 199
preservation (data) 153
*Prevent* 68–9, 164
prison environment: testimony exposing brutality of 65–6
privacy: in interviews 111
proactive resourcefulness 86
probing: in interviews 143
problem-solving framework 162–6
problem-solving technique 136–9
professionals: involved in oral histories 9, 40, 60; as target audiences *121*
Project budget 130, 183
Project Induction Sheet 131
Project Information Sheet 106, 107, 108, 111, 114, 173–4
Project Logbook 132, 153–4
project teams 130

Project Timeline 133–4, 186–7
prosecution of war crimes 60, 61–3
prospective figures: for future funding 156
pseudonyms 108
psychology: use of oral histories in 44–5, 47, 68
public education: publicizing findings as *129*
public good 199
public policy: decision-making 25–6; oral testimony and improved 9; publicizing findings for *129*
publicization: of project findings 128–9; of testimonies through the arts 43–9; of useful messages 86
*Pueblo Sin Fronteras* 39
puppet show 47
purpose: of oral histories 42

quality oral history 165, *see also Four Golden Pillars*
question preparation 136–9, 188

racism 144
radicalization: into military/paramilitary activity 13; oral histories that prevent 68–9; refugee camps, and the 'time bomb' of likely 15; 'second generation' born to refugee parents, Europe and risk of 15
Rahma (refugee) 51
rape 12
rapping 49
rapport 76, 107, 127, 131, 135
re-presenting interviews 147, 149
REACT 44
'receptive following' technique 127
recording: oral histories 140, *see also* audio recordings; video recordings
recording studio: set up by refugees 7–8
records: storing 153
recycling 8
reeducation 23, 24, 74
Reeves, Simon 81
'refereeing' role 127
reframing: in interviews 143
refugee(s): causal relationship between terrorism and 14, 15–16; creativity in the use of language 5; definitions 4, 199; extremes in variation in long-term outcomes *103*; and host communities *see* host communities; hosting other refugees 85–6; innovation and lateral thinking concerning 4–11; numbers forcibly displaced 4; passive connotation of term 67; political and ideological divisions 99; political responses to 37–9; researching available low-cost resources for 102; reversal of preconceptions about 7; socioeconomic contributions 7–8, 23; spectrum of political activity before fleeing 98; as target audiences *121*; typical preoccupations at each stage of journey *122*; as whole populations on the move 11–14, *see also* refugee oral histories
refugee aid 74, 84, *see also* humanitarian aid; international aid
refugee camps: applying histories to improve 'taboo' medical services 64–5; Dadaab, Eastern Kenya 15; and host community grievances, Africa 77–9; interviews in 111; likelihood of radicalization 15; oral histories publicized through the arts 49; subhuman conditions and risk of terrorism and radicalisation 14, 15
refugee crisis: applied oral histories and resolution of 30; climate change and 4, 159–60; effective solutions for 7; Latin America 4, 39; and the need for listening to host communities 22; as a positive opportunity 8; stalled solutions to 38; the unthinkable costs of failing to manage 14–16
Refugee Economy 6, 199
Refugee Flag 6, 48
*Refugee Hosts Project* 75–7
refugee innovators: in host societies 7–8; oral histories with 8–9
refugee journeys: amateur reportage 52; centrality of online connection 51; histories publicized through the arts 46, 47, 49; illegal 39; innovative and online resource for 50; range of traumas that may be experienced on *102*; 'Snakes & Ladders' metaphor 11–14; typical preoccupations at each stage of *122*; using oral histories to design safer 64
refugee landscape 24, 104
Refugee on the Move 49
Refugee Nation 6, 199
refugee oral histories: case studies of 60–9; importance and impact 35; influential 42; interviewers and methods 40–3; publicizing through the arts 43–9; tech industry's innovations with 50–2; tradition of, and evolving methods 36–7, *see also* narrators; oral history interviews; oral history projects

refugee services: design 8, 9
Refugee Studies 37
Refugee Studies Centre (Oxford University) 8
refugee system 5
*Refugee Voice Tours* 67–8
refugeedom 36, 65
*Refunite* 51, 147
Regeni, Giulio 105
registered refugees 4
relationships: of aid agencies with host communities 76; exploring failure in refugee-community 75, 79–83; humanitarian system and the need for new 5; mutual listening and improved host-refugee 78; useful messages *124*, 136, *137*
*The Remake* 5
reorientation program 67
repatriation 199
reporting illegalities 112, 113
research: publicizing findings as academic *129*
resettlement: defined 199; failed projects/programs 9–10, 79–83; and negligible terrorism 14, 15; and sharing of resources 23
resistance to refugees: driven by far right politics 27; host communities' fears as cause of 77; importance of Western vocal 22, *see also* anti-migrant communities
resourcefulness 7, 8, 86, 136
resources: proportionality of benefits in return for refugees' invested 102, 103; recommended 193–6; researching available low-cost 102; resettlement and sharing of 23
respect 102; for host communities rights, freedoms and lifestyles 23; for narrators 111, 122; for refugees' hierarchy of needs 101
Restrictions: on consent forms 107–8
*The Rethink* 5
retirement in Spain 88–9
retrospective figures: for future funding 156
returning tangible benefit 102, 103
reversal of preconceptions 7, 74
reverse-colonization 29
review: of interview material 150–3; of interview topics 143
right-wing politics/politicians 22, 86, 87, 105, *see also* far right; populists/populism
*The Rise of Global Populism* 28
risks: oral history work 104–5
*The Road to Somewhere: The Populist Revolt and the Future of Politics* 28
robots/robotization 165, 166, 199
route maps (digital) 64
*Rule 35* (theatrical play) 44
Russell Hochschild, Arlie 28, 86, 87, 147, 164
Russian refugees *36*, 37
Ruth (refugee) 73–4

safeguarding legislation 110–12, 113
Safeguarding Protocols 111, 177–9
safety: of narrators and interviewers 105, 110–11; of refugees, political stance and 99
Sargunaraj, Wilbur 49
Saudi teenage refugee: asylum in Canada 44, 50
*#SaveRahaf* 50
savings: demonstrating financial *154*, 155
scaling up 9, 199
scripted questions 127, 139, 140
Scubla, Theo 67
sculpture 47
'second generation' born to refugee parents 15
seeking integration: using the theme of 77
self: experience of 165
self-editing (narrator) 100
self-image (host community) 84
self-image (refugee) 142
self-organized marches 39
self-regulation (narrator) 141–2
'self-reliance model for refugees' 7
self-restraint: in doing oral history 104–6
self-sufficiency 80
semi-structured interviews 84
'sensitive' personal data 109
service improvement: applied oral histories and 9, 79; publicizing findings for *129*; useful messages *124*, 136, 137, 138
service providers: listening to 126
shared values: adoption of 5
Shoah Foundation 37, 49, 166
Shrem, Abdullah 63
smuggled oral histories: exposing illegal incarceration 3, 65–6
'Snakes & Ladders' metaphor 11–14
social inequality 39
social justice: oral history for 153
social media 44, 50, 52, 66, 82, 99
socioeconomic contributions: of refugees 7–8, 23
socioeconomic ladder: and coping strategies, Lebanon 83–5

software: for transcribing 152
Somali refugees 15, 46, 51, 66–7
Somalia 21, 67
South Africa 7–8, 47
Spain 88–9
Sparrow, Jeff 28
Speaker Diarization 152
Speaker Recognition 152
Spielberg, Steven 37, 166
stakeholder: defined 200
stakeholder involvement 8, 64–5
stand up comedy 46
*Standing Tall* (art exhibition) 48
*Startups without Borders* 50
'*stay in your own lane*' 98
steering interventions (interview) 140, 141–2, 143–4
stereotypical roles: exploring community oral histories to get beyond 75–7
storytelling coach 68
*Strangers in Their Own Land: Anger and Mourning on the American Right* 28, 86, 147
*Strategic Update* on 'Understanding the Rise of Global Populism' 28
street violence: experience of 12
subhuman refugee camps: and the risk of terrorism and radicalisation 14, 15
Sudan 13
summarizing interview material 141, 143, 144, 148
support: for host communities 76
Syria 13, 21
*Syria: The World's War* 52
Syrian expatriates 5
Syrian refugees 6, 86, 100, 101, 150; impact on Lebanese society 83, 84; oral histories publicised through the arts 45, 47, 48, 49; oral history project *36*, 37; project examining local community experiences of and responses to 75–7; tour guides, Berlin 67–8

'taboo' medical services: using intimate histories to improve 64–5
tactfulness 142
Talya (refugee) 142
Tanzania 77
target audiences 118, 119, 120–1, *124*, 136
tech industry's innovations: with refugee oral histories 50–2, 64, 66
*TechCrunch* 50
*Techfugees* 50
technical illegalities 113–14
teenage refugees: oral histories publicized though the arts 44, 49; using multimedia oral histories as tools for integration 66
territory: shift in concept of 6
terrorism: causal relationship between refugees and 14, 15–16; correct steps for avoiding 14–15; program to prevent homegrown 68–9
testimonial theatre 43
Texas 39
textile arts 48
theatre groups 43–4, 46
therapy: oral histories as 44–5, 47, 60, 68
'*they're cutting in line*' narrative 87
'thinking through oceans' 6, 200
Thunberg, Greta 158
Tibetan refugees 38
time aspect: in refugee oral histories 42
timelines (project) 133–4, 186–7
tolerance 76, 162, 164
torture survivors: trauma story therapy 68
*Traces Project* 48
Trail of Tears 35, 37, 56n1
Training Workshop 111, 131, 184–5
training workshops: for resistant hosts 88, 89; for volunteers 130–1
*Transcribing Oral History* 152
transcription 152
transferable skills 12, *13*
translation: of project documentation 107, 109
'translocal' perspective 6, 200
'transnational' perspective 6, 200
transparency 40, 41, 152
trauma: extremes of variation experienced before fleeing *101*; the refugee experience as a four-stage 100–1; that refugees may experience during escape journeys *102*; theatre and cathartic expression of 43
Trauma Story Assessment and Therapy 68
traumatized refugees: oral interviews with 112
*Travels in Trumpland* 28, 147
*Trigger Warnings: Political Correctness and the Rise of the Right* 28
Trilling, Daniel 82, 142
Trump, Donald 26, 29, 39
Trump voters 28
trust 85
truth(s) 82, 135–6
Turkey 21, 75, 105
Twitter 50

Uganda 7, 21
underclass: testimonies from French 30, 147
unfair competition: white populist voters' perceptions of 87
unfulfilled promises/expectations 80–1
unfunded refugee histories 42
United Arab Emirates 48
United Kingdom 26; data protection 110; Department for International Development 27; mental capacity legislation 112; oral histories, Cambridge 73–4, 88–90; poorest communities housing refugees 85; refugee oral histories 46, 47, 48
United Nations: awareness of grievances of host communities 27; community-refugee boundaries 79; design of future refugee services 8; environmental migration 4; *Global Compact on Refugees* 8; invitation to participate in Humanitarian Innovation 5; oral interviews with women of child-bearing age 65; on Palestinian refugees 37–8; predicted Latin American refugee crisis 39
United Nations High Commissioner for Refugees (UNHCR) 7, 22, 48, 49, 78, 158, 165, 200
United Nations Relief and Works Agency for Palestine Refugees (UNRWA) 38, 200
United States: data protection 110; environmental migration 4; far right movements and terrorist attacks 15; Justice Department 27; Native American refugees 35, *36*, 37, 56n1; neo-Nazis 29; refugees displaced by Vietnam war *36*; refugees' expectations 81, *see also* Charlottesville; Louisiana; Texas; Wisconsin
universities: depositing interviews in 109
unspoken navigation 142
upcycling 8, 200
*US Media and Migration* 81
useful messages: categories *124*, 136; communicating 86; gathering 124–5; questions for capturing specific *137*
user-involvement approach 64–5

values: and citizenship, Canada 5; cultural 23; interviewing those opposed to one's own 128
Vance, J.D. 29, 30, 147
Venezuela 4, 39, 85
verbatim theatre 43
vested interests 126, 163
video links: smuggled histories through use of 66
video recordings 131; advantages 132; project findings 149; refugee journeys 52; refugee oral history 49; transcribing 152; use and equipment 132–3
Vietnamese refugee 46
Village of All-Together 64
violations: physical and psychological 79
violence 12, 39, 49
virtual connections 51, 66
virtual countries 6
virtual reality holograms 49
voice: communities' complaints of lack of 27; refugee oral histories 42; tone of 111
voice recorders 132
volunteers 130–1
vulnerabilities: host communities 79; refugees 11, 12–14, 99
vulnerable people: exposure to grooming by radicalizers 69; interviews with 111; safeguarding legislation 113

war crimes: oral histories and prosecution of 60, 61–3
war refugees 4, *36*, 60, 61–3, 86
Washington, DC 4
weak state institutions 39
wealth: sharing 81
wealthy economies *see* developed economies
WebASR 152
Weiwei, Ai 45, 64, 117, 146
'Welcome 2 Europe' network 64
welcoming: using the theme of 77
Western host communities: categories 22; importance of vocal resistance in 22; leftist interviews with 28; listening to anti-migrant 86–8; the need to inform and reeducate 23; the need to listen and engage with resistant 22; tackling anti-migrant prejudice 88–90
Western politicians: listening to the masses who elect 23
Western working class: current malaise among 160–1; empathy with grievances of 87
white natives: and terrorist attacks 15
white populists 28, 86–8
white supremacists 27, 29, 123
white working class 28, 29
*Whiteshift: Populism, Immigration and the Future of White Majorities* 28

*Who Killed My Father* 30
wicked problems: frameworks for tackling 163–6
Wilde, Oscar 66
win/win solutions 22
*Wintegreat* 67, 147
*Winter Journey* 46
Wisconsin 87
women: and extremist networks 29; likelihood of rape and enslavement 12; tension between refugees and those of host communities 84
women's refugee histories: publicized through the arts 44, 46, 48; using to improve 'taboo' medical services in refugee camps 64–5
World Bank 27
World Humanitarian Summit (2016) 74, 164
World War 2 refugees *36*
The World in a Suitcase 47
writing workshops 76

Yazidi women: oral testimonies and prosecution of ISIS war criminals 61–3
young males: experience of street violence 12
youngsters: interviews with 111, *see also* child refugees; teenage refugees
Yousafzai, Malala 158
Yuval-Davis, Nira 46

Zelenskiy, Volodymyr 29
Zimbabwe 7